THE QUEST FOR ATTENTION

THE QUEST
FOR ATTENTION

NONPROFIT ADVOCACY
IN A SOCIAL MEDIA AGE

CHAO GUO

AND

GREGORY D. SAXTON

STANFORD BUSINESS BOOKS
AN IMPRINT OF STANFORD UNIVERSITY PRESS
STANFORD, CALIFORNIA

Special discounts for bulk quantities of Stanford Business Books are available to corporations, professional associations, and other organizations. For details and discount information, contact the special sales department of Stanford University Press. Tel: (650) 725-0820, Fax: (650) 725-3457

Printed in the United States of America on acid-free, archival-quality paper

Library of Congress Cataloging-in-Publication Data

Names: Guo, Chao, 1971- author. | Saxton, Gregory D. (Gregory Douglas),author.
Title: The quest for attention : nonprofit advocacy in a social media age /
    Chao Guo and Gregory D. Saxton.
Description: Stanford, California : Stanford Business Books, an imprint of
    Stanford University Press, 2020. | Includes bibliographical references
    and index.
Identifiers: LCCN 2019045510 (print) | LCCN 2019045511 (ebook) | ISBN 9781503605015 (cloth) |
    ISBN 9781503613072 (paperback) | ISBN 9781503613089 (ebook)
Subjects: LCSH: Nonprofit organizations—Political activity. | Social media.
Classification: LCC HD62.6 .G845 2020 (print) | LCC HD62.6 (ebook) | DDC 659.2/88—dc23
LC record available at https://lccn.loc.gov/2019045510
LC ebook record available at https://lccn.loc.gov/2019045511

Cover design: Andrew Brozyna

Typeset by Newgen in 10/14 Minion

CONTENTS

ACKNOWLEDGMENTS

It's been a long journey: three years have passed since we started planning the book. In the social media universe, that is probably equivalent to at least a decade. And yet the journey has also been an intellectually stimulating and rewarding one, as it offers a precious opportunity to build on and extend our collective work over the years and to challenge ourselves to step out of our comfort zone and explore the unknown.

Now that the book is complete, we first wish to thank Steve Catalano, Senior Editor at Stanford University Press, for his patience, trust, and advice throughout the writing process. Without him, we would not have brought this project to fruition. We also thank Editorial Assistant Sunna Juhn for all the support and technical guidance that she has offered. Margo Beth Fleming, formerly of the press, saw potential in our original book idea and walked us through the proposal stage, for which we are grateful.

We owe an immense debt of gratitude to the practitioner colleagues at the three nonprofit advocacy organizations who generously shared their experiences, observations, and insights during the interviews. Their identities are concealed in the book for confidentiality reasons, but their contributions are invaluable to our book and deserve special recognition.

The book has benefited tremendously from the thoughtful comments of the anonymous reviewers. Their suggestions helped push us in important new directions while prodding us to improve the clarity and impact of our work. We are also grateful to our colleagues David Campbell (Binghamton University), John McNutt (University of Delaware), and David Suárez (University of Washington), who spent quality time reading through parts of our manuscript and encouraged us to move the book to a higher level.

The book would not have been possible without the participation and contributions of our former and current doctoral students: Seongho An (University of Central Florida), Wayne Xu (University of Massachusetts Amherst), and Viviana Wu (University of Pennsylvania). The numerous intellectual discussions with them and the research assistance they kindly provided have allowed us to include some really fabulous ideas and data in this book. Dominic Noble (York University) also did some excellent last-minute work checking the references and helping with the tables and figures. We also acknowledge the contributions of several visiting doctoral students at Penn: Kunpeng Cheng (Shanghai Jiaotong University), Jinghua Gao (Renmin University of China), Zhuang Sang (Tsinghua University), Meng-Che Yu (National Chengchi University), and Zhe Zhang (Renmin University of China). We would also like to thank our respective academic homes, Penn School of Social Policy and Practice and the accounting area at the Schulich School of Business, for providing us with excellent colleagues, students, and strong support for the pursuit of academic work.

More personally, we are deeply indebted to our loving families: Charlotte and Emma, and Michelle, Riley, and Tyler. They gave us space when we were busy writing, brainstormed with us when we were running out of ideas, and hung out with us when we needed a break. Caffeine also played a supportive role, especially near the end of the editing process. We each spent hours at our favorite coffee houses, probably taking in more caffeine than we realized. So, if the language of the book sounds a bit too energetic in some places, it's the coffee talking.

CHAPTER 1

SOCIAL MEDIA AND NONPROFIT ADVOCACY

The Beginning of a New Paradigm

October 4, 2010. *The New Yorker Magazine*. Canadian journalist and writer Malcolm Gladwell published a short essay titled "Why the Revolution Will Not Be Tweeted." He began with a recount of the 1960 Greensboro sit-in, when a group of African American college students in North Carolina peacefully protested at a segregated Woolworth's lunch counter after being denied service. After comparing traditional activism and its online variant, Gladwell then wrote, "The instruments of social media . . . are not a natural enemy of the status quo. If you are of the opinion that all the world needs is a little buffing around the edges, this should not trouble you. But if you think that there are still lunch counters out there that need integrating it ought to give you pause" (Gladwell 2010).

February 25, 2015. New York City. The annual Social Media Week conference welcomed a special guest: the Reverend Jesse Jackson, prominent American civil rights leader and two-time Democratic presidential candidate. In his keynote speech, Jackson talked about the impact of social media on social justice. His message was unequivocal: social media does not equal social change. He said, "I think sometimes people who use social media think that you can sit there and send the message to people. People need more than information. . . . If you leave here and [see] there's a school in your city that does not teach music or art, there should be a protest" (Dalenberg 2015).

Underlying the above viewpoints is an uneasy feeling that social media may be pushing to the wayside more important "traditional"—meaning offline—

advocacy work. In the United States, advocacy has been in the DNA of non-profit and voluntary action since the genesis of the sector, and has been an increasingly salient function of nonprofit organizations in the wake of World War II. From civil rights to anti-war movements, from women's rights to gay rights, from poverty to the environment, from Occupy Wall Street to the fight for a $15 minimum wage, countless nonprofit organizations and generations of activists have been at the forefront of these causes since the start. They have been seen participating in letter writing, petitioning, lobbying elected officials, running or contributing to political campaigns, and participating in rallies, protests, sit-ins, boycotts, and strikes. Battles fought, causes won, changes made. In doing so, the activists have often risked confronting the authorities, getting injured or arrested, and sometimes even losing their lives.

Then, with the advent of the new millennium came a new age. In just two decades, the Internet and Web 2.0 have quickly become inseparable parts of our lives. Social media channels such as Facebook, Twitter, YouTube, Instagram, LinkedIn, and Google+ have greatly enhanced the ability of both citizens and organizations to engage in meaningful interactions in cyberspace. The nonprofit sector is not immune to these developments, as the way people think of and participate in social change and advocacy has also changed (see Goldkind and McNutt 2014; Guo and Saxton 2014b; Karpf 2012; McNutt and Menon 2008; Suárez 2009). Today, you can have the comfort of sending testimony or signing a petition by email, or showing your support for or against an issue by tweeting, retweeting, commenting and liking on Facebook, posting a photo on Instagram, or watching a video on YouTube. You can engage in a policy debate or attract a huge following on social media without meeting with people face-to-face.

For lifelong activists and seasoned leaders of advocacy groups, it is difficult not to view social media with a skeptical eye. All of a sudden, many nonprofit leaders feel like an old kid in a new town. Are newer forms of engagement replacing demonstrations, sit-ins, meetings with policymakers, and other offline efforts? Will traditional nonprofit advocacy organizations become dinosaurs in this increasingly networked world? Can these "old dogs" be taught new social media tricks?

This book seeks to explore these questions by unpacking the prevalence, mechanisms, and ramifications of a new model for nonprofit advocacy in a social media age. The key word for this new model is *attention*. Advocacy always starts with attention: when an organization speaks out on a cause, it must ensure that it has an audience and that its voice is heard by that audience; it must ensure that current and potential supporters are paying attention to what it has to say before expecting more tangible outcomes. Yet the organization must also ensure that advocacy does not end with attention: attention should serve as a springboard to something greater. In the course of this book we will elaborate how attention fits into contemporary organizations' advocacy work. We will explain key features of social media that are driving the quest for attention. We will develop and then test conceptual models that explain why some organizations and some messages gain attention while others do not. And we will explore how organizations are weaving online and offline efforts to deliver strategic advocacy outcomes.

Nonprofit Advocacy: A Primer

In much of the world, the nonprofit sector plays a key and growing part in fostering a strong civil society (e.g., for recent changes in China, see Guo et al. 2012; Xu and Ngai 2011; for recent changes in Russia, see Salamon, Benevolenski, and Jakobson 2015). Focusing just on the United States, where voluntary civil society organizations have a long tradition (de Tocqueville 1838), America's nonprofit sector has continued to steadily increase in social, political, and economic importance. In the past four decades alone, the number of organizations has jumped from 740,000 in 1977 (Independent Sector 2001) to 1.3 million in 2000 (Blackwood, Wing, and Pollak 2008) and 1.56 million in 2015 (McKeever 2018). These organizations come in a range of sizes and undertake activities in a wide array of areas, covering activities in, among others, health, religion, education, the environment, the arts, politics, human services, and international affairs. Their work can be done by full- and part-time paid employees, volunteers, members, or, more typically, a combination of the above. Some organizations are funded chiefly by government, others are dependent almost solely on individual donations, and others receive funds from private philanthropists or social entrepreneurial activities. In brief, it is a diverse and growing sector.

Advocacy is a core nonprofit function. Through their advocacy work, nonprofit organizations strengthen the democratic process by representing the interests of citizens and promoting changes in public policy. In the United States,[1] certain types of nonprofit organizations have advocacy as their primary purpose; public interest groups and business leagues would fall into this category. However, the most common type of nonprofit is the charitable organization, classified as 501(c)(3) by the Internal Revenue Service (IRS). Charitable organizations—or public charities—cover a wide range of organizations including hospitals, universities, museums, churches, human services organizations, and international and foreign affairs organizations. These groups are often known by the public for their service-provision roles, but they also advance their missions by influencing public policy and empowering the individuals and families whom they serve (Guo 2007; LeRoux 2009; Mosley 2011; O'Connell 1994). As with the corporate sector, the nonprofit community engages in advocacy efforts related to public policies that govern its work, including operational concerns such as benefits for charitable giving and benefits afforded to employers.

In light of the tremendous growth of the nonprofit sector in the United States and worldwide, it is not surprising that scholarly interest in nonprofit advocacy has increased over the past two decades (e.g., Almog-Bar and Schmid 2014; Berry and Arons 2003; Boris and Mosher-Williams 1998; Chen 2018; Child and Gronbjerg 2007; Clear, Paull, and Holloway 2018; Frumkin 2002; Fyall and McGuire 2015; Guo and Saxton 2010; Guo and Zhang 2014; Kim and Mason 2018; LeRoux and Goerdel 2009; Li, Lo, and Tang 2017; Lu 2018; Mosley 2011; Neumayr, Schneider, and Meyer 2015; O'Connell 1994; O'Connell 1996; Prakash and Gugerty 2010; Schmid, Bar, and Nirel 2008; Suárez and Hwang 2008; Zhan and Tang 2013; Zhang 2018; Zhang and Guo in press).

There is no clear consensus, at least in the early literature, regarding the definition of nonprofit advocacy (Bass et al. 2007). Hopkins (1992, 32) defines nonprofit advocacy as action by nonprofit organizations to "[plead] for or against a cause or a position," and "address . . . legislators with a view to influencing their votes." This relatively narrow definition brings it closer to direct lobbying. Jenkins (2006, 308) provides a broader definition, including activities such as "grassroots lobbying (encouraging others to contact legislators to support or oppose specific legislation), attempts to influence public opinion, and educational efforts designed to encourage community and political participation" (see also Boris and Mosher-Williams 1998; Reid 1999). Broad or narrow, both definitions regard the ultimate goal of nonprofit advocacy as influencing government policy. More recent studies seem to take a middle ground, focusing on influencing policy but covering a wide variety of activities. Guo (2012), for example, defines nonprofit advocacy as attempts by nonprofits to influence government decisions through direct and indirect means, including communication with policymakers, grassroots mobilization, and public education.

There is a common misperception that, except for some public interest groups that are often classified by the IRS as 501(c)(4) social welfare organizations, most public charities do not engage in advocacy activities. One key source of the misperception is that people often confuse advocacy with lobbying, which is only one type of advocacy work. Charities are required to report to the IRS "direct lobbying" activities, which are defined as attempts to influence a legislative body on specific legislation, and "grassroots lobbying," which involves encouraging members of the public to take action on specific legislation. Only a tiny percentage of charities actually report this type of activity: for example, Suárez and Hwang (2008) show that less than 3% of operating charities in California lobby in any given year between 1998 and 2003, though some types of charities (e.g., environment, health) lobby more than others (e.g., religion and arts). Despite this low level of participation, charitable organizations can certainly engage in lobbying activities as long as such work does not constitute a substantial part of their activities.

Advocacy, on the other hand, covers a much broader range of activities beyond lobbying (a point we will return to later in this section). Mounting research demonstrates that policy advocacy broadly defined is a common practice of charitable organizations (e.g., Andrews and Edwards 2004; Berry and Arons 2003; Guo and Saxton 2010; Mosley 2011), though research varies widely on the level of participation. In a well-known survey of Indiana nonprofit organizations, Child and Gronbjerg (2007) found that nearly three-quarters of nonprofits in their study did not participate in any form of advocacy activity, and only one-quarter of those organizations that did report participating in some advocacy work devoted substantial resources to advocacy efforts. By contrast, in another influential, multiple-year research project called the Strengthening Nonprofit Advocacy Project (SNAP), Berry and Arons (2003) conducted a national survey of 1,738 public charities. Their findings showed that about three-fourths of these organizations engaged in some sort of advocacy activity, ranging from direct and grassroots lobbying to testifying at a legislative or administrative hearing. Having said that, the frequency of policy participation was generally low among those charities who indicated their engagement in advocacy work.

There are at least two possible explanations for this fairly large discrepancy in the findings from these two studies. The first explanation is methodological:

the Indiana survey includes a less detailed definition of advocacy than SNAP, which might cause the respondents to underreport their participation in advocacy work. The giving and volunteering literatures serve as a useful reference here: prior research indicates that longer, more detailed questionnaires on giving and volunteering led respondents to report higher incidence rates and higher levels than did less detailed surveys (Rooney, Steinberg, and Schervish 2004). The second explanation is conceptual: there is a lack of clear understanding among nonprofit leaders in terms of the nature of advocacy work and what it entails. Berry and Arons (2003) found many charities did not think of themselves as influencing public policy even when they actually engaged in public policy matters. In other words, it is very likely that more organizations are involved in advocacy work—they are just not aware of it.

What does advocacy work involve, then? An organization's advocacy efforts can be understood in terms of its advocacy strategy as well as the tactics it employs to implement the strategy. Berry (1977) pioneered this line of inquiry by making an early distinction between the more general, long-range approaches to influencing public policy (i.e., advocacy strategies) and the specific actions taken to execute a particular strategy (i.e., advocacy tactics). Scholars have since devised various ways of broadly categorizing advocacy strategies: Gais and Walker (1991) characterized inside and outside strategies; Gormley and Cymrot (2006) theorized insider versus outsider strategies; while Mosley (2011) conceptualized insider and indirect strategies. Despite the minor differences in preferred terminology, these studies share a concern with distinguishing working "inside the system" (e.g., legislative lobbying, legislative testimony) from working "outside the system" (e.g., public education efforts, mass media campaigns, and protests and demonstrations).

The existing literature has also compiled a long and comprehensive list of advocacy tactics nonprofit organizations use to execute their chosen strategies. In an earlier study (Guo and Saxton 2010), we drew upon existing typologies (e.g., Avner 2002; Reid 1999) to identify eleven advocacy tactics: research, media advocacy, direct lobbying, grassroots lobbying, public events and direct action, judicial advocacy, public education, coalition building, administrative lobbying, voter registration and education, and expert testimony. In that study, we did not explicitly relate these advocacy tactics to broader strategies, but one can reasonably infer that direct lobbying, judicial advocacy, administrative advocacy, and expert testimony would fall under the umbrella of the "insider" strategy, while the other tactics would fall under the "outsider" strategy.

In summary, prior research has highlighted the importance of advocacy work for nonprofit organizations and identified the broad strategies and specific tactical forms these organizations employ offline to reach their public policy goals. Next, we turn to how social media are quietly changing the ways in which advocacy work is done by nonprofit organizations.

The Challenges of Advocacy in a 2.0 World

Nonprofit organizations today face two fundamental and interrelated challenges: the resource challenge and the relevance challenge. Both have implications for understanding the new attention-focused model we posit for advocacy organizations in a social media age. Before elaborating our model, we explore the two challenges in turn.

The Resource Challenge

In the past quarter century, resource scarcity has become an increasingly pressing challenge for nonprofit organizations in general and advocacy organizations in particular. One important source of this resource challenge lies in the concentration of financial resources: a small number of leading public charities in the United States control a lion's share of private contributions. In a population-level analysis that covers a two-decade span (1991–2013), Cleveland (2015) found that the growth of charities slowed down in terms of both the number of organizations and total revenue, while the largest fundraising charities continued to grow in terms of receiving a disproportionate share of overall donations and revenue.

Similar patterns emerge from several other studies (e.g., Galaskiewicz and Bielefeld 1998; Lecy 2010) that have observed a trend of increasing concentration of revenues in a cross section of nonprofit organizations. This trend raises an important concern that the biggest players are taking a disproportionate share of resources at the price of smaller organizations in an increasingly top-heavy industry. In his study of US-based international nonprofit organizations[2] from 1989 to 2007, Lecy (2010) found that the international subsector grew 600% in terms of revenues during the study period but the number of organizations only increased by 350%. A simple comparison of the two statistics suggests that international nonprofits were growing in size (as reflected in revenues) during the 20-year period, which appears to be the case if we look at the mean size of organizations. If we look at the median size of organizations, however, it was actually decreasing from annual revenues of $190,000 to $170,000 in nominal dollars; the decline would be even steeper if we use inflation-adjusted rates. In short, the growth in average size was driven by increased revenues among larger organizations; the income inequality between the "haves" and the "have-nots" effectively increased from 1989 to 2007.

A direct implication of this finding is that resource concentration within a small number of the largest organizations leads to more intense competition for resources among the smaller organizations, which in turn will likely have a negative effect on organizational performance. Previous research seems to corroborate this argument. For example, Rose-Ackerman (1982) found that competition for donors led to increased fundraising expenses "crowding out" expenditures on services, while Thornton (2006) found that when a competing organization increased fundraising expenses, the overall effect was to "steal" the other organizations' donors rather than expand the market for charitable donations.

To make things more complicated, the problem of resource concentration is not necessarily equally distributed across different subsectors or types of nonprofits. For example, "commercial" nonprofits with client relationships that are the most customer-like tend to rely most on program service revenue and least on private contributions, whereas donative nonprofits, such as advocacy groups, international nonprofits, and youth development organizations, tend to rely most on private contributions and least on program service revenue (Horne 2005). If we consider these subsector-specific patterns, then the problem of resource concentration might be even more severe among nonprofit advocacy organizations.

On the donor side, charitable giving in the United States has reached an all-time high, with a total of $410 billion in donations to nonprofits in 2017. While this growth in absolute dollars is certainly encouraging news, it needs to be taken with a grain of salt: the total amount of giving accounts for about 2.1% of gross domestic product (GDP), which as a share of GDP has remained almost unchanged in the past four decades. Moreover, the percentage of households making donations has actually decreased: in 2000, more than two-thirds of households gave to charities; but the number dropped to 55% in 2014 (Osili and Zarins 2018). This could be troubling news, as it suggests that on average a nonprofit organization now has fewer donors from whom to solicit funds.

Resource shortage is not limited to financial concerns. A notable trend is that nonprofits are experiencing unprecedented pressure to recruit and retain volunteers, due not only to the decline in the number of volunteers in recent years but also to the growing popularity of "episodic" or short-term volunteering (see Cnaan and Handy 2005; Hyde et al. 2016). Although there is little empirical evidence to confirm our prediction directly, it seems reasonable to suspect the negative consequence of episodic volunteering would be felt most strongly among advocacy organizations. The United States has been described as a nation of volunteers, but not all volunteers are equal. Volunteers for advocacy organizations appear to be "marching to a different drummer" than typical "good-deed doers" (Guo et al. 2013), such that the volunteer pool for such organizations might be especially small. In a study of social change volunteering based on the 2005 wave of the Center on Philanthropy Panel Study (COPPS) supplement to the Panel Study of Income Dynamics (PSID), Guo and colleagues (2013) found that only 3% of household heads volunteered with advocacy and social change organizations; by contrast, 27% of the household heads volunteered for any charitable cause. Similarly, Nesbit (2017) found only 5.4% of all volunteers in the United States donate their time for a civic organization, compared to 34% who volunteer for religious organizations, 26% for education-related organizations, and 15% for social service–focused charities.

The Relevance Challenge

Even before the dawn of the social media age, Pablo Eisenberg, a renowned American scholar and a leading social justice advocate, had already lamented, "One can reasonably argue that, despite its enormous expansion, the nonprofit world has become less influential in shaping the direction, priorities, and policies of our society. . . . We may be larger and more effective deliverers of social services than we were 30 years ago, but we are more fragmented than ever before, often finding it difficult to collaborate with others to engage in the policy battles that threaten our collective well-being" (Eisenberg 2004).[3]

Recent studies echo this observation. Using a unique data set that includes 1,779 policy issues, Gilens and Page (2014) found that, compared to their business counterparts, advocacy organizations and public interest groups have little or no independent influence on US government policy. The authors interpreted their finding as evidence for theories of biased pluralism, which hold that public policies as an outcome of interest group competition tend to favor the wishes of business interests at the price of citizen groups. More broadly, in their recent book *The Unheavenly Chorus: Unequal Political Voice and the Broken Promise of American Democracy*, Schlozman, Verba, and Brady (2013) revisited the issue of inequalities in political activity, which was the focus of their early influential work (Verba, Schlozman, and Brady 1995). They examined the political participation of individual citizens as well as the advocacy work of numerous organized interests ranging from unions and citizen groups to trade unions and large corporations. Their findings powerfully demonstrated the persistency of participatory inequalities in American civic life: the most affluent and best-educated citizens are consistently overrepresented, while the voices of the disadvantaged remain unheard. In addition, according to a recent survey of 600 gender equality advocates around the world, nearly half (49%) of the advocates noted that gender equality had neither improved nor worsened but had remained stagnant for the past five years. The survey also revealed significant variations between genders: more than half (55%) of male respondents felt the gender equality situation in their country had improved, whereas only one-third (33%) of female respondents felt the same way (Equal Measures 2030, n.d.).

The above studies raise a serious question: Is nonprofit advocacy work still relevant? Put differently, does nonprofit advocacy make a difference? An important source of the relevance challenge lies in the difficulties associated with evaluating advocacy effectiveness. Although sophisticated tools have been developed over the years for evaluating the effectiveness of service delivery programs, these tools are often not helpful in evaluating an organization's advocacy efforts (Teles and Schmitt 2011). This is partially due to the influence of political context and other factors beyond the control of any organization and the difficulty in establishing the causal link between advocacy efforts and intended policy outcomes. The situation is further complicated by the presence of multiple objectives and intangible long-term impacts of advocacy efforts (Guo 2012).

Another important source of the relevance challenge lies in the interdependent relationship with governments, which serve as an important financier to nonprofit contractors. In a prior study (Guo and Saxton 2010), we raised concerns about the consequences of this interdependence for the advocacy work of nonprofit contractors: To what extent would they actually advocate for their disadvantaged constituents rather than their own interests? To what extent would they be willing to challenge the status quo (see also Alexander, Nank, and Stivers 1999; Berry and Arons 2003)? There is mounting evidence to confirm such concerns. For example, a study of safety-net providers in the state of Connecticut (Grogan and Gusmano 2009) found that, as the dynamics of government contracting changed from collaboration to competition (i.e., competitive contracting under Medicaid Managed Care), service providers increased advocacy efforts to secure a favorable role at the price of compromising their ability to act as representatives of poor and vulnerable populations. Another study of advocacy involvement in the field of homeless services (Mosley 2012) also showed that the dependence on government funding threatened to alter the nature of nonprofit advocacy: an organization's advocacy work drifted away from substantive policy change or client representation to brokering resources and promoting organizational interest. Similarly, a study of Australian nonprofits in the human services and environmental fields (Onyx et al. 2008) indicated the difficulty in maintaining an advocacy program while receiving significant government funding.

Along the same lines, relevance becomes more challenging in the face of pressure to modify the mission in ways that are more appealing to funders or donors. More often than not, nonprofits are constrained by financial support, such that they tend to conduct work they think donors will be willing to fund, which is arguably a different set of priorities than those shared by the general public. Nonprofits have thus found themselves increasingly pulled further away from the poor groups that they claim to represent and in whose name many now raise huge funds (Wallace and Porter 2013). This is an important point, given that organizations with missions that pertain to serving specific populations are more likely to advocate on behalf of those populations than organizations with missions to serve the general public (MacIndoe and Whelan 2013).

More than ever, achieving relevance and impact through advocacy work requires that organizations go beyond their organizational boundaries and comfort zones. Indeed, the recent advances in information and communication technologies have greatly empowered the development of grassroots community initiatives and "do-it-yourself" democracy-type movements, such as the numerous activist petitions launched on Change.org (which, by the way, is a for-profit business). When advocacy work is increasingly being done without the leadership or even the involvement of established advocacy organizations who used to be the major players in the game, what kind of role can these organizations play—and should they play—in influencing public policy?

When Advocacy Meets Social Media

The Internet and social media have significantly changed how politics operates in the United States and around the globe. In particular, the use of social media in political campaigns began at the end of the twentieth century, when George W. Bush and John McCain started accepting donations online during the 2000 presidential campaign. Yet it was the success of the Howard Dean presidential campaign online in 2003–2004 that turned the use of social media into a topic of mainstream discussion. Later referred to by some as "the first viral moment in American politics" (Murray 2019), Dean's use of social media for political mobilization and fundraising in his campaign vividly demonstrated the impact that ordinary citizens could directly have on a national election.

Similarly, nonprofit organizations have been at the forefront of this technological wave to engage in advocacy work. Long before the birth of social media, advocacy organizations had begun to use emails, bulletin boards, geographic information systems, and numerous other applications as early as the 1980s (Downing et al. 1991; Schwartz 1996; Wittig and Schmitz 1996; Yerxa and Moll 1994). The emergence of the Internet and the first generation of the World Wide Web (i.e., Web 1.0) led to the growth of serious efforts by advocacy groups and social movement organizations to apply technology to advocacy (Bennett and Fielding 1999; Davis 1999; McNutt and Boland 1999). For example, technology was heavily used in the 1999 anti–World Trade Organization protests, often termed the "Battle in Seattle," to coordinate groups in the effort. Then Web 2.0 entered the scene in the early 2000s, allowing greater user interactivity and user-generated content. Accordingly, organizations began to use social media such as Facebook and Twitter to raise awareness, mobilize supporters, facilitate collective action, and influence public policy (see McNutt et al. 2018 and Chapter 2 of this book for more detailed discussions).

Only recently have researchers begun to explore social media use by nonprofit organizations in their policy advocacy work, and yet the pace of research on the subject has been extraordinary. One stream of research focuses on the adoption and frequency of use of social media by nonprofit organizations for advocacy work. For example, Bortree and Seltzer (2009) examined the Facebook profiles of 50 environmental advocacy groups, whereas Greenberg and MacAulay (2009) analyzed 43 Canadian environmental organizations' use of websites along with social media such as Facebook, Twitter, and blogs. Edwards and Hoefer (2010) examined the current levels of Web 2.0 use on the websites of 63 social work advocacy organizations. These studies showed that nonprofit organizations were indeed adopting social media to enhance their communication, organization, and fundraising strategies; not surprisingly, these early studies also indicated that they had not fully utilized the affordances of social media for their advocacy work. Overall, in terms of the prevalence of social media use, advocacy organizations seem to be ahead of the game as compared to other types of nonprofits. For example, recent studies of public and nonprofit human services showed that social media use by these organizations was still rather modest, and that most of the users either lacked a long-term vision for social media or held a narrow view that barely went beyond marketing or raising community awareness (Campbell and Lambright 2019; Campbell, Lambright, and Wells 2014).

The other stream of research considers why, how, how often, and how well social media is being incorporated into nonprofit advocacy work. For example, Obar, Zube, and Lampe (2012) found most of the 53 US-based advocacy groups in their study were using social media for their civic engagement and collective action work on a daily basis. Other studies (e.g., Brady, Young, and McLeod 2015; Goldkind and McNutt 2014) have subsequently expanded on such work and explored both how advocacy organizations are using social media and the benefits and challenges of social media use for engaging in advocacy. Taking an event-centered approach, Merry (2013, 2014) examined how environmental organizations used Twitter to conduct advocacy work in the aftermath of the 2010 oil spill in the Gulf of Mexico. In a national study of 4,615 homelessness-related nonprofits in the United States, An (2019) found that two in three organizations were using social media, and, when it comes to Twitter, around 30% of their messages were related to "calls to action" for the homeless. Overall, social media appears to be an increasingly relevant tool for the nonprofit sector's advocacy efforts. An emerging issue in the literature is the role of communication and building awareness. For instance, Petray (2011) found that a key element of Australian Aboriginal activists' social media efforts was focused on bringing awareness of their struggle to a wider audience. Johansson and Scaramuzzino (2019), meanwhile, found that a key goal of a sample of Swedish advocacy organizations was to boost their political presence through a series of interconnected online and offline activities.

To better understand the role of social media in advocacy work, recent studies have also begun to focus on micro-level analyses by examining the messages advocacy organizations are sending on social media. Communication and public relations scholars have pioneered the effort to provide message-level analyses (Lovejoy and Saxton 2012; Waters and Jamal 2011). For example, Waters and Jamal (2011) examined the presence of four different public relations models in tweets—public information, press agentry, asymmetrical communication, and symmetrical dialogue. Lovejoy and Saxton (2012), meanwhile, coded nonprofit organizational tweets according to whether the message was primarily aimed at providing information, engaging in dialogic community-building, or mobilizing followers through a "call to action." Subsequent research has expanded this *information-community-action* framework to social media messages by advocacy organizations (e.g., Auger 2013; Bürger 2015; Xu et al. 2014). Gupta, Ripberger, and Wehde (2018), meanwhile, coded the presence of policy narratives in tweets by pro- and anti-nuclear advocacy groups. Using an unsupervised machine learning approach (latent Dirichlet allocation topic modeling), An (2019) extracted seven themes on Twitter discussed by US-based homelessness-related nonprofits, and found most of their tweets were mission related. These studies offer useful frameworks and typologies for examining nonprofit advocacy in the social media environment.

Social Media–Driven Attention and the Resource and Relevance Challenges

Given the nature and magnitude of the resource and relevance challenges discussed above, it is somewhat surprising that the extant academic literature has been relatively quiet on understanding and tackling these challenges. Although these challenges are not necessarily initiated by the growth of social media, they are certainly propelled by it.

Social media brings some exciting opportunities to the nonprofit advocacy world. Congressman Joaquin Castro says that for him, social media has greatly changed advocacy by placing him in a "surround sound" environment where he can hear from and engage with advocates from all perspectives (Ory 2017). On the one hand, nonprofit organizations utilize social media to reach out and keep in contact with their stakeholder targets more easily (Carboni and Maxwell 2015; Guo and Saxton 2014b). Social media also offers new tools for nonprofits to raise awareness and conduct outreach (Boles 2013). The rapid diffusion of social media applications also potentially "changes the game" with respect to the types of resources and capacities organizations need and the strategies they may adopt to successfully capitalize on their social media presence (Lovejoy and Saxton 2012). Our read of this collective literature hints at how the advocacy "game" on social media is one in which gaining attention and "being seen" lays the foundation for follow-up advocacy work. For instance, an organization may devote the bulk of its social media messages to increasing awareness of the organization's causes among both current and potential supporters and use only a small but important minority of messages to convert social media interactions into more substantive forms of advocacy actions, such as asking recipients to sign a petition or contact an elected official (e.g., Guo and Saxton 2014b). In effect, the attention paid to social media messages appears to constitute an important mobilizable (or convertible) resource for advocacy organizations.

On the other hand, social media–driven attention also shows signs of limitations. First, social media provides useful tools for advocates to engage with their stakeholders, but these tools are not necessarily enough to mobilize people and turn attitudes into collective action. Skeptics of online advocacy campaigns have charged that this is not real grassroots organizing, but instead "AstroTurf" advocacy (see McNutt and Boland 2007), while others deride it as a lazy form of commitment or "slacktivism" (Karpf 2010). Second, though social media helps strengthen interorganizational connections of some nonprofits, it remains unclear how nonprofits can take advantage of social media to facilitate collective action in policy advocacy. The usual pattern for individual groups interested in forming a new coalition is that the groups get together early on, sit down, figure out their priorities and resources, then find a way to work together to be mutually supportive even as they are going down parallel tracks (Casey and Mehrotra 2011). For existing partnerships, nonprofits can "scratch each other's back" by cross-promoting one another on social media— for example, liking each other's content, reposting each other's posts, promoting each other's events, sharing news and tools from one another's sites, and recognizing and congratulating each other's work (Hou and Lampe 2015). Yet beyond such cross-promotion and information-sharing activities, it remains an open question as to whether and how social media is replacing and/or supplementing the in-person organizing and coordination efforts traditionally required for successful collective action.

In Chapter 2 we delve into the social media context in more depth. Our point here is to argue that the issue of attention—social media–driven attention—holds the key to understanding and tackling both the resource and relevance challenges. First, attention constitutes an important but often over-looked component of the resource challenge faced by a nonprofit advocacy organization. The worldwide proliferation of information and communica-tion technologies has brought in an age characterized by a 24-hour news cycle, powerful Internet search engines, and countless social media outlets. In this altered informational landscape, attention has arguably become a scarce or-ganizational resource. Nonprofit organizations must acquire it in order to at-tract and sustain donors, volunteers, and supporters. The challenge is particu-larly salient when nonprofits begin embracing social networking technologies. Recent research shows the great majority of large and most medium-sized nonprofits are using these information channels. The problem is, if everyone is doing social networking, who is paying attention to your nonprofit? There are no first-mover advantages for adopting these technologies, and just having a Facebook profile is not enough to make your organization unique. With so much to look at but a limited information-processing capacity, how should donors and supporters direct their attention? And what must organizations do to grab and hold it?

Second, the apparent "easiness" of social media attention has led it to be-come a common scapegoat for the perceived shortcomings of contemporary advocacy work. Brady, Young, and McLeod (2015, 270) write, "[People] may become confused or come to believe that simply liking something, sharing something, or signing something via social media will lead to definitive social change." They further argue that "[we] do not believe that social media, by itself, leads to sustainable, long-term social change or attainment of concrete goals. . . . If not for the boots-on-the-ground work of many key people in this effort, the desired outcomes may not have been achieved." Similarly, Harlow and Guo (2014, 463) suggest that "technologies are perhaps pacifying would-be activists, convincing them they are contributing more than they actually are," and thus creating a false sense of impact. Casey (2011) also argues that the ability to "spread the word" electronically has diminished the use of more traditional means such as mass mailings, print media campaigns, and "hit-ting the streets."

In this book, we examine the resource and relevance challenges faced by nonprofit advocacy organizations through the lens of attention. In the re-mainder of the chapter, we set the stage by defining attention, establishing its theoretical and practical significance, and developing a theoretical framework using the concept of attention as the basic building block.

May I Have Your Attention, Please?

Social media offers an alternative broadcast and communication medium for nonprofit organizations, a low-cost and interactive tool for them to speak out and to educate, engage, mobilize, and build rapport with large audiences of supporters. In the meantime, ironically, social media has ushered in a "noisy" information environment that renders it more difficult for nonprofits to make their voices heard. With so much information available through numerous venues, donors and supporters today are better equipped to assess a wider variety of causes and organizations than at any time in the past. However, this abundance of information comes at a price. As Herbert Simon (1971, 40) points out, "a wealth of information creates a poverty of attention." In effect, we find ourselves drowning in information but short of the attention to make sense of it (Lanham 2006). For this very reason, *attention* is regarded by some as the scarcest resource in today's organizations (Davenport and Beck 2001; Ocasio 2011).[4]

Though it has yet to be studied explicitly, the attention deficit problem would appear to be especially critical for advocacy organizations, for whom the capture of public attention is often a prerequisite for achieving any more tangible strategic outcomes (see Tufekci 2013). We maintain that in the context of information overload, a critical (and immediate) measure of the effectiveness of any policy advocacy effort—whether offline or on social media—is the level and type of attention it receives. While offline such attention has been difficult to capture, social media (as a form of Big Data) makes it publicly visible, testable, and comparable (Clark and Golder 2015; Saxton and Waters 2014).

As researchers begin to look into the role of attention in nonprofit advocacy and social movements, it is important to review some of the insights from the existing literature on policy agenda setting that illuminate the dynamics of public attention and its role in enacting social change. In particular, the notion of public attention is at the heart of two influential agenda-setting theories: policy windows and punctuated equilibria. Policy window theory (Howlett 1998; Kingdon 1984) discusses how agenda-setting opportunities (i.e., "policy windows") serve to focus public attention on certain policy issues and move them onto formal government agendas. Punctuated equilibrium theory (Baumgartner and Jones 2010; Jones and Baumgartner 2005) suggests there are extended periods of policy stability when issues receive little attention followed by short periods of increased attention and dramatic policy changes. Both approaches share the view that governments and the public have limited attentional capacities and that they only pay attention to a limited number of issues while ignoring others.

Most of the agenda-setting models operate at the macro level, with the nation or public as their main unit of analysis (Wood and Vedlitz 2007). A general implication of these macro-level theories is that social movements and advocacy organizations influence policy agenda setting by reacting to broad shifts in public attention. In this chapter as well as Guo and Saxton (2018), however, we aim at developing a micro-level approach that complements the macro-level theories. Namely, within the current policy agenda context, what drives the public's attention to an organization and its cause? In short, while advocacy organizations certainly adapt to policy windows and macro-level changes in public attention when promoting their causes, we are interested in how a particular organization garners attention for the messages it sends on social media by connecting and engaging with its target audiences.

The point of departure of a micro-level attention-based theory of nonprofit advocacy is the information overload/attention deficit problem. We argue that public attention is a necessary step for achieving social outcomes, for it is through attention that advocacy organizations are able to convince, connect, counteract, recruit, and mobilize. Within this context, social media presents a valuable tool for mobilizing and garnering attention for nonprofit advocacy organizations, and a growing number of studies have begun to explore whether, why, and how these organizations are using various Web 2.0 and social media tools (Bortree and Seltzer 2009; Edwards and Hoefer 2010; Greenberg and MacAulay 2009; McNutt and Menon 2008; Petray 2011). Among other things, these studies have highlighted the decentralized nature of social media with its highly participatory structure and low barriers to entry, where controlling the organization's message presents a formidable challenge (Edwards and Hoefer 2010; Farrar-Myers and Vaughn 2015). At the same time, the sheer amount of (often redundant) information made available by social media has resulted in a substantial *signal-to-noise* problem (Hermida

2010) whereby it is increasingly difficult for the recipients of information to distinguish useful, desirable information ("signals") from irrelevant information ("noise").

On social media, the "signals" come in the form of the series of brief dynamic updates, or more simply *messages*, the organizations send to their followers. It is through their messages—their tweets, pins, videos, and status updates—that advocacy organizations seek to bring awareness to their struggle (Petray 2011), tighten ties with their community of followers (Guo and Saxton 2014b), and mobilize constituents to collective action (Obar, Zupe, and Lampe 2012). Social media is, in effect, used for a variety of strategic purposes, yet the achievement of each purpose is dependent on the public paying attention to what the organization is saying. Therefore, a key immediate resource for the organization—and measure of the effectiveness of its work on social media—is the level of attention the public pays to its messages.

Differently put, if we want to understand whether organizations' actions on social media are working, we need to zero in on the audience's reaction to the key tools the organizations use—the messages. The audience's immediate reactions to organizations' messages—their sharing, liking, and commenting behaviors—reflect the level of attention they are paying to these messages. Because these reactions are publicly visible and in a standardized, accessible format (Saxton and Waters 2014), we are able to employ quantifiable and comparable measures of the attention different organizations are acquiring from their social media efforts.

Despite this, existing research focuses almost exclusively on either the adoption or organizational uses of social media (e.g., Bortree and Seltzer 2009; Campbell, Lambright, and Wells 2014; Edwards and Hoefer 2010; Greenberg and MacAulay 2009; Guo and Saxton 2014b). Scholars have yet to examine the extent to which advocacy organizations—or, indeed, nonprofit organizations in general—are *effective* in their social media use. We maintain that, in the context of information overload, a critical (and immediate) measure of the effectiveness of any given message—whether online or offline—is the level and type of attention it receives. Yet offline such attention has been difficult to capture. In effect, while attention has always been a key organizational resource, social media (as a form of Big Data) makes visible—and testable—certain phenomena that were previously invisible or not amenable to testing (Clark and Golder 2015). Thus we are able to examine audience attention to social media messages in a context where individual pieces of organizational communication are related to specific, visible, comparable indicators of public attention. In so doing, we are able to capture and test arguments about what determines variation in this key immediate resource. Given the time and effort needed to roll out a social media advocacy campaign, it is imperative that we develop an understanding of what makes these campaigns more or less successful.

The Conceptual Framework

In this section, we present a conceptual framework for understanding the strategies of seeking, sustaining, and transforming attention as nonprofit advocacy organizations work to bring awareness to their struggle, tighten ties with the community of their followers, and mobilize constituents to engage in collective action, both online and offline.

As Figure 1.1 makes clear, the concept of attention serves as a linchpin that connects the main elements of the model and that holds the dynamic process of social media advocacy together.

Network Characteristics

The first dimension of our conceptual model is a recognition that the amount of attention an organization receives depends on the nature of the organization's social media network. The set of characteristics of the organization's audience network has consistently proven to be one of the central determinants of

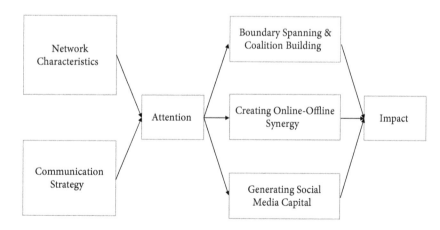

FIGURE 1.1 Attention and impact strategies of nonprofit advocacy organizations

the extent to which the audience reacts (e.g., Bakshy et al. 2011) to new messages. Most research has focused on the size of the network, finding that larger audiences are more likely to generate audience reactions (e.g., Saxton and Waters 2014); however, Liu-Thompkins and Rogerson (2012) have extended this to look at the size of the *audience's* networks as well as the density of the audience network in influencing the diffusion of user-generated network content. Lipsman et al. (2012), in turn, looked at how content interactions were affected by the audience demographics of consumer brands' Facebook page fans. Still other potential characteristics of an organization's social media network come from the field of study known as social network analysis, particularly density, centrality and, more broadly, network position (e.g., Debreceny, Rahman, and Wang 2017). With social media, all of the above measures can be observed by accessing the various platforms' application programming interfaces (APIs), where the number of followers, the number of friends, the number of people engaging with or talking about the organization, and other indicators become directly observable "behavioral traces" that tap the size of the network, however defined. Other features, notably centrality and density, become discernible by applying social network analysis tools to the matrix of dyadic connections of all those comprising that network. The central point is that, in a social network–driven environment like social media, audience effects are mediated by the characteristics of the audience. For this very reason, *network characteristics* have a prominent position in our conceptual model.

Communication Strategy

An organization's overall strategy for social media communication includes three dimensions: timing and pacing, targeting and connecting, and content. First, in light of the dynamic and real-time nature of social media, timing and pacing concerns when and how often an organization sends social media messages. The second dimension, targeting and connecting, directly flows from the importance of social networks in the social media context; through direct and unmediated targeting and connecting efforts, social media greatly expand an organization's potential for interacting and building relationships with its multiple stakeholders while implicitly asking for attention from those targeted by these actions. The third dimension, content, is a recognition that what is said matters. The content of a social media message can be approached and measured in many different ways; in this book, we look at both visual content (e.g., videos and images) and textual content (e.g., value-based language).

Garnering Attention

In our conceptual model depicted in Figure 1.1, attention flows from network characteristics and communication strategy and comes before strategic impact. For nonprofit advocacy organizations, garnering public attention—whether offline or on social media—is a necessary first step for achieving any more tangible strategic outcomes, because it is through attention that advocacy organizations are able to convince, connect, counteract, recruit, and mobilize. As in prior research (Guo and Saxton 2018; Webster 2011), public attention to an organization on social media is defined as "the extent to which multiple audience members (individuals and organizations) react to the messages sent by an organization on its social media platform(s)" (Guo and Saxton 2018, 8).

Boundary Spanning and Coalition Building

As shown in Figure 1.1, in our model the end point is *impact*. Attention is prominently in the middle, in explicit recognition of the fact that it is a means to an end and not an end in itself. To build on attention and reach strategic outcomes, our overarching conceptual model identifies three pathways. A first pathway to impact is *accelerating attention* through boundary spanning and coalition building. Coalition building is one of the key advocacy tactics adopted by nonprofit organizations. The networked nature of social media platforms makes them a natural partner as an organization joins forces with others across organizational and sector boundaries to engage in advocacy work.

Generating Social Media Capital

A second pathway to impact is *transforming attention* garnered on social media by turning it into a new, novel, and highly valuable organizational resource. Labeled as "social media capital" (Saxton and Guo 2014), this new resource is a special form of social capital that is accumulated through an organization's formal online social media network. Organizations generate this key immediate resource through their social media–based activities. Nonprofits cannot expect to get donations, find volunteers, or mobilize constituents for advocacy action simply by being present on social media; rather, they must first build their stock of social media capital through growing and nurturing their networks of social media followers. And they cannot grow and nurture their networks of social media followers without obtaining and sustaining the attention of followers.

Creating Online-Offline Synergy

A third pathway to impact is to *leverage attention* by creating online-offline synergy in the organization's advocacy work. In view of the existence of "an advocacy mix"—a mixture of online and offline advocacy tools—that is at the disposal of any organization, we examine the different ways nonprofit advocacy organizations combine the use of online and social media tools with traditional offline advocacy tactics to influence public policy. We also examine how social media advocacy work is organized and managed in an established organization, and the extent to which the use of social media has added value to and transformed how policy advocacy is done.

Chapter Overviews

In the main body of this opening chapter, we first provided a primer to non-profit advocacy. We went on to identify and discuss two fundamental challenges faced by nonprofit advocacy organizations; namely, the resource challenge and the relevance challenge. Then, after a brief review of the existing literature on social media advocacy, we introduced the concept of attention and highlighted its key role in nonprofit advocacy in a social media age. Finally, we presented a conceptual framework for understanding how nonprofit advocacy organizations seek and sustain attention on social media and how they transform this attention into tangible and strategic organizational outcomes.

With the conceptual framework in mind, in this section we present a short outline of the main chapters of the book. Our subsequent chapters follow the theoretical framework closely: We begin with a discussion of the context of social media advocacy, followed by organizational and message-level analyses of the attention problem and the various strategies that nonprofit advocacy organizations implement to address the attention problem. We then discuss how this quest for attention affects the relevance and impact of nonprofit organizations as they engage in policy advocacy work.

More specifically, in Chapter 2 we provide a conceptual understanding of the social media context. We discuss the evolution of social media, the main types, and their prevalence among nonprofit advocacy organizations. We provide a framework for understanding the central tools available to advocacy organizations for building attention on social media. Regardless of which social media platforms they choose, organizations usually have two main tools at their disposal: making connections and sending messages. Connecting tools are designed to make, build, foster, or maintain ties to a specific member (a particular individual or organization) within an organization's network. Messaging tools are designed to provide value-added content to an organization's audience; over time, the repeat use of message-based connecting also serves to develop ties with new users or strengthen ties with existing users.

In Chapter 3, we present and test an expanded explanatory model for understanding why some advocacy organizations get attention on social media while others do not. The amount of attention an organization receives is modeled as a function of two factors, network characteristics and communication strategy. In colloquial terms, we argue that the extent to which an organization is "being heard" (i.e., the attention it receives) depends on the size of the audience, how much and how the organization speaks, and what it says. Most significantly, in terms of textual content, we find that the inclusion of values-based language has a positive effect on attention. This finding suggests that value framing is a useful strategy for organizations to generate public attention.

In Chapter 4, we extend the organizational-level model presented in Chapter 3 in two important ways: we bring the model down to the message level and we expand the number of variables. We seek to do so in a new way—a way that incorporates machine learning and data analytic methods into the social scientific enterprise. In so doing, we provide a template for scholars similarly interested in using data science methods to expand existing models. More importantly, we use this method to bring insights to bear on what drives attention to individual organizational messages.

Chapter 5, in turn, is concerned with the following question: Does the attention gained by the organization lead to any tangible or intangible organizational outcome? It considers whether and to what extent this social media attention can create a "real" impact for the organization. In this chapter, we discuss three possible pathways by which organizations can turn attention into impact: *accelerate attention* through boundary spanning and coalition building; *transform attention* by generating social media capital; and *leverage attention* by creating online-offline synergy in their advocacy work.

Chapter 6—the concluding chapter—summarizes the preceding chapters while further discussing the theoretical, methodological, and practical implications of the research presented in this book. A key takeaway for the book is to highlight "attention" as a key intermediate goal and an important spring-board for advocacy organizations. Yet we also acknowledge that attention is not the end game: in order to effectively promote their causes, not only must these organizations obtain and sustain public attention on social media, but they also must be able to turn that attention into action and impact.

CHAPTER 2

THE CONTEXT OF SOCIAL
MEDIA ADVOCACY

Chapter 1 has given us a conceptual framework that will guide our subsequent efforts in identifying the variables that are the key drivers, processes, and outcomes of attention in the new social media environment. The goal of this chapter is to provide a deeper understanding of this environment. A core premise of our book is that social media has provided a different context—a more participatory and collaborative and decentralized and communicative context—in which to do advocacy work (e.g., Bortree and Seltzer 2009; Goldkind and McNutt 2014; Guo and Saxton 2014b, 2018; Obar, Zube, and Lampe 2012). It is also a context in which a wide array of different platforms are available on which to do this work. And, it must be said, it is also a context in which attention works differently than in the offline environment. In effect, in order to understand attention on social media—and why our conceptual framework in Chapter 1 is structured as it is—it is necessary to have a solid conceptual understanding of the social media context.

The present chapter is devoted to providing that understanding. To that end we cover four main topics. First, we provide a definition of social media and discuss how it differs from earlier forms of new media. Second, we provide up-to-date empirical data on current adoption rates of the major social media platforms by US-based nonprofit advocacy organizations. Third, we cover the core attention-building tools available on social media; the goal here is to provide a conceptual way of thinking about these tools that facilitates holistic thinking and comparisons across platforms. Last, we discuss the key characteristics of attention on social media, including the nature of the social media "attention market." Upon completing this chapter, the reader should have a good sense of what social media is, how widely it is used, the attention-building tools available to advocacy organizations, and the basics of the social media attention economy.

What Is Social Media?
An Overview of the Context

Web 1.0: The Early Phase of the Web (1993–2003)

In our highly connected world, it is sometimes easy to forget that the emergence of online communication technologies is a relatively recent phenomenon. Though the Internet was initially developed for military and research purposes in the 1960s, popular Internet *services*,[1] particularly the World Wide Web and email, did not become widely available until the 1990s. The World Wide Web (the "Web") went live in 1991, yet free public access to the Web did not begin until 1993.[2] This is also the same year access to email became broadly available to the public through such providers as AOL and Delphi, improving on the efforts of early Internet Service Providers (ISPs) that had begun offering email access as early as the end of the 1980s through the launch of paid services such as CompuServe in 1989. The first widely available free Web browsers were launched in 1993 (Mosaic) and the end of 1994 (Netscape Navigator).

Save for nascent bulletin board systems (BBS), Internet technologies during the first decade of popularity (roughly 1993–2003) featured largely one-way communication, with websites chiefly being static, non-interactive "brochureware."[3] With its dearth of dynamic content and interactivity, this first phase later became denoted as Web 1.0. Despite the lack of interactivity and dynamism, websites and email proved to have great possibilities for, among other things, transparency, accountability, and civic engagement (Saxton, Guo, and Brown 2007; Saxton and Guo 2011; Suárez 2009).

Nonprofit researchers were also quick to pick up on the organizational opportunities for using these early technologies for advocacy purposes (McNutt and Boland 1999). The first wave of research dealt with how predominant Web 1.0 technologies, such as websites and email, were changing advocacy and activism practices (Hick and McNutt 2002; McNutt and Boland 1999; Suárez 2009). Scholars explored the advocacy opportunities and challenges presented by these electronic media (McNutt 2008a) and sought to develop an understanding of the determinants of e-advocacy activities (Goldkind 2014) as well as what makes for effective use of the website for electronic advocacy efforts (Edwards and Hoefer 2010). A now large body of research shows how Web 1.0 technologies have changed the nature of advocacy work (Saxton et al. 2015).

Web 2.0 and Social Media (2003–present)

Toward the end of the 1990s, new digital technologies emerged—particularly instant messaging, blogs, and Internet Relay Chat (IRC)—that contained a greater capacity for *interactive communication* than websites and email (Cameron and Webster 2005; Macias, Hilyard, and Freimuth 2009; Quan-Haase, Cothrel, and Wellman 2005).[4] At the same time, another set of platforms emerged that facilitated the widespread diffusion of *user-generated content*, including blogs, RSS feeds, social bookmarking platforms, image-sharing sites, and wikis (e.g., McNutt 2008b). Given the heightened interactivity and user-generated content, all of these technologies—along with social media—came to be known as Web 2.0 (McNutt 2008b).

Our focus is on what is arguably the most important subset of Web 2.0 technologies: social media. The emergence of a new era of the Internet was heralded by the launch of such sites as LinkedIn and MySpace in 2003, Facebook in 2004, Qzone and YouTube in 2005, Twitter in 2006, WhatsApp in 2009, Instagram and Pinterest in 2010, and WeChat in 2011. Collectively known as *social media*, these sites are distinguished from first-generation (Web 1.0) Internet technologies in terms of the substantially heightened opportunities for direct interactivity, two-way exchange of information, network connectivity, and the creation and exchange of user-generated content (boyd and Ellison 2007; Kane et al. 2014). It is the combination of these features that makes them different from other Web 2.0 platforms—and it has proven to be a powerful combination, with use of social media sites exploding over the past decade and a half. Social media platforms now have a vast audience, with 250 million users on Pinterest, 326 million on Twitter, 303 million on LinkedIn, 1 billion on Instagram, 287 million on SnapChat, 803 million on China's Tencent QQ, and over 2.27 billion users on Facebook (Statista 2019a). In the United States, 79% of adults now use social media (Statista 2019b). Globally, the average social media user spends 2 hours and 22 minutes per day on social media platforms and has 8.5 social media accounts (GlobalWebIndex 2018). Moreover, by one estimate "1 in every 3 minutes spent online is devoted to social media" (GlobalWebIndex 2018) and, overall, 98% of people who are online regularly use social media, such that "being an internet user means being a social media user" (GlobalWebIndex 2018). In brief, the individual, organizational, and societal relevance of social media is huge.

With the widespread adoption of social media platforms by nonprofit organizations has come a growing body of research exploring the role of social media in advocacy work. Studies have successively looked at whether advocacy organizations were using social media (e.g., Bortree and Seltzer 2009), perceptions of the benefits and challenges of social media use (e.g., Goldkind and McNutt 2014; Obar, Zube, and Lampe 2012), and the different ways nonprofit advocacy organizations were using social media in their advocacy work (e.g., Guo and Saxton 2014b). This literature is covered in more detail in other chapters. In this section we are more concerned with outlining what is unique about the social media context and how these unique qualities influence the ways organizations seek and obtain attention. Before delving into that content, in the next section we provide up-to-date data on the prevalence of social media use by nonprofit advocacy organizations.

Nonprofit Participation in the Main Social Media Platforms

In this section we will cover nonprofit participation rates on the major social media platforms. Previous studies of nonprofit organizational adoption of social media have generally shown a steady increase in adoption rates. At the same time, adoption rates have varied widely from study to study depending on the time period, the platforms examined, and the type and size of organizations studied. For example, looking at the nonprofit sector in general, Lovejoy and Saxton (2012) found that in 2009, 73% of the 100 largest nonprofits had a Twitter account. Campbell, Lambright, and Wells (2014), meanwhile, found that in 2012 only 49% of human service organizations had adopted Facebook and only 9% YouTube.

Looking specifically at advocacy organizations, adoption rates have also varied widely depending on the sample. Greenberg and MacAulay (2009), analyzing 43 Canadian environmental organizations in 2009, found 49% of organizations publicized a Facebook account and only 21% a Twitter account. Looking at 48 US-based advocacy groups, Obar, Zube, and Lampe (2012), using a survey-based method that likely reports higher social media usage, found Facebook use was reported by 98% of groups, Twitter by 96% of groups, YouTube by 77% of groups, and LinkedIn by slightly under 40% of groups.[5] Around the same time, looking at the 188 advocacy organizations listed on Charity Navigator in 2012 (Guo and Saxton 2014b), we found 86.7% had a Facebook profile, 79.8% a Twitter account, 71.8% a YouTube channel, and 93.1% any social media account.

Looking at these data, it is somewhat difficult to have an accurate sense of social media adoption by nonprofit organizations and, particularly, advocacy nonprofits. In order to have a robust and up-to-date view of the landscape, we gathered 2019 data on three different samples of organizations. For our first sample, we obtained data from GuideStar on all 4,847 organizations that had set up a valid GuideStar profile. The data shown in the *Sample 1* column of Table 2.1 indicates the percentages of organizations that listed each social media platform in their GuideStar profile.[6] The benefit of this sample is that it represents a broad cross section of the nonprofit sector. Here we see that 70% of nonprofits have any social media account, with 69.3% having a Facebook account and 59.3% a Twitter account. Moreover, on average, each organization has 2.77 social media accounts. This sample also shows adoption rates for additional social media platforms, including Instagram (36.3% of organizations), LinkedIn (34.0%), Pinterest (11.3%), and Google+ (9.7%).

Our second sample (*Sample 2* in Table 2.1) restricts the GuideStar sample to 55 of these nonprofits that have an "advocacy"-related National Taxonomy of Exempt Entities (NTEE) code. What is interesting here are the generally much higher rates of social media adoption for these advocacy organizations. Notably, for Facebook (89.1%), Twitter (78.2%), YouTube (63.6%), and LinkedIn (52.7%), adoption rates are roughly 20% higher than in the general population of nonprofits, and adoption of Google+ is almost double (18.2%) that seen in Sample 1. Pinterest, however, shows a much lower rate of adoption by advocacy nonprofits, being used by only 3.6% of the organizations. Vimeo and Tumblr have similar adoption rates compared to the general population.

Our third sample pertains to the core sample we examine in Chapters 3 and 4 of this book: the 188 advocacy nonprofits rated by the Charity Navigator website. Given that we also looked at these organizations in Guo and Saxton (2014b), this sample has the added benefit of facilitating a cross-temporal comparison in adoption rates for the same set of organizations.[7] These data thus give us the best sense of not only how many medium- and large-sized

ABLE 2.1   Social media adoption rates in three samples of nonprofit organizations

Platform Adoption	Sample 1: All GuideStar Profiles (N = 4,847)	Sample 2: GuideStar "Advocacy" Nonprofit Profiles (N = 55)	Sample 3: Charity Navigator Advocacy Orgs (N = 188)	
			2012 Data	2019 Data
Facebook	69.3%	89.1%	86.7%	97.3%
Twitter	59.3%	78.2%	79.8%	96.8%
YouTube	42.4%	63.6%	71.8%	59.9%
Instagram	36.3%	38.2%	–	43.3%
LinkedIn	34.0%	52.7%	–	25.7%
Pinterest	11.3%	3.6%	–	7.5%
Google+	9.7%	18.2%	–	8.0%
Flickr	6.1%	7.3%	–	5.9%
Vimeo	5.3%	5.5%	–	2.1%
Tumblr	2.4%	3.6%	–	3.7%
Other Account	–	–	–	1.6%
Any Social Media Account	70.0%	89.1%	93.1%	98.9%
Average No. of Social Media Accounts	2.77	3.60	–	3.55

NOTE: This table shows percentage of organizations in three different samples of nonprofit organizations that have adopted each social media platform. Sample 1 comprises all 4,847 organizational profiles on GuideStar for which valid data are available. Sample 2 constitutes the 55 GuideStar organizations with an "advocacy" industry code (in the National Taxonomy of Exempt Entities system). Sample 3 comprises the 188 advocacy organizations listed on Charity Navigator that constitute our primary sample for Chapters 3 and 4. For the 2012 data in Sample 3, not shown is that 42.0% of organizations had an "other" social media account, generally Google+, LinkedIn, Instagram, Vimeo, or Pinterest. Given that we did not gather detailed data on this "other" category and that what is considered "other" is different from the 2019 sample, we have left this off the 2012 column.

advocacy organizations are using social media, but also the change in adoption rates over time.

For the first time period, given the social media landscape at the time, in Guo and Saxton (2014b) we reported the data from 2012 for a more limited set of platforms and found that 86.7% of the 188 organizations had a Facebook account, 79.8% had a Twitter account, 71.8% were on YouTube, 42.0% (see Table 2.1 note) had an account on some other platform such as Google+ or LinkedIn, and 93.1% of the organizations had any social media account. These data are shown in the *Sample 3—2012 Data* column of Table 2.1.

In the *Sample 3—2019 Data* column, in turn, we see the 2019 adoption rates for the 188 advocacy organizations. Overall, we see significant changes in adoption rates in the seven years between data gathering. Facebook adoption increased from 86.7% to 97.3%—a 10.6% increase—which means there is close to universal adoption of Facebook. Twitter saw an even bigger increase, jumping from 79.8% adoption in 2012 to 96.8% in 2019. Interestingly, YouTube adoption dropped, with only 59.9% of organizations using the channel in 2019. Also notable is how in 2019 Instagram has become a popular channel for advocacy work, being used by 43.3% of the organizations. LinkedIn is used by roughly a quarter of the organizations (25.7%). Much less commonly used are Google+ (8.0%), Pinterest (7.5%), Flickr (5.9%), Vimeo (2.1%), and Tumblr (3.7%). Three organizations (1.6%) used other social media platforms; namely one each for SoundCloud (used by the Acton Institute for the Study of Religion and Liberty, https://soundcloud.com/actoninstitute), Medium (American Civil Liberties Union Foundation of Northern California, https://medium.com/@ACLU_NorCal), and Snapchat (Judicial Watch, http://www.judicialwatch.org/snapchat/). Finally, we see that on average each organization has accounts on 3.55 different social media platforms and that, overall, 98.9% of the organizations employ some form of social media channel. From all appearances, we have reached the stage of near-universal adoption of social media—at least by medium- and large-sized advocacy organizations. Social media use no longer appears to be optional.

How Attention Is Acquired: Understanding Social Media's Attention-Building Tools

Each of the social media platforms is unique in some respects: some allow asymmetrical network ties (Twitter, Facebook Pages, Instagram, YouTube, Pinterest) and others not (Facebook for individuals, LinkedIn), and each may focus on text (Twitter), videos (YouTube), images (Instagram, Pinterest, Snapchat), or some combination (Facebook). Nevertheless, we argue there is a common set of overarching affordances, or tools, available on social media sites. In order to understand how organizations garner attention on social media, it is critical to have a solid understanding of the primary attention-building tools. In this section we present a conceptual framework that outlines the three primary tools shown in Figure 2.1: architecture, messages, and connecting actions.

Architecture

At the top level of Figure 2.1 is the *architecture*. It is by far the least important element on social media platforms, but architecture is still important to discuss insofar as it determines how communication is organized and presented

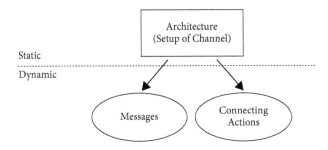

FIGURE 2.1   Primary static and dynamic tools available on social media

to stakeholders and how stakeholders interact with the organization in the online context. In effect, just as classroom interactions with students take place in contexts with different lighting and decorations, room sizes, seating configurations, and technological enhancements—that is, with different architectural choices—online engagement and communication with stakeholders takes place within a specific "architectural" framework.

The notion of architecture is best explained by comparison to a website. When designing a website, the organization needs to consider what information will be shown. It also needs to decide how that information will be organized—including how menus and submenus, folders and subfolders, and pages and subpages will be organized. The decision also includes how—and how extensively—individual pages will be linked. On the back end, the organization needs to decide who is in charge of communication on the website, such as updating information on the website, as well as the technological means (FTP, web-based GUI, etc.) by which the new communication will be added to the site. At the same time, the organization needs to consider how the public will interact with the website. For instance, is the organization interested in having a link to the CEO's email account, a feedback page, or a live online chat? Will there be a search tool on the home page to find a local affiliate? A "donate now" button? What about links to its social media accounts? Or an email or newsletter sign-up box? Will it show off its Charity Navigator or Better Business Bureau (BBB) ratings on the home page? Where does the organization wish to place (if at all) its latest IRS 990 form? Does the organization wish to hide information from nonmembers and require log-in credentials, or even hide the website behind a paywall? How often does the organization wish to update information on the website? Does the organization wish to add widgets to the home page that include the organization's Twitter and/or Facebook feeds? And does the organization wish to have a blog-style website that features the latest blog posts? All of these decisions are *architectural* in nature. They set up the way the organization and users interact with the website content.

The information systems literature would refer to this, more specifically, as the *information architecture* of the organization's website (Allen and Boynton 1991). Generally speaking, the information architecture covers the setup, policies, and rules that relate to an information system; it "specifies how and why the pieces fit together as they do, when they're needed, and why and how changes will be implemented" (Allen and Boynton 1991, 445).[8] In terms of information architecture, websites provide a meaningful contrast to social media. The information architecture of a website is a blank slate. On social media, in contrast, much of the architecture is fixed by the platform; variation in architecture occurs across but not so much within platforms. In effect, after deciding to adopt a particular social media platform, most of the organization's decisions are taken at the dynamic, messaging and connecting, level, which we discuss in the following section.

On certain platforms, such as YouTube, Instagram, Snapchat, Pinterest, and Twitter, the architectural choices available to the organization are minimal and mostly cosmetic. The organization may choose whether to upload a background image, provide a link to a website, provide location information, and give a description of its mission, key activities, or favorite hashtags. The organization may also be able to "pin" certain information or messages on its profile page. All other architectural decisions are predetermined by the platform.

In contrast, other social media sites, notably Facebook, are architecturally fairly rich. On Facebook, similar to designing a website, the organization has considerable flexibility in setting up its Facebook Page. Here the organization makes choices about including features that foster dialogue, interactivity, and community building. For instance, on Facebook, organizations have been able to make choices about whether to open the "Wall" to fan statuses, allow fan picture uploads, or allow replies to fan comments. They could also add a wide range of unique content and third-party apps that foster stakeholder relationships. Extending the notion of information architecture noted above, and incorporating notions of website design and architecture in a variety of fields (e.g., Faiola and Matei 2005; Kwon, Kim, and Lee 2002; Simon and Peppas 2005), we refer to these static elements as architectural, insofar as they create the "design," "framework," "venue," "setting," or "space" within which engagement and dialogic interactions can take place; these relatively static features constitute the environment within which relationship building may occur.

The most basic aspect of the architecture on a Facebook page, or any of the other main social media platforms, is what we might think of as *informational choices*, where we can consider relevant any information that organizations make available that might help facilitate engagement with stakeholders. If we were following early social media literature, here we might consider relevant contact information or basic details of the organization's mission or history. With few exceptions almost the entire early "engagement" literature (save for the survey-based and experimental studies) focused on this static informational component, with both website and social media studies commonly employing the Kent and Taylor (1998) framework to code details such as the presentation of staff email addresses on websites (Taylor, Kent, and White 2001) or profiles on Facebook (Bortree and Seltzer 2009; Waters et al. 2009) or Twitter (Rybalko and Seltzer 2010). However, on platforms with strong, built-in two-way communication capabilities such as Facebook, such informational features only weakly indicate an organization's relationship-building intent. More relevant for social media is a relatively new type of information we found on the Boy Scouts of America's Digital Community Contract, a code of conduct that describes the types of comments that are encouraged or discouraged, the types of comments that will be deleted, and the actions that will cause a fan to be "defriended."

Yet architectural choices go beyond the provision of information. For example, on the Nature Conservancy's Facebook fan page, in addition to constant features of "liking" statuses and becoming a "fan" of the organization, visitors could, among other things, "join" an Earth Day picnic, post comments and statuses, donate money, invite friends to donate to or to join the cause, sign up to receive email, create a "birthday wish," or post a supporter "badge" in their newsfeed. Other dialogic or interactive features and settings can also be enabled during the setup of the organization's Facebook channel. For instance, in a previous review of nonprofits' Facebook pages we found meaningful variation around several key settings related to the sharing and tagging of visual content and to the ability of fans to make posts and replies. In short, a number of architectural features beyond information provision serve to structure the space in which public interactions and hence relationship building can take place.[9]

Though it takes minimal effort on the organization's part to enable these features, they can make a difference in a site's dialogic and interactive potential, which in turn could influence the amount of attention the organization receives. Still, it is worth reiterating that all of the above are facets of the static architecture of Facebook. We should thus think of them as reflecting the organization's *intent* to engage in relationship building, but they do not directly represent communicative efforts. For that, we now turn to the dynamic elements of relationship building on social media.

Dynamic, Communicative Actions: Sending Messages and Making Connections

Juxtaposed to the static architectural features of a social medium are the day-to-day steps an organization takes to connect and communicate with the public. Here organizations have the ability to dynamically engage in interactive relationship-building activities by sending messages and through a variety of communicative and network-based "connecting" behaviors.

It is here that social media adds something not seen on websites. Compared to websites, which are sometimes pejoratively referred to as "brochure-ware," social media platforms are inherently more dynamic. While a more static website may be developed by a Web developer with input from organizational staff, the day-to-day content that appears on an organization's Facebook or Twitter account reflects the active communicative, connecting, and relationship-building decisions made by organizational staff (Saxton and Waters 2014). The audience's reactions to and engagement with the organization's content are similarly dynamic and publicly visible (Saxton and Waters 2014; Smith 2012). In effect, social media facilitates the capture of the day-to-day communicative interactions by a given entity or within a given network.

How attention is acquired on social media is also distinct from offline settings. Whereas offline attention may be gained in a hugely diverse number of settings—ranging from golf outings to dinner parties, investment clubs, church attendance, and postcards—attention on social media can only emerge from the two specific sets of actions available on social media platforms: sending messages and formal or informal connecting behaviors. The term *communication network* (Monge and Contractor 2003) thus fits social media platforms perfectly: they are, fundamentally, dynamic *networks*, with actors dynamically connecting with and disconnecting from other actors;

and what flows through these networks is *communication*, in the form of the stream of messages that are sent.

In brief, regardless of which social media platforms they choose, organizations only have two notable day-to-day tools at their disposal: sending messages and making connections. It is these two actions that comprise the heart of what is afforded by social media and separate them from earlier, more static forms of new media. We discuss each of the two tools in turn.

Sending Messages

A key feature of social media is its dynamic updating and messaging capabilities. The videos on YouTube, photos on Instagram, pins on Pinterest, messages on LinkedIn, tweets on Twitter, and status updates on Facebook can all be thought of discrete dynamic updates or, more succinctly, "messages" the organization is sending to its public audience—and it is these messages that comprise the chief communicative activity on social media (de Vries et al. 2012; Lovejoy and Saxton 2012; Saxton and Waters 2014; Swani, Milne, and Brown 2013). They represent the continual, dynamic steps an organization takes to engage with the public and hence acquire, maintain, and mobilize resources. In contrast to the static architecture element of social media sites, it is the messages that represent the continual, dynamic steps an organization takes to engage with the public and hence acquire, maintain, and mobilize resources.

Figure 2.2 shows sample messages on three different platforms from one of our core sample organizations: the ACLU. The Instagram message contains an image accompanied by text, the Facebook message contains text and a video, and the Twitter message contains text and a reference to another tweet (which has both text and an image) by *@thehill*.

The messages the nonprofit sends are designed to provide value-added content to the organization's strategically identified ideal audience. The extent to which the organization can effectively develop and maintain a social media network depends on whether the messages are meeting and exceeding what the network wants from the organization.

Making Connections: Message- and Network-Based Connecting Actions

The preceding section dealt with messages an organization crafts to engage or connect with members of the public. Organizations are also able to employ a number of other dynamic tools for forging ties with new or existing community members. As with messages, these are not static features of the medium,

FIGURE 2.2 Sample messages by the ACLU on Instagram, Facebook, and Twitter

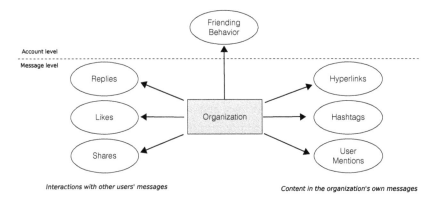

FIGURE 2.3 Types of "connecting" actions organizations can take on social media

but rather dynamic actions the organization undertakes on a continual basis to foster community ties. We therefore refer to these collectively as *connecting actions*. These connecting behaviors are relationship building because they are discrete actions that make or solidify a connection to another user. They are, in effect, a means of establishing a new tie or, if to a user with whom the organization already has a connection, of boosting tie strength (Gilbert and Karahalios 2009; Granovetter 1973; Worrell, Wasko, and Johnston 2013). Each new connection effectively adds to the size of the network, while repeated interactions can bolster tie strength, foster stronger community norms and values, and ultimately help improve the organization's network position. They build relationships by forging ties to specific members of the public.

Social media provides a much richer connecting environment than prior forms of new media. Figure 2.3 shows seven types of connections to outside users, groups, and movements that organizations can make on Twitter and Facebook: friending, hyperlinks, hashtags, user mentions, replies, likes, and shares. As shown in the figure, these behaviors occur at two different levels: the account, or organizational, level and the message level.

Friending Behavior

As shown in Figure 2.3, the only account-level, or network-based, connecting action is that which might typically come to mind when thinking of social networking sites: the organization's friending and following behavior. On all social media sites, organizations have the ability to follow and/or be followed by other users of the site. An organization's decision to follow (aka "friend") another user reflects the decision to make a *formal* connection to that user (Lovejoy, Waters, and Saxton 2012; Westerman, Spence, and Van Der Heide 2012).

Organizations' following behaviors are important for a key reason: they show the organization's interest in listening to, gathering information from, and connecting to and engaging with other individual and organizational users. As argued by Lovejoy, Waters, and Saxton (2012), following users that follow an organization gives the impression the organization is interested in what its followers are talking about, even if it never actually reads this information. In signaling the organization's interest in establishing a *reciprocal* relationship, organizations that actively create mutual ties with followers are sending a signal of their interest in creating an online community.[10] Overall, organizations' following behavior effectively helps the nonprofit build a form of *attention network*—a community of users who will be the first to see the organizations' messages.

There are two key features of these formal social network connections. First, on all social media sites they are *binary*: either you are connected or you are not. At the level of individual connections, it is thus a decision that the organization makes only once. Yet at the organizational level it is fundamentally a dynamic part of the social media context insofar as it represents the organization's day-to-day decisions about whom to follow. That said, there are important differences among platforms regarding a second key feature of these connections: their *symmetry*. On some platforms, such as Twitter or Instagram, the connection can be asymmetrical: the organization does not need to "friend" any of its followers if it does not wish to. By the same token, the organization can follow any other user it chooses. On other platforms, such as LinkedIn, a connection can be made only if it is symmetrical: both parties must agree to a simultaneous friend/follower relationship. Second, on certain platforms, notably Facebook, friending/following behavior by the organization is not possible. For example, in early 2019 the ACLU's Facebook page was liked or followed by more than 2 million other Facebook users, yet because of the Facebook system's architecture for organizational pages, the ACLU page was not able to follow any other Facebook users. The friend/follower relationships on Facebook are fundamentally asymmetrical (fans "like" the organization, but not vice versa).

In short, on all major social media platforms save for Facebook, the binary formal connections a nonprofit makes demonstrate the organization's interest in engaging with other users and signal its interest in creating an online community. Yet there is tremendous variation in how organizations use the formal connecting tool.[11]

Message-Based Connections

As shown in Figure 2.3, the remaining six connecting actions occur at the message level—in the messages users send on a social media platform. Each of these actions serves to foster a *message tie* with other targeted user(s) on the platform. Depending on the "target," these connections can serve either to strengthen the organization's ties to its current follower base or to develop ties with new users and expose the organization's current followers to new information, ideas, movements, actors, or events. Furthermore, these connecting actions typically serve as calls for attention themselves, insofar as the automatically triggered notifications to the targeted user(s) implicitly ask for a reaction. As reflected in Figure 2.3, three of these actions—hyperlinks, hashtags, and user mentions—occur in the organization's *own messages,* while the other three—sharing, replying, and liking/"emoting"—occur in the organization's interactions with *other users' messages.* What binds all of them is that they serve to forge a message tie with other users on the platform.

To shed light on the six actions, we will focus on Twitter. In the early stages of the social media era there were notable differences in which message-level tools were available depending on the platform, but there has been a marked convergence over time, such that now all six actions are typically available on each of the main platforms.

Hyperlinks. Three of the message-based connecting behaviors are made through the messages the organizations send on social media. The first of these is the hyperlink. It is the oldest and most established tool and, by extension, the most "Web 1.0" of all the connecting tools. The hyperlink is the crudest of all connecting actions for a simple reason: it is difficult for the target of the connection (the user or organization to which the hyperlink points) to be aware that a connecting action has been made. Hyperlinks are, in other words, less important (though still useful) as connecting tools, and more important as informational tools. Namely, when the link is to an external source, hyperlinks indicate the organization's efforts to connect its current followers to outside information (Lovejoy, Waters, and Saxton 2012). The use of hyperlinks thus serves as a way of infusing new information into the online community. For example, the following tweet by the advocacy organization OpenSecrets.org contains a link to an article from the *Dayton Daily News* (the linked article becomes embedded at the bottom of the tweet).[12]

> *.@daytondailynews* finds the net worth of Ohio's members of #Congress grew by an average of 78% since first elected https://t.co/JlG6huAwAZ

User Mentions. The second connecting tool is the user mention. User mentions are a means of formally linking a message to specific Facebook, LinkedIn, Instagram, or Twitter user(s) and thus forming a *message tie* between the sender and the mentioned user, often a form of public acknowledgment or recognition. User mentions are now a standard feature on all of the major social media platforms.[13] Messages containing user mentions can potentially serve to strengthen the relationship between the organization and the identified user, especially insofar as the target of the user mention will receive a notification that the user mention has occurred. For instance, in the sample tweet above, the advocacy organization OpenSecrets starts the message with a user mention of the *Dayton Daily News*'s Twitter account by prepending the @ symbol to the account username *daytondailynews*. The inclusion of *@daytondailynews* indicates that OpenSecrets is "talking about" the *Dayton Daily News*. The newspaper will receive a notification that it has been mentioned in a tweet by @*OpenSecretsDC*; moreover, anyone who follows or searches for messages mentioning the *Dayton Daily News* will also be able to find and read the message. In effect, when an advocacy organization includes a user mention in one of its social media messages, it is initiating or engaging in a public conversation either with or about the mentioned user.

Hashtags. The third message-based tool organizations can employ is the hashtag. While they were originally unique to Twitter, they are now a standard feature of major social media platforms.[14] Denoted by the # sign, such as in the #Haiti hashtag used in the aftermath of the 2010 earthquake in Haiti, hashtags help build a community of users around something abstract, such as disaster-relief efforts (*#WeAreAlabama*), academic conferences (*#arnova19*), social movements (*#IranElection*), companies (*#Apple*), concepts (*#healthcare, #CharityFraud*), and public-health campaigns (*#DontFryDay*). By including the hashtag *#Congress* in the sample message above, OpenSecrets.org seeks to engage in a conversation with those interested in that US political institution.

The use of hashtags serves to foster organization-public relationships by strengthening existing ties or by broadening the community—all users employing the same tag form an ephemeral yet potentially important hashtag network (e.g., Chang 2010) or *ad hoc public* (Bruns and Burgess 2011). At the same time, when a hashtag is related to a specific event, it focuses the community's attention, such that the use of the hashtag can serve to rapidly mobilize a community into a transitory yet effective force. When the hashtag pertains to a concept, in turn, the hashtag can serve to either widely diffuse information throughout a set of interconnected networks, or it can serve as the means through which information is *aggregated* from a diffuse network of interested constituents. Overall, the use of hashtags is a connecting action insofar as it helps connect the organization to the other members of the ad hoc communities that form around the hashtag (Saxton et al. 2015).

Liking. The remaining three connecting tools are used in interacting with *other users' messages.* They are, in effect, indications that the organization has been paying attention to these other users' messages. The first of these tools is what we call a "like," using the name from Facebook, Twitter, Instagram, and LinkedIn. This action sends a signal to the target (the original message sender) that the organization views the message as valuable, important, or informative. On some platforms, liking also serves as an archiving function (Lovejoy, Waters, and Saxton 2012). On Pinterest, for example, the archiving element is explicit, with the liking function (called *pinning*) accomplished through a "Save" button. Facebook is also somewhat unique in its liking capabilities; since 2016, the Like function allows users to hit the Like button and then choose from six "emoji reactions": *Like, Love, Haha, Wow, Sad,* or *Angry.* All of these actions indicate that the organization has paid attention to the message and that it has some nonneutral reaction to it.

On Twitter, the name of anyone who marked a message as a favorite (officially called a "like" since 2015) is visible through the "heart" icon (as with Instagram) underneath a given message.[15] For example, a Twitter user tweeted the following message that mentioned one of our advocacy organizations, the Chicago Foundation for Women (*@ChiFdn4Women*):

> *The agenda for Chicago's next mayor for women and girls from @ChiFdn-*
> *4Women What Chicago's first female African-American mayor can do for girls,*
> *women https://t.co/tysocuynua*

This tweet received one like, which was from the *@ChiFdn4Women* account.[16] In line with our earlier discussion, the original message sender will receive a notification that the organization has liked the message. This message connection serves to help build a relationship with the targeted user. It is also worth reiterating that this message tie will also be publicly visible to any other user.

Sharing. The second form of message interaction is to share or repost a message to all of an organization's followers. Sharing suggests the organization believes the other user's message has "pass-along" value (Cha et al. 2010). On Facebook and LinkedIn this is known as sharing, and on Twitter it is a retweet. On Pinterest the functionality is more limited, though a pin can be "sent" to other (specific) users. On Instagram, meanwhile, *reposting* or *regramming* is not an official part of the platform's architecture but can be done through third-party apps. On the sites with full sharing capabilities (especially Facebook, LinkedIn, and Twitter), the sharing action is more powerful than the liking action; for a retweet being sent out to all of the organization's followers, the threshold of value needs to be higher in order that the organization not be seen as "polluting" its feed with irrelevant messages.

In any case, when an organization does choose to share information created by an external user (one that does not follow the organization), the organization's followers potentially become exposed to new information. And when the original tweet was sent by one of the organization's current followers, it helps strengthen ties to the current user. In effect, what makes this a form of *connecting action* is the fact that sharing a message is an implicit endorsement of the user who originally posted the message, forging a message tie between the originator and disseminator. The following is an example of a tweet that one of our organizations, Connecticut Legal Services, chose to retweet:

> *Even better news—DHS to release both CT children and parents today, for immediate reunification and freedom! @WiracYis @CTLegal . . .*

Replying. The final connecting tool is what is known on Twitter as a reply and on Facebook, LinkedIn, and Pinterest as a comment. In replying to or commenting on a message, the organization indicates it is interested in initiating dialogue (Kent and Taylor 1998; Unerman and Bennett 2004) with the message sender. Of the three interactions, a reply represents the highest level of effort. In terms of public attention to organizational messages, in the sample tweet shown earlier in Figure 2.2 we can see that the organization's tweet received close to 4,000 replies. The following is an example of an advocacy organization's replying action. Replying to a tweet from the Oakland Literacy Coalition (*@oaklandreads*), the Taproot Foundation (*@taprootfound*) tweeted:

> *Thanks for helping us spread the word! We're looking forward to connecting with you or your partner orgs w/ #skilledvolunteers for projects in mktg, finance, tech, and more.*

Summary of Connecting Tools

Connecting actions are designed to make, build, foster, or maintain ties to a specific individual or organizational member within an organization's strategically determined network. Each connecting action to a new target adds to the size of the organization's *attention network,* while future interactions serve to strengthen the bond. In addition to being a building block of network creation, each connecting action also implicitly serves as a call for attention.

As described above, organizations can employ a variety of different connecting tools at a number of levels. At the account level, friend/follower ties establish a formal link between organization and user. At the message level, in interacting with other users' messages, the organization has three tools at its disposal: liking, sharing, and replying. Three additional connecting actions—hyperlinks, hashtags, and user mentions—are used by the organization within its own messages; these tools are not mutually exclusive, such that organizations can include more than one in a given message. What binds all seven types of connecting actions is that they comprise distinct ways of connecting or linking an organization to another user, with the effect that the bond between users is either established or strengthened.

Whenever an organization retweets or shares another user's message, replies to or comments on that message, likes a message, or includes in one of its messages a hyperlink to or a mention of another user, it is forming a message tie to that other actor. Reciprocal use of these ties can foster greater reciprocity and thus further develop tie strength (Gilbert and Karahalios 2009; Worrell, Wasko, and Johnston 2013). The use of hashtags can similarly help connect the organization to the other members of the ad hoc publics (Bruns and Burgess 2011) that form around the hashtag. Each of these connecting tools can either bolster the organization's ties to its current follower base or develop ties with new users, all while exposing the organization's followers to new people, ideas, information, or events.

All of these tools are important given the power of the social network on social media. In order to garner attention, the organization needs to strategically build a social network—a community of social media users—and it builds such a network through relationship-building connecting actions. These relationship-building activities are reflected in the seven connecting tools available to organizations on the social media platforms. The organization's friending actions, retweets/shares, likes, replies, user mentions, hyperlinks, and hashtags are the "digital footprints of the organization-stakeholder relationship" (Smith 2012, 842).

The framework above presents an expanded and more theoretically precise conceptualization of how an organization can make connections with members of the public on social media. Prior research looking at websites had looked at hyperlink connections (Park, Barnett, and Nam 2002), but the meaning of these connections was somewhat vague and, with the advent of syndicated content and other changes, has become less clear over time. On social media the nature of connections is different. To start, in line with what others have studied at the individual level (e.g., Valenzuela, Park, and Kee 2009), there are the formal, binary social network connections available on social media sites. This is something that was not possible on a large scale with organizational websites, yet is a central feature of Twitter and Facebook, among other platforms. To the extent that social networking tools become further integrated into new media applications, this element of organization-public relations will become increasingly central. We have incorporated these social network links into the concept of relationship-building connections while also expanding the idea with the notion of message-based connecting actions. In effect, the nature of connecting with other users on social media goes beyond the binary social network links that others have studied. The framework we have presented takes into account the way that organizations are able to form a connection with other users through the sharing, liking, and discussion of other users' messages and the inclusion of external hyperlinks, user mentions, and hashtags in their own messages. All in all, social media platforms such as Twitter and Facebook represent a rich connecting environment.

Summary of Social Media Architecture and Attention-Building Tools

We have argued here that there are three main components to organizations' relationship-building efforts on social media: the static features, or *architecture*, of the site, the dynamic *messages* sent, and the organization's dynamic *connecting actions*. While the static elements set up the "space" in which relationship building can occur, the dynamic elements serve as visible, day-to-day manifestations of an organization's attempts at engaging and interacting with new and existing constituencies. It is through these dynamic social media tools that the organization seeks to garner attention from the public.

The explicit delineation of relationship building into static and dynamic elements is important, for it better represents how social media applications facilitate dialogue, interactivity, and relationship building. On social media sites such as Facebook and Twitter, the relationship-building and attention-building "action" is not in the static design of an organization's page, but rather in the discrete, day-to-day actions the organization takes through the sending of messages and the active linkages it makes to individual and group members of its online community.

In short, engagement with the public on social media is unique in terms of how it comes about almost wholly through a set of two specific communicative actions—what we refer to as messages and connecting actions. It is these two actions that comprise the heart of what is afforded by social media. It is these two actions that separate social media from earlier, more static forms of new media. It is these two actions—and these two actions alone—that capture the day-to-day relationship-building decisions made by organizations on social media. And it is these two actions that enable organizations to acquire resources—and garner attention—through their social media–based efforts.

Understanding Attention in the Social Media Environment

Up to this point in the chapter we have covered the definition and characteristics of social media, the adoption rates of social media by nonprofits, and the primary attention-building tools available on social media sites. We now turn our attention to attention; here we will discuss the key characteristics of the social media "attention economy."

The Zero-Sum Attention Economy

Because of the unique nature of social media, attention is also unique in this context. In Chapter 1 we provided an overview of the centrality of attention for contemporary advocacy organizations. Here we will elaborate on several key points that are specific to the social media context. The first important point to understand, reiterating a point from the previous chapter, is that attention is a *scarce resource.* Even in a social media era there are, after all, still only 24 hours in a day and 7 days in a week. Moreover, one can only pay attention to one thing at a time; at any given moment in time, if you are paying attention to one piece of information, it means all the other pieces of information have "lost." For this very reason attention, unlike, say, altruism, is a *zero-sum* game. If one organization "wins" the attention of a consumer, all other organizations have "lost" during that specific period of time.

Because of these fundamental qualities, it is helpful to think of attention by using the analogy of the "attention economy" (Davenport and Beck 2001). An attention economy certainly existed before the rise of the Internet and social media, and furthermore exists offline as well as online. Yet it is precisely because of the Internet that this analogy has only recently become popular—chiefly due to the explosion of information engendered by the rise of the Internet. With its low barriers to entry, lack of gatekeepers, and decentralized structure (boyd and Ellison 2007; Kane et al. 2014; Tufekci 2013), almost anyone could become a producer and disseminator of information. With the daily tsunami of information flowing into people's inboxes and social media screens, it has become common to talk about feelings of information overload (see Eppler and Mengis 2004). It is within this context that the economic analogy has taken root; with so much choice about which information to consume yet limited time, the analogy of an attention economy makes sense.

Moreover, the pace of data creation is increasing. In 2013, it was suggested that over 90% of the data in existence had been created in just the previous two years (Jacobson 2013). Another estimate predicted that by 2020, for every person on the planet, 1.7 MB of data would be generated per second (Domo 2018). Just focusing on social media, the scale of this "market" is huge. To help lend some context to this, we can refer to our focal platform Twitter. A rough estimate is that 473,400 tweets are sent each minute (Domo 2018). Using the analogy of the attention economy, the minute an advocacy organization sends a tweet—offering a new message for consumption in the attention market—it is competing with 473,399 other messages for the consumer's attention. Unless the organization is strategic, the odds are low that the message will win a significant market share.

How Does the Social Media Attention Market Work?

To recap: the participants involved in sending and receiving social media messages are the producers and consumers of an enormous global attention market. The first key to understanding this market for attention on social media is to understand the fundamental role of the social network.

The Primacy of the Social Network

Perhaps the defining feature of social media, and what differentiates it from prior forms of new media such as websites and blogs, is the primacy of the formalized social network (e.g., Kaplan and Haenlein 2010; Kietzmann et al. 2011).Whereas a website can be viewed by anyone with an Internet connection, few activities occur on social media without being mediated by a formal friend/follower relationship. Messages are the key social media tool (Lovejoy and Saxton 2012; Saxton and Waters 2014), and who reads these messages—whether they be tweets or status updates or photos—is largely determined by the set of users who have formed a formal, typically binary (on/off) friend or follower relationship with the message sender. On social media, the social network is key.

The privileging of the social network—and the extremely tight relationship between the social network and organizational outcomes—is distinct from what occurs offline. Offline, a nonprofit organization could, for instance, hold a fundraising event that would be attractive enough to raise funds in the absence of a large preexisting network, and in many cases a lasting network would not be built as an offshoot from the fundraising event. Similarly, offline, a TV ad could reach millions without a firm having any substantial social capital or preexisting social network; at the very least, the size of the audience is divorced from the organization's social capital. This would be highly improbable on social media: without a preexisting (even if extremely new) network, a message would simply not reach a large enough number of followers to be successful. In short, offline, the relationship between social capital and audience outcomes is tenuous; on social media, it is paramount.[17]

For these reasons, social media theoreticians have posited we are becoming a network society (Castells 1996), where being "networked" is "the new social operating system" (Rainie and Wellman 2012, 3). Wellman's (2002) hypothesis is that *networked individualism* constitutes a new form of social arrangement, one where people are networked as individuals as opposed to members of densely knit, hierarchical traditional groups, communities, families, or bureaucracies. Ties are built around looser, more diffuse, more ephemeral, and more diverse communities of interest to the individual or organizational user. The implication is that networks are more purposive and, by extension, more instrumental. Organizations' attempts at building strategic networks are thus ever more important in this new, networked social environment. Ultimately, there is compelling evidence that the primacy of networks is the new normal. The strong implication for attention is that the attention a given organizational message receives will be heavily influenced by the characteristics of the network in which it is sent—meaning not only the size of the network but also the organization's position within that network, the density and structure of the network, the type of users belonging to it, and the strength of the organization's ties to community members (e.g., Gilbert and Karahalios 2009; Kane et al. 2014; Worrell, Wasko, and Johnston 2013; Xu et al. 2014). In brief, on social media messages are sent and attention is acquired within a heavily networked context. The quality of the network an organization builds is therefore a critical factor in determining how well the organization fares in the attention economy.

Characteristics of Social Networks on Social Media

In effect, attention is garnered in a particular form of social sphere: the public, formal online social networks described above (Hanna, Rohm, and Crittenden 2011; Kaplan and Haenlein 2010). This is important, for the nature and characteristics of the networks that are formed on social media are distinct, which in turn influences how attention is gained. The differences are many. To start, in line with Wellman's (2002) arguments, social media–based networks are generally more purposive, more instrumental, and less hierarchical. These social networks are also often more geographically dispersed as spatial boundaries become less important barriers.

More important from a resource development perspective is that, unlike in the offline world, on social media one's network position—and the amount of social capital and attention accrued—is generally public, transparent, and eminently measurable (Anger and Kittl 2011; Bakshy et al. 2011; Bruns and Stieglitz 2012; Cha et al. 2010). The size of the attention network built by an organization—and the amount of attention ultimately garnered—is public and quantifiable.

Network resources—and the attention those networks give—are also formed at a different pace (Bakshy et al. 2011; Meeder et al. 2011; Myers and Leskovec 2014). Both the networks and the network-driven attention are gained and lost more quickly online than offline. With the low costs and low barriers to entry, social networks on social media sites are more variable, with a more ephemeral, ever-changing, fluid network composition. Yet the social media network does not have to be enduring for it to be effective. The rapid conglomeration of individuals for a temporary, focused effort is what Bruns and Burgess (2011) call "ad hoc publics." The ALS Association's #Ice-BucketChallenge of 2014 (Miller 2014) provides a salient example. Here, via a series of fortuitous celebrity connections, a far-reaching, temporary social network centered on the #IceBucketChallenge hashtag rapidly developed, through which viral messages and fundraising actions quickly spread.[18] Similarly, though the #ARNOVA19 network dissipated rapidly after the conference participants left San Diego, the network served a temporally, geographically, and topically meaningful purpose. The point is that both the primacy and the ephemerality of the socially embedded network resources on social media are distinctive.

A corollary of the more ephemeral, more loosely knit, more diverse, and less hierarchical and bureaucratic nature of the social media–based social networks (Wellman 2002) is that they are based on *weak ties* (Granovetter 1973). The networks primarily form around communities of interest rather than geography, family, or bureaucracy (Castells 1996; Rainie and Wellman 2012; Wellman 2002). These communities of interest can center on a hobby, a brand, an idea, a social movement, an organization, a knowledge community, a social identity, or countless other facets of daily existence. Just as important is how new media facilitates the development of communities of interest in the *long tail* (Anderson 2004; Brynjolfsson, Hu, and Smith 2006); communities that are specialized and/or hyperpersonalized in terms of topic, location, or time are now commonplace. The flourishing of brand communities, specialized knowledge communities, ice bucket challenges, social support systems for rare diseases, and viral marketing campaigns all flow from the ease with which hyperspecialized communities of interest take shape on social media.

Social media hence provides a mechanism by which organizations can rapidly form weak ties with a specialized and often geographically dispersed audience. In this way, social media provides a communication channel that helps an organization reach a broader array of *diffused* stakeholders at a much lower cost (Saxton and Guo 2014). The stakeholders are diffused in that none of them "has command over a significant proportion of the (stakeholder) group's total resources" and in that the ability of stakeholders to act collectively is constrained by the prohibitive cost of coordination among them (Hill and Jones 1992, 140). For instance, for a nonprofit organization, these might be the general members of the public; for a business-to-consumer firm, these could be the members of a brand community. In both cases, social media is what renders feasible sustained and/or concentrated managerial attention on such diffused stakeholders.

A final distinctive characteristic of social media networks is that they are categorically a specific form of social network: the *communication network* (Monge and Contractor 2003; Vergeer, Lim, and Park 2011). The linkages made between individuals in the network are centered around the communication flows engendered by sending, receiving, and interacting with social media messages. Offline, what links any two nodes in a social network could be kinship, sharing a disease, lending a book, a piece of gossip, belonging to the same criminal organization, or attendance at the same church; differently put, what flows through the offline social network could be marriage, membership, disease, books, money, rumors, or almost any social or physical artifact. On social media, though, the fundamental tie is communicative.

A corollary is that *communication-based activities* are privileged in social media networks. Fundamentally, each social media platform is comprised of networks designed to facilitate the flow of communication. Anything that can be communicated—information, rumors, messages, knowledge, ideas, memes, emotion, sentiment, affect, greetings, insults, compliments, and opinions—is fertile ground for making its way rapidly through these geographically dispersed, loosely connected networks. It is thus that social media possesses a singular ability to fulfill the informational needs of users (Hargittai 2007; Shirky 2011), a key ingredient for strengthening weak ties and promoting collective action (Kenski and Stroud 2006; Shah, Kwak, and Holbert 2001). It is also why (with the easy ability to publicly target and converse with individual users) notions of conversation, dialogue, and community building have garnered considerable attention in social media–based public relations, stakeholder relations, and corporate social responsibility research (Bruning, Dials, and Shirka 2008; Kent and Taylor 1998; Lovejoy and Saxton 2012; Rybalko and Seltzer 2010; Saxton and Guo 2011; Saxton and Waters 2014; Unerman and Bennett 2004). A final, interesting side note from the organizational perspective is *what* and *who* is involved in the production of social networks in the context of social media. It is communicative activities and it is communication experts rather than, say, socializing skills and those who excel on the golf course or the conference circuit.

In sum, almost any outcome of importance on social media—attention included—is mediated by social networks. Moreover, the nature of these networks is different on social media than it is offline. Understanding this funda-mental social network context is of utmost importance if one is to understand how attention works on social media.

Empirical Observability of Attention: An Open, Transparent Market

The social media attention economy is also notable for its transparency. On the major social media platforms, each organization's performance in the atten-tion market is in the public domain. The reason lies in the fact that the amount of attention the public pays to an organization and its messages is visible in the "digital footprints" of organization-stakeholder relationships (Smith 2012). Most concretely, attention is visible in the audience's interactions with the orga-nization and its messages. In fact, the same connecting tools we noted earlier are available for members of the public to interact with the organizations' mes-sages. When the public follows the organization and likes, shares, or replies to its messages, we are able to observe these interactions and take them as indications of public attention. Interested members of the public—academics, potential donors, collaborators, grantmakers, competitors, and others—can all examine these visible "digital footprints."

Attention Goes to the Dramatic

The attention market features competition among millions of content produc-ers. This market generates pressure to "sell" messages that stakeholders are willing to consume. In this context it is perhaps not surprising that some orga-nizations would seek to highlight content that is more exciting or dramatic.

On the "demand" side, the literature provides some initial evidence of this. Looking at nonprofit crowdfunding on Facebook, Saxton and Wang (2014) found qualitative evidence of more exciting projects being fully funded, such as those sponsored by celebrities, those featuring creative endeavors (e.g., movie production), and those involving the construction of buildings, playgrounds, etc. On the "supply" side, none of the nonprofits examined in the study posted requests to fund pressing yet mundane concerns such as an audit, computer replacement, staff training, or updating an organization's ac-counting information system.

There is also evidence that the architecture of social media platforms may be pushing more exciting and extreme content. Notably, the suggestion algo-rithms of certain platforms, especially YouTube (Tufekci 2018) and to a lesser extent Facebook, push the user to more and more "radical" content, such as conspiracy theories. Overall, there appears to be some evidence that the market for attention has a preference for the dramatic.

The Power Law: Either Everyone Knows You, or No One Knows You

The last major feature of the social media attention market we highlight is how it is distributed. Simply put, one cannot understand attention in the social media context without understanding the power law. On social media there is not an equal or a "normal" (i.e., bell curve) distribution of attention across organizations or their messages. Instead, it is a power law–driven phenomenon that makes it seem as if, on social media, either everyone has heard of you or no one has heard of you. We will get back to this point shortly.

Also called the Pareto distribution, the *power law* distribution (e.g., Shirky 2003) has the general shape $y = 1/x$. Because of how frequently it occurs in the consumption of new media—the number of website visitors, online book sales, etc.—discussion of the power law has moved into the mainstream (Anderson 2006).[19] It tends to arise under conditions of variety in content, inequality (some content is better than others), and the presence of network effects, which suppress the bad and promote the good (Anderson 2006).

Conditions of content variety and content inequality are present equally on websites and newer social media, but the network effects condition holds even more strongly in the network-based social media environment (e.g., Saxton et al. 2015). Figure 2.4 illustrates this at the organizational level with a histogram of the number of followers of the Twitter accounts of 167 advocacy organizations in 2017. This serves as a rough proxy for the aggregate level of attention the organization has garnered on Twitter.[20]

What immediately stands out is how the distribution of followers among these 167 organizations looks nothing like a normally distributed bell curve and instead shows a clear power law–like distribution. Why is this important? To start, in contrast to the normal distribution, in a power law distribution a large number of organizations have low levels of attention, while a few organizations generate very high levels of attention. In fact, as can be seen in Figure 2.4, the mean value of 52,763 followers (dashed vertical line) conveys little information in such distributions.[21] Of the 167 organizations, 133 have fewer than the mean value; these 133 "low attention" organizations have an average of 14,027 followers. By contrast, the 34 "high attention" organizations (those with values higher than the mean) have an average of 204,293 followers. While

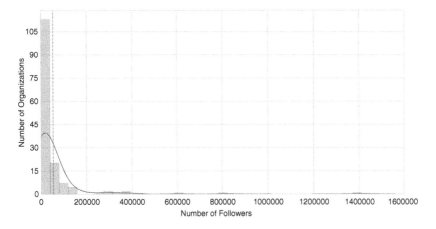

FIGURE 2.4 Histogram of number of Twitter followers per advocacy nonprofit in 2017 ($N = 167$)

NOTE: Solid line indicates kernel density estimation line; dashed vertical line indicates mean value of 52,763.45 followers.

the follower count is an admittedly blunt measure of aggregate attention, the contrast between the low- and high-attention organizations is stark. In effect, while such things as test scores, commute times, blood pressure, wait times, and height tend to follow a normal distribution, a large number of relevant social media phenomena—attention included—do not. Instead, they follow the power law distribution. Why is this important? The answer, briefly put, is that such distributions are notable for the small number of "winners" and the relatively large number of "losers." The notion of "average" conveys much less information in the "rich get richer" context of these nonnormal distributions. It is these characteristics that make it seem that on social media, either everyone knows you or no one knows you. At the same time, it is difficult to forecast performance in an environment characterized by power law distributions. The degree to which a fundraising campaign is successful is dependent on the "X factor" that is the network effect (Saxton and Wang, 2014); for instance, no one could have foreseen the ALS Association's *#IceBucket-Challenge* reaching such a massive audience in 2014; reaching that level of success was equivalent to winning the attention lottery. At the practical level, organizations and their social media managers need to familiarize themselves with the power law if they wish to fully appreciate the nature of attention in the social media context.

Discussion

In this chapter we have sought to provide an overview of the social media environment. Beyond simply defining social media, we have provided up-to-date data on participation rates in various social media platforms by advocacy organizations; with 98.9% of our advocacy organizations having one or more accounts, these organizations seem to believe social media is no longer optional.

More importantly, we have provided a framework for understanding the central tools available to advocacy organizations for building attention on social media. The key communicative action an organization takes to build attention is the sending of messages. In addition to offering content to establish an organization's strategic role, messages can also be used for connecting purposes through the use of replying and commenting, liking, sharing, user mentions, hyperlinks, and hashtags. These connecting actions form message ties that can be reciprocated, and over time the repeated use of message-based connecting also serves to develop ties with new users or strengthen ties with existing users. Fostering such ties is essential if the organization is to develop an attention network that will consume the organization's messages. To be clear, while the connecting actions are crucial for developing network resources, the key tool is the messages. It is the organization's dynamic stream of social media messages that constitute the central "product" an advocacy organization offers to the social media attention market.

Finally, we have covered important aspects of the nature of attention in the social media context. We noted the centrality of the social network and covered several unique and/or salient features of social networks on social media. We further noted how attention on social media is eminently observable, has a preference for drama, and is regulated by the power law distribution. Overall, the reader should now have a good sense of what social media is, how widely it is used, the attention-building tools available to advocacy organizations, and the nature of the social media attention economy. With this contextual understanding in mind, we can now turn in the next chapters to an examination of what makes advocacy organizations and their messages more or less successful in garnering attention.

CHAPTER 3

GETTING ATTENTION

An Organizational-Level Analysis

When it comes to the information environment in which nonprofit advocacy organizations operate today, technological advances are a double-edged sword. On the one hand, the widespread adoption of information and communications technologies (ICTs) has created new platforms on which nonprofit organizations can promote their causes. They can launch organizational websites to highlight their work and demonstrate accountability, and they can make an appearance on social media to broadcast information and engage with a wide range of stakeholders. Indeed, at the turn of the twenty-first century it was common for community organizations and grassroots advocacy groups to have zero Internet presence; nowadays it is rare to encounter an organization that does not have a website and some social media presence such as a Facebook page or a Twitter handle. In addition, in the pre-Internet age, the organization itself was the primary information source for the public: if you wanted to look at the organization's annual tax returns or audited financial statements, you would have to contact the organization directly and make a request. Now people can obtain information from intermediaries such as GuideStar (now part of a new organization called Candid), rating agencies such as Charity Navigator, and decentralized "word of mouth."

On the other hand, with information flowing from so many different sources and in so many different formats, it becomes more difficult for nonprofits to make their voices heard amid all the noise. As Herbert Simon (1971, 40) famously declared, "a wealth of information creates a poverty of attention." Operating in a world that is flooded by an endless inflow of information but lacks the capacity to effectively process it, organizations suffer from an attention deficit. For this very reason, attention, defined as the allocation of "information-processing capacity . . . to environmental stimuli over time" (Sproull 1984, 10), has become a scarce organizational resource (Davenport and Beck 2001; Ocasio 2011; Ren and Guo 2011). This attention deficit problem has several characteristics with broad potential implications for nonprofit organizations. For one thing, people are more attracted to new issues and initiatives than old ones (Scurlock, Dolsak, and Prakash, 2020). Today, they are reading about the wildfires in California; tomorrow, a tsunami in Indonesia holds their attention. Thus, whatever attention the public gives to an issue is fleeting and not sustainable: people notice an issue and then forget about it. Furthermore, people seem to be obsessed with drama. Donors and supporters are often drawn to dramatic stories and spectacular events, but their attention soon recedes or shifts to the next big thing. In September 2015, the image of the drowning in the Mediterranean Sea of a three-year-old Syrian boy made global headlines and drew public attention to the Syrian refugee crisis; at the end of 2019, while the largest refugee crisis of our time had no signs of coming to an end, our attention to it seemed to have faded away.

While the attention deficit problem is not unique to nonprofit advocacy organizations, this issue holds special significance for them because they often must draw public attention to a policy or issue first in order to achieve more tangible strategic outcomes (Tufekci 2013). In this regard, the level and type of public attention an organization receives serves as an immediate and key indicator of the effectiveness of its policy advocacy effort, regardless of whether it occurs online or offline. When using social media to speak out about a cause, organizations must ensure that their voice reaches audiences of current and potential supporters before they can achieve more tangible goals. However, as discussed in the previous chapter, prior research, which heavily focuses on the prevalence of social media use by nonprofit organizations, has paid very little attention to the effectiveness of that social media usage.

In a recent study (Guo and Saxton 2018), we began to address this research gap by asking a simple question: How does an advocacy organization gain supporters' attention with its social media messages? Given the dearth of existing theory, we have developed an original explanatory model for understanding why some organizations get attention on social media while others do not. More specifically, we argue that the extent to which an organization is "being heard" (i.e., the attention it receives) depends on the size of its audience, how much and how it speaks, and what it says. We tested our hypotheses with a panel data set that collapsed by month and organization the 219,915 tweets sent by 145 organizations over the entire 12 months of 2013. Using *number of retweets* and *number of likes* as proxies of attention, we found that attention had a positive association with the size of an organization's network (i.e., number of followers), its volume of speech (i.e., number of tweets sent), and how many "conversations" it joined (i.e., number of hashtags employed).

This chapter is a continuation of the conversation we began with that study (Guo and Saxton 2018). Here, we extend and test the original explanatory model proposed in our previous work with additional variables and newer and richer data. Adding new variables to an existing model or theory is one of the fundamental ways of doing innovative research (Slater and Gleason 2012; Voss 2003).[1] For instance, if one is interested in what drives giving to nonprofit organizations, the influential "economic model of giving" developed by Weisbrod and Dominguez (1986) proposed three key determinants: price (proxied by the program spending ratio), quality (proxied by age), and advertising (proxied by fundraising expenses). One could thus expand the model by *adding a new independent variable* to the existing model (whether a direct determinant, a moderator, or a mediator), as others have done with website disclosure (Saxton, Neely, and Guo 2014), third-party ratings agencies (Gordon, Knock, and Neely 2009), or financial stability (Trussel and Parsons 2007). In much of our own work, we have taken this approach, although ideally the addition of new variables is paired with a refining of the existing model and/or reconceptualization of the existing relationships in a way that deepens and/or makes more precise our understanding of the core nonprofit organizational context.

While the above approach works well in some situations (like the "economic model of giving") where there exists a well-defined explanatory model, such models are often not available in other situations. For instance, take the case of our 2018 *NVSQ* article, where we began by asking how nonprofit advocacy organizations garner attention on social media. Advocacy on social media was a relatively new phenomenon at the time we began the study in 2013. A number of studies up to that point had looked at *how* organizations were using electronic and social media for advocacy efforts (e.g., Guo and Saxton 2014b; McNutt and Boland 1999). Studies of what types of social media messages were effective had also started to appear (e.g., Saxton and Waters

2014; Swani, Milne, and Brown 2013). There was also a long line of research on nonprofit advocacy (see Chapter 1 for a brief review), including how organizations conduct advocacy and how they achieve success. Yet the lack of research on our specific context meant there was no model to explain levels of attention obtained by nonprofit advocacy organizations on social media.

Accordingly, our efforts to build an explanatory model were chiefly deductive.[2] Domain-specific knowledge was essential, such that the first guide for our deductive efforts was the identification of what we considered to be our domain.[3] We considered our domain to have three main elements: (1) nonprofit organizations, (2) advocacy, and (3) social media. Casting a wide net on our collective understanding of these literatures, we ultimately developed a relatively parsimonious cross-disciplinary model that posited that attention was driven by 10 variables across four main conceptual categories: *network characteristics* along with three elements of communication strategy—*targeting and connecting, timing and pacing,* and *content.*

Chapter 3 started from a different place. We already had an existing model to build on. The situation is thus analogous to that faced by researchers looking at aggregate nonprofit donations—we have already encountered our equivalent to Weisbrod and Dominguez's (1986) three-variable "economic model of giving." Accordingly, building on the point made earlier, we could be "innovative" (Slater and Gleason 2012; Voss 2003) by taking a primarily deductive approach that incrementally improves the existing model by drawing on recent work conducted in the domains of social media and nonprofit advocacy. Given that such findings provide additional explanations that are relevant to our context, this is that path we take. In effect, we innovate by taking an existing model (from Guo and Saxton 2018) and updating the data (from 2013 to 2017), adding new variants of the dependent variables (including the number of replies), and adding independent variables designed to measure different elements of an existing conceptual category (especially content). In essence, the model we develop in this chapter represents one of the paradigmatic (and likely most popular) approaches to innovative, theory-driven quantitative research in the social sciences (see, among others, Voss 2003).

In the next section of this chapter, we will present the expanded framework and a set of testable hypotheses. The third section covers the methods and data. In the fourth section, we then test the model with a series of logit regressions. In our final section we discuss the findings and their implications for future research.

Expanded Framework and Hypotheses

In this section, we provide a framework for understanding the factors that facilitate or hinder the ability of advocacy organizations to gain attention on social media. We build on our previous arguments (Guo and Saxton 2018) to present an expanded four-factor explanatory model, proposing that attention derives from four main sets of factors: network characteristics, targeting and connecting strategies, timing and pacing, and content. The four factors fall into two broad categories. The first factor concerns audience- or network-level characteristics, while the remaining three—timing and pacing, targeting and connecting, and content—cover message-level characteristics that reflect the organization's communication strategy. Using this framework, we then present a set of hypotheses to be tested in the next section.

Network Characteristics

First, the level of attention an organization receives on social media depends on characteristics of the organization's social media network, particularly its size. There is much intuitive sense in this assertion, and a growing line of research has found evidence of the resources that can accrue to organizations from their social networks. For instance, Eng, Liu, and Sekhon (2012) found that informal and personal relationships—so-called relationally embedded network ties— are strongly linked to resource acquisition such as donor or volunteer support. Meanwhile, Reddick and Ponomariov (2013) found that people who are members of voluntary associations are more likely to donate online. In turn, Saxton and Wang (2014) found the *social network effect* to be one of the most important determinants of the amount of donations received by organizations on the crowdfunding site Facebook Causes.

The positive relationship between network ties and resource acquisition is not limited to tangible financial or human resources. Entrepreneurship research provides evidence that social networks can also generate intangible resources such as access to information, advice, and new ideas (e.g., Hills, Lumpkin, and Singh 1997). In the online context, social network size (i.e., number of followers) is found to help accrue intangible resources such as an individual's perceived attractiveness (Antheunis and Schouten 2011) and an organization's perceived legitimacy (Lee, Yoon, and O'Donnell 2018). We consider attention a vital intangible resource, with a potential that hinges on the size of an organization's social media network. More specifically, we posit that the informal belonging to an online network implied by following an organization makes a given user more likely to afford attention to that organization in the form of retweeting, liking, or replying to that organization's messages. In fact, individual-level research on Twitter has found that network size has a strong relationship with retweeting and message popularity (e.g., Bakshy et al. 2011). This reasoning leads to our first hypothesis:

> H1: *The level of attention an organization receives will be positively associated with the number of followers the organization has.*

Communication Strategy

Network characteristics aside, it is also critical to consider an organization's overall communication strategy as reflected in features of the messages that it sends. We identify three salient dimensions of communication strategy: timing and pacing, targeting and connecting, and content.

Timing and Pacing. Timing and pacing concerns when and how often an organization communicates. In particular, we argue that the extent to which an organization is "heard" depends on how loudly it "speaks," as reflected in the volume and frequency of messages sent. We can find evidence for this argument by examining the literature on, among other issues, medical research advocacy. For example, findings from a study of the relationship between funding by the National Institutes of Health and the "burden" of various conditions or diseases show that some (AIDS, breast cancer, diabetes mellitus, and dementia) receive disproportionate funding and that these diseases happen to be the same ones that have the most vocal advocates (Elman, Ogar, and Elman 2000; Gross, Anderson, and Powe 1999).

On social media, an organization's advocacy work is essentially message-based: Through the continual sending of brief messages, the organization promotes a cause, an issue, or an event, makes new connections, and strengthens its ties with existing communities of interest and networks of supporters (Guo and Saxton 2014b). As such, the volume and frequency of an organization's speech is instrumental to its ability to get the word out and get attention from the audience. For Twitter in particular, its most important technological feature is the ability to send short messages, or tweets, historically of 140 characters or fewer. To capture speech volume and frequency, we therefore concentrate on the number of tweets an organization sends in a given month. We predict that, all other things being equal, organizations that tweet more frequently will be more likely to receive attention. Thus our second hypothesis:

H2: *The level of attention an organization receives will be positively associated with the number of tweets sent by the organization.*

Targeting and Connecting Strategy. A second dimension of an organization's communication strategy is relationship building through *targeting* of and *connecting* with its existing or potential audience members. Bonk (2010) discusses the crucial role that strategic communications can play in developing nonprofits—with a particular emphasis on targeted audiences reached through targeted messages. Such ideas have their roots in the "relational turn" that has occurred in public relations since the late 1990s, wherein theorizing has shifted from an emphasis on managing communication toward building and maintaining relationships (Broom, Casey, and Ritchey 1997; Ledingham and Bruning 1998). Dovetailing with this idea, in our previous work (Guo and Saxton 2010) we have found evidence suggesting a positive relationship between stakeholder communication and the scope and intensity of nonprofit advocacy activities, at least within the offline context. In the online context, evidence is mounting that social media has greatly expanded organizations' potential for interacting and building relationships with stakeholders through direct and unmediated targeting and connecting efforts (e.g., Waters et al. 2009). We develop separate hypotheses to examine these two interrelated efforts.

First, with respect to targeting, communication directed at specific audience members is more likely to receive attention from those audience members, as targeted communication both fosters a sense of reciprocity and conveys a perception of personalness. The former, as highlighted by social exchange theory (Homans 2013), triggers an obligation to reciprocate in a social interaction, while the latter signals trust and intimacy, which motivates those audience members to respond to the communication (Jang and Stefanone 2011). On Twitter, targeted messages are indicated by the use of the "@USER-NAME" convention at the start of the message; these *public reply messages* are a form of "public email" that represent a departure from "broadcast" messages in that they are directed at a specific audience member. A good example is the following tweet from Freedom Works:

@EdSturgill1 Today is important for #TaxReform. Tell Ron Johnson and Bob Corker to support tax relief in their hearing today! Click here: http://fwact .org/lKvN8tK

Sending a public reply message demonstrates responsiveness and establishes a dialogue between the organization and a specific Twitter user. Users can direct questions and comments to the organization using a public message, and organizations can acknowledge and respond to these messages. As such, public reply messages reflect an organization's explicit attempts at dialogic conversation with a specific user or set of users (Lovejoy and Saxton 2012). This leads to our third hypothesis:

H3: The level of attention an organization receives will be positively associated with the number of public reply messages sent by the organization.

In a related manner, we posit that a relationship exists between an organization's *connecting* behavior and levels of audience attention. This assertion conforms with marketing research that finds audience engagement in social media to be linked to increased advertising effectiveness (Calder, Malthouse, and Schaedel 2009). On Twitter, four types of tweeting behavior reflect organizations' efforts to engage and connect with specific Twitter entities. First, organizations can connect with *messages* (and message senders) by sharing or retweeting an existing message. Indicated by RT, the retweet function allows one user to repost a tweet from another user while acknowledging that user by adding "RT@[username]" to the beginning of the message. For example, People for the American Way retweeted a message from @United4Democracy:

RT @United4Democracy: The hearing on D.C. fair Elections is starting! Lots of great folks speaking up about the need for citizen-funded elections! #fairelections

Retweeting a message sent by another user shows the organization is paying attention to that user; retweeting amounts to a form of connection in that sharing a message is an implicit endorsement of the user who originally posted the message, forging a message tie between the originator and disseminator (Guo and Saxton 2014b).

Second, organizations can connect to existing *topics* by including a specific hashtag in their tweets. Represented by the pound sign (#), hashtags denote that a message is relevant to a particular topic (often an abstract concept), including political and social movements (#kony2012), conferences (#Home-sWithinReach), places (#Haiti), and knowledge bases (#womenshealth). In one of the tweet examples mentioned earlier, a hashtag (#TaxReform) is included in the body of the message. This convention allows for easier searching as well as aggregation of information on a particular topic, which renders hashtags particularly important for advocacy organizations in aggregating knowledge, in rapidly disseminating information during crises, and in mobilizing their support base during advocacy campaigns and social movements.

Third, an organization can connect to existing *content* through the inclusion of URLs (Internet addresses, which serve as hyperlinks to other sites). Hyperlinks play a key role in microblogging services such as Twitter: By including a (typically shortened) external link, organizations can bypass character limitations (particularly Twitter's previous 140-character restriction) and share longer textual passages, as well as photos and videos, with their user community. Again, in the tweet example mentioned earlier, an external link (http://fwact.org/1KvN8tK) is provided to direct the reader to additional information.

Fourth, an organization can connect to specific *people* through the use of user mentions, which occur when the organization includes a username ("@USERNAME") anywhere except at the start of a tweet (tweets that *begin* with "@USERNAME" are, as described in the discussion of H3, a form of public email coded separately as *public reply messages*). The following tweet sent by the Brady Campaign to Prevent Gun Violence (@BradyBuzz) actually mentions multiple users:

> Press conference w/ @Dan_at_Brady, @GabbyGiffords and more about to begin w/ gun violence prevention advocates on the Hill. #SaferSolutions

Such messages indicate that the sender is "talking about" another user, and are thus useful ways of acknowledging or making connections with other Twitter users.

Each of these four tools represents a different facet of the connecting quality of a social media message. We therefore posit the following four hypotheses:

H4a: The level of attention an organization receives will be positively associated with the number of the organization's tweets that are retweets of other users' tweets.

H4b: The level of attention an organization receives will be positively associated with the number of hashtags included in the organization's tweets.

H4c: The level of attention an organization receives will be positively associated with the number of URLs included in the organization's tweets.

H4d: The level of attention an organization receives will be positively associated with the number of user mentions included in the organization's tweets.

Content. The third dimension of an organization's communication strategy focuses on the nature of the information it delivers in its messages: the extent to which an organization is "heard" depends on what it communicates; in other words, *content* matters. There are numerous ways of approaching and measuring the content of a message. First, we look at *visual content*—videos and images—which have been shown to relate to the retweetability of messages on Twitter (Guo and Saxton 2014b). In marketing and advertising research, pictorial illustrations are considered the most important element in print advertisements for capturing consumers' attention (Pieters and Wedel 2004). Recent social media research similarly documents that the inclusion of visual content increases the likelihood of a message being shared on social media. For example, in a study of vaccine imagery in health communication, Chen and Dredze (2018) found that vaccine tweets with images were more likely to be retweeted than their text-only counterparts. Considering both sets of evidence, we expect social media messages with visual content to receive greater audience attention.

On Twitter, images and videos can be included in a tweet, such that when a tweet is viewed, the image or video will appear automatically. We thus formulate two hypotheses to capture the inclusion of the above two forms of visual content:

H5a: The level of attention an organization receives will be positively associated with the number of an organization's messages that include a photo.

H5b: The level of attention an organization receives will be positively associated with the number of an organization's messages that include a video.

In addition to visual content such as images and videos, it is equally important to look at *textual content*. More specifically, we look at an organization's "value framing" as reflected in its use of ethical or value-based language in its messages. According to framing theory, how a piece of information is presented to the audience affects the choices the audience makes about how to process that information (Goffman 1974). Through framing, the messenger draws the audience's attention to an issue by making a certain aspect of the issue more salient. In particular, the audience tends to pay more attention to a message if the message is designed to frame an issue in a way that activates core values (Gollust, Niederdeppe, and Barry 2013; see also Nelson and Garst 2005; Taber and Lodge 2006). Psychologists define a value as "a conception . . . of the desirable" (Kluckhohn 1951, 395), "the dominating force in life" (Allport 1961, 543), and "an enduring belief that a specific mode of conduct or end-state of existence is personally or socially preferable" (Rokeach 1973, 5). Political scientists emphasize the nature of values as "general and enduring standards" that are central to citizens' belief systems (Kinder and Sears 1985, 674), "personal statements regarding the individual's priorities" (Hurwitz and Peffley 1987, 1105–1106), or "each individual's abstract, general conceptions about the desirable and undesirable end-states of human life" (Jacoby 2006, 706).

In political communication, the appeal to values has long been regarded as a key rhetorical tactic for policy entrepreneurs to use in promoting their causes (e.g., Nelson, Wittmer, and Shortle 2010; Sniderman and Theriault 2004). This strategic use of the rhetorical framing of political issues in terms of specific values is often termed "value framing," a concept that "involve[s] linking value positions to the construction of political debate" (Schemer, Wirth, and Matthes 2012, 335). Value framing can be identified by words such as *ethics, moral, faith, fair,* and *transparency* that appear in a message. For example, read the following two tweets (the first from the American Civil Liberties Union and the second from the American Civil Rights Union) that contain the values-based words "right" and "integrity," respectively:

> The government can't tell its employees to denounce the #BDS movement. An individual's right to boycott is protected. #1A https://t.co/LDHFA4ADMz

> Will the Senate finally vote on Jeff Sessions and bring back voter integrity to DOJ @judicialnetwork @JCNSeverino https://t.co/3OzHQeG2Nu

These linguistic signs indicate that the topic in a message concerns normative questions of right and wrong (Briggs and Bauman 1992, 144), and at the same time the signs appeal to preexisting value systems (Keane 2011, 174). Through these linguistic signs, the organization communicates to the audience its "evaluative and intentional commitment . . . towards states of affairs" (Kockelman 2004, 142; see also Neu et al. 2018).

We argue that, in the nonprofit advocacy context, value framing would be the most likely framing tactic to generate attention from the audience.

H5c: The level of attention an organization receives will be positively associated with the value framing of the organization's messages.

Data and Methods

Sample and Data Collection

To maintain continuity with our previous study (Guo and Saxton 2018), our sample was drawn from all 188 "civil rights and advocacy" organizations rated in 2011 and 2017 by Charity Navigator, an independent nonprofit organization that evaluates the financial health of U.S. charities. To be evaluated, an organization had to be a 501(c)(3) charitable organization, have at least four consecutive years of IRS Form 990 available, have received public support greater than $500,000, and have total revenues exceeding $1,000,000. The average organization had $8.7 million in total revenues and $8.8 million in total expenses in the most recently completed fiscal year. Organizations in the sample covered a range of sizes and advocacy issue areas, including health, education, civil rights, the environment, and others (information about each organization's name, location, size, industry, and Twitter profile are provided in a Web appendix).[4]

In this test, we focused on organizations' use of Twitter. We first determined each organization's Twitter adoption profile through a review of its website supplemented by queries on the Google and Twitter search interfaces. We identified 167 organizations with an active Twitter profile (i.e., organizations that had a Twitter account and sent at least one tweet over the course of 2017). In 2017, these organizations on average had $15.8 million in total assets, and the number of years they had been in operation ranged from 11 to 93. We then gathered detailed Twitter data for all organizations by writing Python code (available upon request) to access the Twitter API and download all Twitter activities of each organization over the entire 12 months of 2017. Our analysis is based on the 261,127 original (non-retweeted) tweets sent in 2017 by the 167 advocacy organizations.

Variables and Methods

We operationalized three dependent variables that served as proxies for attention: (1) *Number of Retweets*, defined as the total number of retweets of an organization's tweets by other users in a given month, (2) *Number of Likes*, defined as the total number of likes of an organization's tweets by other users in a given month, and (3) *Number of Replies*, defined as the total replies to an organization's tweets by other users in a given month. A retweet is a reposting of someone else's tweet; it is a popular feature for spreading news or sharing information on Twitter. A like is represented by a small star icon below a tweet; this feature is used when a user likes a particular tweet and/or would like to save it for later. A reply is a tweet that a user posts in response to a particular tweet posted by the organization. All three features indicate that a user has paid some attention to a particular tweet.

We also operationalized the following 10 independent variables, all measured monthly for each organization. To start, H1 was operationalized with *Number of Followers*, which indicates the organization's number of Twitter followers. H2, which relates to the timing and pacing of the organization's communication strategy, was operationalized with *Number of Tweets*, a count of the total number of tweets sent by the organization. The targeting element of the communication strategy, reflected in H3, was operationalized through *Public Reply*, a measure of the total number of public reply messages (tweets starting with "@USERNAME") sent by the organization. The connecting element of the organization's strategy (H4a–d), meanwhile, was operationalized through four variables: *Retweets of Other Users*, measured as the total number of an organization's messages that are retweets of other users' tweets; *URL*, the total number of hyperlinks (URLs) included in an organization's tweets; *Hashtag*, the total number of hashtags included in an organization's tweets; and *User Mention*, the total number of user mentions included in an organization's tweets. Finally, the content aspect of communication strategy (H5a–c) was operationalized through two variables that denote the inclusion of visual content and one variable that captures the inclusion of values-based words in an organization's messages: *Photo*, which measures the total number of an organization's messages that include one or more photos; *Video*, which measures the total number of an organization's messages that include one or more videos; and *Value Framing*, which, using a "dictionary-based" approach (e.g., Suddaby, Saxton, and Gunz 2015), indicates the total number of an organization's messages that contain one or more "ethical" words as listed in the Harvard IV/Lasswell *RcEthic* dictionary, a dictionary containing words related to moral rectitude, values, and ethics (see Suddaby, Saxton, and Gunz 2015; Tetlock 2007; Tetlock, Saar-Tsechansky, and Macskassy 2008).[5] We logged all the variables to account for their skewed distribution.

Finally, we added month dummies as control variables to account for any trend-related time effects. For some models, we controlled for *Organization Size*, which was measured as an organization's reported annual revenue for the year 2017. We also included *Organization Age*, which was measured as the difference between the year 2017 and the year when the IRS granted the organization 501(c)(3) status.

For our data analysis, we used one-way (organizational-level) fixed effects to account for any time-invariant organizational heterogeneity. To address the possibility that error terms correlate with observations involving the same organization, we reported robust standard errors clustered at the organizational level.

We also conducted the data analysis using two alternative methods. One is random effects regression. An advantage of this method is that it allows us to add time-invariant organizational-level controls such as *Organization Size* and *Organization Age*. We added both controls when we ran random effects regression analysis. Hausman tests showed that the fixed effects model is more appropriate than the random effects model when *Number of Retweets* and *Number of Likes* are the dependent variables, but the random effects model is preferred when *Number of Replies* is the dependent variable. Since we have the same set of independent variables and three different dependent variables, which are likely correlated with each other, we also used seemingly unrelated regression (SUR) models to account for potential correlations of the errors across the *Number of Retweets, Number of Likes*, and *Number of Replies* equations. Overall, our results were largely similar with each of the three estimation methods.

Results

Descriptive Statistics

Before we discuss the descriptive statistics for the variables used in our regressions, it is useful to observe some general trends at the sample level. First, recall that the primary tool used on social media is the message—or on Twitter, the tweet. To provide a sense of how frequently our sample organizations are sending out these social media messages, Figure 3.1 shows a histogram of the number of tweets sent in 2017 by the 167 Charity Navigator advocacy organizations

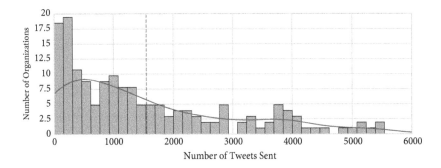

FIGURE 3.1 Histogram of number of tweets sent per advocacy nonprofit in 2017 (*N* = 167)

NOTE: Solid line indicates kernel density estimation line; dashed vertical line indicates mean value of 1,551.2 tweets.

that had a Twitter account. The average organization sent 1,551 tweets over the course of the year, though the range was broad, from a minimum of 4 tweets in 2017 by Connecticut Legal Services (@CTLegal) to a maximum of 5,541 sent by Jobs with Justice (@jwjnational). Moreover, replicating what we see with the follower count in Chapter 2, the figure highlights the nonnormal nature of the distribution of tweeting efforts.

We also believe it is worthwhile to provide some details of the general use of the six tweet-level connecting tools: hyperlinks (URLs), user mentions, hashtags, likes, replies, and retweets. To start, hyperlinks used to be the most common connecting tool, though there was evidence its popularity was decreasing.[6] In our sample, however, we found no such evidence of a decrease: 85.2% of all tweets sent by these organizations contained a hyperlink. We also found that 37.4% of the 261,127 tweets sent by the advocacy organizations contained a user mention, and that 48.7% of them contained a hashtag.

Turning to the organizational use of likes, replies, and retweets, we see that, collectively, by the end of 2017 the 167 organizations had liked slightly over 450,000 tweets. We found that 24,248 (9.3%) of the 261,127 tweets sent were "replies" to either other users or tweets, with 19,230 (7.4%) of these being replies to specific tweets and the remaining 5,018 (1.9%) being generic user replies. As for retweets, while we cannot see what proportion of the messages an organization reads that it decides to share, we can determine how frequently an organization decides to retweet other users' messages. We found that the 167 advocacy organizations sent 377,497 tweets in 2017, of which

TABLE 3.1   Descriptive statistics: January–December 2017 for 167 advocacy nonprofits

Variables	Obs.	Mean	S.D.	Min.	Max.
Number of Retweets	1890	5,917.47	35,000.29	0.00	548,420.00
Number of Likes	1890	9,883.57	65,224.20	0.00	1,072,781.00
Number of Replies	1832	207.48	1,488.09	0.00	37,856.00
Number of Followers	1890	44,090.30	118,328.60	40.00	1,409,521.00
Number of Tweets	1890	137.07	146.58	1.00	1,213.00
Public Reply	1890	6.21	13.88	0.00	173.00
Retweets of Other Users	1890	60.77	88.14	0.00	947.00
URL	1890	116.83	128.76	0.00	1,155.00
Hashtag	1890	66.62	91.35	0.00	915.00
User Mention	1890	51.32	71.13	0.00	1,083.00
Photo	1890	14.91	28.90	0.00	625.00
Video	1890	0.50	1.82	0.00	24.00
Value Framing	1890	26.71	34.52	0.00	346.00
Organization Size (logged)	1875	15.38	1.67	10.81	19.61
Organization Age	1890	35.55	14.18	11.00	93.00

NOTE: This table provides the descriptive statistics for the variables in our model. All of our variables, except for Organization Size, are the unlogged values at the organization/month level. All the variables are logged. Obs., number of observations; S.D., standard deviation.

261,127 were original and the remaining 116,370 were retweets. This means 30.83% of all messages the organizations sent were retweets of other users' messages.[7]

With the above general observations, we present the descriptive statistics for the variables in our model in Table 3.1. While all of the variables used in our regressions are the logged values at the organization/month level, for ease of understanding we show the unlogged versions here.

Proxies for Attention: Retweeting, Liking, and Replying. In terms of the amount of attention garnered, an examination of the data reveals some interesting patterns in the number of retweets, likes, and replies made by the Twitter community to the messages sent by the organizations. Each month in 2017, an organization received on average 5,917 retweets (median = 326), 9,883 likes (median = 431), and 207 replies (median = 1) from its audience. The range was wide, varying from zero to 548,420 retweets, from zero to 1,072,781 likes, and from zero to 37,856 replies. By comparison, an organization received on average 2,183 retweets (median = 350) and 210 likes (median = 34) from its audience each month in 2013; the range was similarly dramatic, ranging from zero to 206,624 retweets and from zero to 14,895 likes. The substantial difference between the mean and median scores and the wide range of results suggest that the distributions of these data approximate a *power law* distribution (Barabási and Albert 1999) rather than a normal bell curve distribution. We thus see a large number of organizations garnering low levels of attention and a smaller subset generating extremely high levels of attention.

Network Size. The average organization in our sample had 44,090 followers (median = 12,731). Their sizes spanned a vast range, from a low of 40 followers for the National Child Safety Council in January 2017, to a high of 1,409,521 for the American Civil Liberties Union Foundation in December. By comparison, the average organization in 2013 had 15,057 followers (median = 5,349), ranging from a low of 22 for the National Child Safety Council in January 2013 to a high of 334,949 for the Human Rights Campaign Foundation in December 2013.

Volume of Tweets. The organizations in our sample with Twitter accounts sent a total of 259,039 tweets during the 12 months of 2017. On average, an organization sent about 137 tweets per month during the 12-month period, roughly 4.6 tweets per day. This represents a slight increase from 2013, when an organization sent about 131 tweets per month during the 12-month period, roughly 4.4 tweets per day. Still, compared to the 2.3 tweets per day sent out by the *Non-Profit Times* (NPT) Top 100 organizations (Lovejoy et al. 2012) in 2009, these advocacy organizations have been relatively heavier tweeters.

Targeting and Connecting Strategy. When making tweets, organizations have access to a number of technological tools that allow them to connect with and target specific constituencies: public reply messages (also known as direct messages), retweets, hyperlinks, hashtags, and user mentions. We found that 9.29% (*n* = 24,248) of all tweets were direct messages, well below the 16% by nonprofits on the NPT Top 100 list (Lovejoy, Waters, and Saxton 2012) or the 22% of individuals studied by Hughes and Palen (2009). As shown in Table 3.1, the average organization sent about six public reply messages in a typical month. While our analysis here focuses on the 261,127 original (non-retweeted) messages sent by the organizations, we found the organizations also made 116,370 retweets (30.83% of the 377,497 total messages sent), with the average organization sending 60.77 retweets each month. This volume of retweets exceeds the 16.2% found by Lovejoy, Waters, and Saxton (2012) for NPT Top 100 organizations, yet it is only slightly more than the 28% found by Hughes and Palen (2009) for individuals during natural emergencies.

Three remaining tools—hyperlinks, hashtags, and user mentions—are available *within* tweets and are not mutually exclusive. Hyperlinks were included in 85.19% of the tweets ($n = 222,446$), with the average organization sending 117 tweets with a hyperlink over the course of a month. Hashtags were included in 48.70% of all tweets ($n = 127,174$), with the average organization sending around 67 tweets with at least one hashtag each month. We found that 37.42% of the tweets ($n = 97,720$) contained at least one user mention, and the average nonprofit sent 51 such messages each month.

Content. Organizations are able to include a variety of different media in their tweets. We found that 10.9% ($n = 28,435$) of all tweets sent contained a photo, with a typical organization sending out 15 such tweets in an average month; 0.95% ($n = 2,079$) of all tweets contained a video, with the average organization sending out 0.50 such tweets in a typical month. We also found that 19.48% ($n = 50,864$) of all tweets sent contained one or more ethical or values-based words, with a typical organization sending out about 27 such tweets in an average month.

Analysis Results

Prior to the multivariate regression analysis, we conducted a correlation analysis to examine the possible relationships among independent variables (the correlation matrix of all of our variables will be provided in a Web appendix). There were no unusually high correlations between most variables used in the same model. To further ease the concern about multicollinearity, we examined the variance inflation factor (VIF) values of our regression models, which range from 3.92 to 4.00, suggesting that multicollinearity is not a threat in our data analysis.

Table 3.2 reports the fixed effects regression results found using three models. To recap, each of the independent variables is associated with a specific hypothesis related to one of the four primary factors in our model. In line with our hypothesis testing, we present our results here briefly factor by factor before discussing the most important implications of these findings in the Discussion section. Because the regression analysis reported here is based on an extension of the original explanatory model proposed in our previous work (Guo and Saxton 2018) and on newer data from the same set of organizations, we also compare the results from both studies to observe what changed from 2013 to 2017.

TABLE 3.2 Determinants of audience attention to social media messages

	Model 1	Model 2	Model 3
	Number of Retweets	Number of Likes	Number of Replies
Estimation Method	Fixed Effects	Fixed Effects	Fixed Effects
Number of Followers	0.117**	0.154***	0.947***
	(0.050)	(0.058)	(0.292)
Number of Tweets	0.681***	0.879***	0.613**
	(0.130)	(0.139)	(0.241)
Public Reply	0.002	−0.001	−0.129**
	(0.018)	(0.020)	(0.057)
Retweets of Other Users	0.047*	0.040	−0.047
	(0.026)	(0.031)	(0.072)
URL	0.034	−0.195	−0.158
	(0.106)	(0.131)	(0.207)
Hashtag	0.077**	0.073*	0.092
	(0.038)	(0.039)	(0.111)
User Mention	0.025	0.071*	0.027
	(0.043)	(0.039)	(0.077)
Photo	0.033	0.051**	−0.012
	(0.026)	(0.026)	(0.060)
Video	0.032	0.054*	0.034
	(0.029)	(0.031)	(0.086)
Value Framing	0.105**	0.088**	0.038
	(0.045)	(0.039)	(0.075)
Constant	0.879*	0.737	−10.828***
	(0.483)	(0.579)	(2.810)
Month Dummies	Yes	Yes	Yes
Cluster (Firm)	167	167	162
R^2	0.796	0.587	0.637
F Statistics	$F(21, 166) =$ 45.83***	$F(21,166) =$ 44.46***	$F(21,161) =$ 24.02***
N	1890	1890	1832

NOTE: Parentheses contain heteroskedasticity-adjusted robust standard errors (clustered at firm level).
$^*p < 0.10$
$^{**}p < 0.05$
$^{***}p < 0.01$

Hypothesis 1 proposed that the level of attention an organization received would be positively associated with the organization's number of followers. In Models 1–3, the coefficients of the variable *Number of Followers* were positive and significant, suggesting a positive and significant relationship between network size and all three measures of attention (*Number of Retweets, Number of Likes,* and *Number of Replies*). Thus, Hypothesis 1 was supported. By comparison, the results of our previous study (Guo and Saxton 2018) only partially supported this hypothesis: A positive and significant association was found between number of followers and number of likes, but not between number of followers and number of retweets. In that study, we had not considered number of replies as a measure of attention.

Hypothesis 2 predicted that the level of attention an organization received would be positively associated with the number of tweets sent by the organization. The coefficients of the variable *Number of Tweets* were positive and significant across all models, suggesting a positive and significant relationship between the volume and frequency of messages sent and all three measures of attention. Thus, the results supported Hypothesis 2. This result is consistent with the findings we reported previously (Guo and Saxton 2018), wherein we found a positive and significant relationship between the number of tweets sent by an organization and two measures of attention—number of retweets and number of likes.

Hypothesis 3 pertained to the effect of targeting strategy. It predicted that the level of attention an organization received would be positively associated with the number of public reply messages (i.e., "@USER" messages) sent by the organization. Interestingly, the regression analysis only showed a significant relationship for Model 3, and the direction of the relationship was opposite that of our prediction. More specifically, one measure of attention (number of total replies to an organization's tweets by other users) was negatively associated with the number of public reply messages sent by the organization. Hypothesis 3 thus was not supported. By comparison, our previous work (Guo and Saxton 2018) revealed a negative relationship between the number of public reply messages by the organization and the number of retweets of an organization's tweets, but a positive relationship between the number of public reply messages by the organization and the number of likes of the organization's tweets.

Next, we created four hypotheses to examine the effect of connecting strategy. Hypotheses 4a through 4d described positive relationships with attention for the number of an organization's tweets that were retweets of other users' tweets, as well as for the number of hashtags, hyperlinks, and user mentions included in an organization's tweets. The results were mixed. Our analysis showed a significantly positive association between the number of an organization's tweets that were retweets of others' tweets and the attention received by an organization when we measured attention by the dependent variable *Number of Retweets* (Model 1). Thus, our findings partially supported Hypothesis 4a. The coefficients of *Hashtags* were positive and significant in Model 1 and Model 2, lending partial support to Hypothesis 4b. Hypothesis 4c received no support, as the coefficients of *URL* were not significant in any of the models. We found a positive and significant relationship between the number of user mentions and the number of likes received by an organization, but this positive relationship was not significant when organizations captured attention via *Number of Retweets* and *Number of Replies*. This finding suggested that Hypothesis 4d was only partially supported.

By comparison, we previously reported (Guo and Saxton 2018) a positive relationship between an organization's tweets that are retweets of others' tweets and the number of retweets of the organization's tweets, but a negative relationship between an organization's tweets that are retweets of others' tweets and the number of likes of the organization's tweets. Our findings (Guo and Saxton 2018) revealed a positive and significant relationship between the number of hashtags included in an organization's messages and two measures of attention (number of retweets and number of likes). We (Guo and Saxton 2018) also reported no significant relationship between URL and attention, while revealing a negative and significant relationship between the number of user mentions and one measure of attention (number of likes).

Hypotheses 5a and 5b proposed that two types of visual content—tweets with photos and tweets with videos—would have a positive relationship with all dependent variable measures. In general, the results were consistent with our hypotheses. The regression analysis revealed a positive and significant relationship between *Photo* and the number of likes of the organization's tweets, thus providing some support for Hypothesis 5a. We found the variable *Video* to have a positive and significant effect on the dependent variable *Number of Likes*, but not on *Number of Retweets* and *Number of Replies*, thus lending partial support to Hypothesis 5b. Similarly, we previously reported (Guo and Saxton 2018) a significant relationship between *Photo* and the number of likes of an organization's tweets.

Finally, Hypothesis 5c predicted that the inclusion of values-based language would reflect a positive relationship with all measures of attention. We found a positive association between *Value Framing* and the attention received by an organization when attention was measured by *Number of Retweets* and *Number of Likes*. Thus, Hypothesis 5c is partially supported.

Discussion

Examining 261,127 tweets sent in 2017 by 167 diverse advocacy organizations, we built and then tested an organizational-level model of public attention to organizational messages on social media. What have we learned here about organizational-level attention?

Our model has four main conceptual categories: network characteristics, timing and pacing, targeting and connecting, and content. In each of these categories, we have found one or more variables to be significant. This finding lends support to the overall theoretical model.

More specifically, an organization's network size on social media (measured by its number of followers) has a positive effect on the level of attention the organization receives, regardless of which measure of attention (retweets, likes, or replies) is used. For the same set of organizations, network size appeared to play a more prominent role in driving public attention in 2017 than it did in 2013. This suggests the presence of a network effect (or network externality): As more followers join an organization's social media network, each existing member of the network becomes more likely to pay some level of attention to the messages sent by the organization.

In addition, communication strategies also play a role in determining the level of attention an advocacy organization receives. In terms of timing and pacing, we found that the volume and frequency of an organization's speech (measured by the number of tweets sent by the organization) had a positive effect on the level of attention the organization received, regardless of which measure of attention (retweets, likes, or replies) was used. This finding is generally consistent with that from our 2013 data. Taken together, our findings highlight the importance of speech volume and frequency for acquiring attention: an organization that broadcasts messages at a faster pace tends to garner more attention from its audience. One interpretation is that, as speech volume and frequency climb, the value of the speech as perceived by the followers also increases, which in turn results in a higher level of attention to the messages sent by the organization.

In terms of targeting, quite contrary to our prediction, we found that the number of public reply messages sent by an organization has a negative effect on one measure of attention (replies) and no effect on the other two attention measures (retweets and likes). Analysis of our 2013 data also generated conflicting results. All things considered, the findings seem to indicate that the targeting strategy is not as effective in helping obtain public attention for the organization. This finding is interesting, as the ineffectiveness of the targeting strategy is likely caused by a unique aspect of the function of social media: it enables the organization to communicate with diffused stakeholders, or stakeholders whose power to influence the organization is diffused (Hill and Jones 1992). This diffusion of power increases the coordination costs among individual stakeholders and thereby limits "the ability of stakeholders to act collectively" (Hill and Jones 1992, 149). Due to their inability to engage in collective action and the prohibitive cost for the organization to communicate with them, diffused stakeholders tend to receive relatively little organizational attention in offline settings, but social media allows the organization to reach a broader array of stakeholders at a much lower cost (Saxton and Guo 2014b). The flip side of this ability to reach out to diffused stakeholders, however, is that it might not be as effective at garnering public attention if used as a targeting mechanism. That said, while targeted public reply messages may not be effective in garnering mass attention in the form of retweets, they may serve to strengthen ties with the users targeted in those messages, as reflected in liking behavior.

In terms of connecting, one strategy stands out as most effective at garnering public attention for the organization: including hashtags in an organization's tweets. To a lesser extent, another two strategies—retweeting other users' tweets and including user mentions in an organization's tweets—also help garner public attention in some way. Including URLs in an organization's tweets does not seem to be effective at all. The use of hashtags as a connecting strategy to garner attention deserves some further discussion here. The hashtag has become one of the most popular tools made available on social media sites such as Twitter, Facebook, Instagram, Pinterest, Tumblr, Vine, and YouTube. The power of hashtags lies in the multiple benefits they offer users: they classify messages, enhance searchability, and allow organizations to link their messages to existing knowledge and action communities (Saxton et al. 2015). Our finding adds to the existing evidence that encourages the increased use of hashtags as part of a nonprofit organization's strategy for social media advocacy.

In terms of visual content, we found that the inclusion of photos and videos has a positive effect on one measure of attention (likes) but no effect on the other two attention measures (retweets and replies). For the same set of organizations, visual content appears to have played a consistent role in driving one aspect of public attention (likes) from 2013 to 2017. Thus, across both studies, we found that visual content matters: as far as getting public attention is concerned, people are fond of photos and videos.

Finally, in terms of textual content, we find that the inclusion of values-based language has a positive effect on two measures of attention (retweets and likes), but not on the third attention measure (replies). This finding suggests that value framing serves as a useful strategy for organizations to generate public attention. While it is beyond the scope of this research to explore the mechanisms by which value framing attracts attention, a useful starting point can be found in the notion of *value representation* (Guo and Marietta 2015; Marietta 2010). Value representation refers to the extent to which an organization embodies the values of its constituents: the organization delivers value representation when there is a congruence of values between the organization and its constituents. This value congruence serves as a foundation for organizational legitimacy—constituents trust the organization because it displays values they share, which in turn drives up attention.

This study carries a number of practical implications. Our findings suggest that to garner attention, nonprofits should seek to grow their follower base, speak often, join conversations (by employing existing hashtags), provide visual content, and include values-based language in their social media messages. They should also be aware that different levels and forms of attention are gained from various tweeting activities. Of course, our three chosen measures are not intended to provide a complete picture of how organizations can gain attention; rather, we are interested in forms of attention that are more "intense" or "interactive" than simply reading messages. Future research should look for ways to further operationalize the notion of audience attention.

One promising and largely untapped area concerns the examination of textual content. In our 2018 article, we initiated the focus on content of organizational messaging on social media, yet limited the examination to visual content, and found images were related to retweetability. In this chapter, we have extended the idea of content to examine the signaling role of "value framing"—the inclusion of ethical and values-based words in social media messages—in getting attention. In addition to value framing, another possible signal lies in what may be labeled as "sentiment framing," or the presence of sentiment in social media messages. A core finding from this emerging stream of research is that emotionally charged Twitter messages tend to receive more attention than neutral ones (see Stieglitz and Dang-Xuan 2013). Thus, if an organization sends more emotionally charged messages, it is likely to receive an increasing amount of public attention. In the next chapter, we will bring this textual examination down to the message level.

Finally, the elephant in the room is whether the attention gained by an organization leads to any tangible or intangible organizational outcomes. For advocacy and social movement organizations, the ultimate long-term goal is not attention but instead spreading awareness, building coalitions, or mobilizing supporters in order to achieve some broader societal or policy goal. We propose that attention is a crucial first step toward such meaningful advocacy actions and outcomes, but this proposition needs to be investigated further. We will revisit this idea in Chapter 5, after presenting the results from our message-level analysis on garnering attention.

CHAPTER 4

BUILDING AN EXPLANATORY MODEL
AT THE MESSAGE LEVEL

In searching to explain what drives attention to individual messages, Guo and Saxton (2018) as well as Chapter 3 of this book provide us with excellent starting points. Both those studies argue that organizational-level attention derives from four main sets of factors: network characteristics, targeting and connecting strategies, timing and pacing, and content. Given that these existing models were developed to explain organizational-level attention, we are still in need of a framework for better understanding what drives attention at the message level. While it is likely that many if not most of the same features will be relevant, we cannot be sure. Moreover, as both prior studies admitted, the goal was to present a parsimonious model and not a comprehensive list of all potentially relevant variables.

In this chapter, we thus aim to extend the existing model in two ways: (1) bring the model down to the message level and (2) expand the number of variables. Moreover, we seek to do so in a new way—a way that leverages recent methodological advances in the emerging field of data analytics, a loosely defined discipline that overlaps with data science, machine learning, and artificial intelligence. Specifically, we devise a novel approach that adapts data analytics methods to the social scientific enterprise. In so doing, a secondary goal is to provide a template for scholars similarly interested in using these methods to expand existing models.

In the first section of this chapter we outline our analysis plan and methodological approach. In the second section we then cover *feature engineering,* where we describe our creation of potential variables for analysis. The third section covers the three levels of *feature selection* techniques that we employ sequentially to narrow down the potential variables for analysis; the end result in the section is an augmented conceptual model with 24 proposed variables. In the fourth section we then test the model with a series of logit and negative binomial regressions. In the final section we discuss the findings and the implications for future research of our novel methodological approach and expanded theoretical model.

Analytical Method and Analysis Plan

Traditional Model Building Approaches in the Face of Big Data and Data Science

For the empirical quantitative researcher, there are two primary approaches to constructing a theoretical model that explains the dependent variable of interest. One is used in the minority of cases in which no relevant model of the phenomenon exists, which may occur when new issues, new media, new groups, new policies, or new situations have arisen that challenge and stretch existing theories to the point that no preexisting model is sufficient. In such situations the researchers need to draw on considerable domain knowledge in order to generate their own parsimonious and rigorous explanatory model. An example is the study described in our 2018 *NVSQ* article (Guo and Saxton 2018), where the absence of a model of attention to advocacy organizations' social media efforts led us to develop an original, 10-variable model using a deductive approach built on our understanding of the literatures in three interrelated domains: nonprofit organizations, advocacy, and social media.

In the second approach, used in the majority of cases, the researcher takes an existing model and modifies or adds one or more model variables. As discussed in the preceding chapter, adding a new variable to an existing model—whether a mediator, moderator, or existing explanatory factor—is one of the fundamental ways of doing "innovative" social scientific research (Slater and Gleason 2012; Voss 2003). This was our approach in Chapter 3, where we expanded the Guo and Saxton (2018) model by adding new variants of the dependent variable as well as several new independent variables.

In short, the well-trained quantitative social scientific researcher, whether a regression-focused scholar or an experimentalist, typically has two main choices in model building: (1) build a new model or (2) incrementally add to an existing one. This brings us to the present chapter. As in Chapter 3, we are again presented with an existing explanatory model. Yet the situation is not fully analogous. We are interested in what drives attention at the message level rather than at the organization/month level; therefore, we cannot be certain all of the variables will translate to our message-level context. Moreover, the goal in both our 2018 *NVSQ* article and Chapter 3 was to present a parsimonious model.

By contrast, in the present chapter our aim is both to bring the model down to the message level and to develop a more comprehensive list of potentially relevant variables. Yet we wish to do so in a novel way; namely, by incorporating machine learning methods based on data science into the social scientific enterprise. Why would we want to do this? Big Data. Simply put, Big Data presents the researcher with new opportunities as well as challenges (e.g., Lecy and Thornton 2016; Vasarhelyi, Kogan, and Tuttle 2015). The opportunity lies in the large number of available cases as well as variables. The challenge lies in how to go about choosing those cases and variables. Recent advances in computer science–based disciplines present new possibilities on this front. At the heart of this development is machine learning. Machine learning has been around for decades in computer science, yet it has exploded in popularity with the rise of Big Data and the newer, overlapping disciplines of what are commonly called data science, data analytics, and artificial intelligence.[1] One of the fundamental tasks of machine learning is *feature selection* (Blum and Langley 1997; Guyon and Elisseeff 2003; Yu and Liu 2004), which comprises numerous procedures, steps, and algorithms used for one key purpose: to take a large number—often thousands—of "features" (i.e., variables) and reduce them to a more manageable or parsimonious or informative level.

There is a key constraint, however. Typically, machine learning approaches are too atheoretical to be applied directly to more theory-driven social scientific problems such as ours. We must therefore modify these approaches to help us find a multimethod, theory-relevant machine learning approach. We now turn to an overview of our methodological solution to this problem.

Overview of a Novel Analytical Approach

Leveraging the opportunities presented by Big Data and the advent of data analytics and data science techniques, in this chapter we employ a novel analytical approach to theory building. As described in detail in the methodological appendix to this chapter, this approach is unique first in how it explicitly contains a mix of inductive and deductive logic; namely, it combines the logic of traditional qualitative inductive approaches to theory building (e.g., Miles and Huberman 1984) with analytical approaches driven by Big Data and machine learning (e.g., Evans 2014). The former comes into play in the strong role of letting the data guide the identification of relevant variables, concepts, and relationships. The latter comes into play in the use of quantitative feature selection techniques designed to help determine which of a large number of variables should be retained for a final empirical model (e.g., Verikas, Gelzinis, and Bacauskiene 2011). What is unique about this is how it is effectively an inductive, qualitative theory-building effort in which we also rely heavily on quantitative machine learning to help make model-building decisions; in fact, we believe it is best to characterize the process as "Inductive-Quantitative," or inductive analysis aided by quantitative feature selection techniques. As we argue in detail in the appendix, to do this well requires both domain expertise (in our case, in-depth knowledge of nonprofit advocacy) as well as the quantitative skills of the data scientist.

Analysis Stages

There are three main stages to our analysis.[2] In line with machine learning terminology, we call these stages (1) feature engineering, (2) feature selection, and (3) model testing. In our first stage, feature engineering, we generate, or "engineer," a set of 133 variables, or "features," for inclusion in our analyses (Dong and Liu 2018) using a range of traditional social scientific as well as newer data analytics techniques. In our second stage, feature selection (see Saeys, Inza, and Larrañaga 2007), we employ an array of univariate, bivariate, and multivariate dimensionality-reduction techniques to help select the most relevant of the 133 features. Feature selection is designed to help determine which of a large number of variables should be retained for a final empirical model (Verikas, Gelzinis, and Bacauskiene 2011). In line with our aim to lift the data to a conceptual level, the feature selection stage ends with the presentation of a theoretical model comprising seven conceptual categories based on the final slate of 24 selected variables. Finally, our third stage, model testing, involves testing the model we have built. This stage is familiar to the typical quantitative researcher, who first develops a model and then tests it through (for instance) a multiple regression technique. We do the same here in running logistic and negative binomial regressions on our 24-variable model.

Data

As in Chapter 3, our analyses are based on the 261,127 tweets sent in 2017 by the 167 advocacy organizations rated on Charity Navigator that had a Twitter account and sent at least one tweet over the course of 2017. Following machine learning convention, we used an 80/20 train/test split and split the data into randomly generated *training* (N = 208,901) and *testing* (N = 52,226) data sets (Amani and Fadlalla 2017; Guyon and Elisseeff 2003). The feature selection stage uses the training portion of the data, while the model testing stage uses the testing portion of the data.

Feature Engineering

The goal of the first two stages of the analysis is to develop a theoretical model of the determinants of public attention to organizations' social media messages. It is a mixed-methods approach that integrates data mining and machine learning techniques into the inductive theorizing process. In our first stage, feature engineering, existing theory (deduction) and data (induction) guide our efforts to generate 133 variables for potential inclusion in the final model. To start, we use deduction in deliberately creating message-level "translations" of all the organization/month variables tested in Chapter 3. We also use deductive reasoning to include variables that our knowledge of the social media, advocacy, and nonprofit domains suggested might be relevant to our dependent variable (attention). On the other hand, we also include variables on a purely inductive basis—they are available and potentially relevant, so we examine them. Yet even here we do not have a "data fishing" expedition; instead, we use the logic of the qualitative inductive theorist to develop and refine the list of variables.[3]

Developing the Set of Possible Features

Concretely, in the feature engineering stage we inductively identify and analyze a large range of potentially interesting variables. Building on insights from Chapter 3, and to help focus the development of inductive insights, we organize our presentation of the 133 variables into seven different categories, including the four highlighted in Chapter 3—network characteristics, targeting and connecting, timing and pacing, and content—and three new inductively driven categories—organizational features, account-level characteristics, and social media sophistication. In line with the iterative inductive process outlined above, within each category the starting point is existing theory.

The methodological appendix contains a detailed description of the 133 variables, including a reference table (Table A.2) showing the data source for each variable and, where applicable, a description of where in the feature selection process the variable is dropped. In this chapter we focus on the most relevant details and leave additional details to the appendix.

Network Characteristics. To start, we consider three network variables taken from the *user* object of the Twitter application program interface (API).[4] In addition to the *Number of Followers*, which was included in our Chapter 3 tests, we include *Number of Friends,* which is the number of other Twitter users the organization is following; and *Number of Lists,* which indicates the number of public "lists" other Twitter users have placed the nonprofit on. The latter is an indication of authority or influence. All three have been found to be positively related to audience reactions (e.g., Nesi et al. 2018; Saxton and Waters 2014).

Communication Strategy: Targeting and Connecting. We next examined 12 *targeting and connecting* variables. Five of the variables tap diverse features of the "@[USER]" convention found in social media messages that reflect different aspects of *whom* the organization is targeting in its tweets. Prior research has generally found such targeted messages to be associated with public reactions (e.g., Saxton and Waters 2014; Swani, Milne, and Brown 2013). Using data found in the *entities* object of the Twitter API, we also generated a suite of binary and continuous variables tapping whether the message is a "quote tweet" and the existence of URLs, hashtags, and user mentions in each tweet. Such variables are commonly included in tests of message effectiveness (e.g., Saxton et al. 2015; Saxton and Waters 2014; Swani, Milne, and Brown 2013), including Chapter 3 of this book and our 2018 *NVSQ* article (Guo and Saxton 2018).

Communication Strategy: Timing and Pacing. We examined four *timing and pacing* variables. As in Chapter 3, we first measure the cumulative number of messages sent by the organization, given its positive association with the number of retweets (Saxton et al. 2015). Given that organizational tweets may be more likely to receive a response during business hours and on business days (Saxton 2016), we also generate three variables based on the tweets' time stamps.

Communication Strategy: Content. We generated 20 content variables. To start, as in Chapter 3, two binary variables for visual content, *Photo* and *Video*, are included. Next, 14 variables are generated using a "dictionary"-based approach that has become increasingly common in social science and management research (e.g., Suddaby, Saxton, and Gunz 2015; Tetlock 2007; Tetlock, Saar-Tsechansky, and Macskassy 2008). In Chapter 3 we argued that, in the nonprofit context, ethical appeals would be most likely to generate attention and thus generated a variable, *Value Framing*, based on an ethics dictionary. Because of this variable's strong relationship with audience attention, we expand the approach here to include 14 dictionary-based variables. Collectively, these variables reflect tweets that convey ethical content, positive content, emphatic content, and political and action content. We next operationalize two miscellaneous content variables that indicate, respectively, tweets that have content truncated due to length and tweets with (according to Twitter) "possibly sensitive" links. Given the growing popularity of "tweet chats" (Budak and Agrawal 2013), we also generate a binary variable indicating tweets that contain a "chat" hashtag. Finally, we create a binary indicator of whether the tweet contains a user mention of a "celebrity fish." The idea for this variable lies in a practice we identified through inductive analysis of our data in Guo and Saxton (2014b). Celebrities are influential on social media in the sense that their tweets almost immediately reach an audience of hundreds of thousands, or even millions, of followers. A nonprofit that can capture the attention of a celebrity can receive a huge payoff in terms of geometrically increasing the diffusion of its message or call to action. For instance, *@PublicCounsel* targeted Oprah Winfrey by tweeting

@oprah in tribute video to Elie Wiesel: "you survived horror without hating"

The nonprofit using this tactic is, to continue with the metaphor, "fishing" for Oprah to take the "bait" offered by a mention of her username by replying to, retweeting, or liking the organization's tweet. We coded a binary variable, *Celebrity Fishing*, to indicate those messages that reference (using an @USER mention) any Twitter user with one million or more followers. We found that roughly 6% of tweets contained such a mention. Collectively, they referenced 832 different Twitter users, with the top ten being @POTUS, @RealDonaldTrump, @NYTimes, @FoxNews, @WashingtonPost, @TheHill, @BenShapiro, @ACLU, @CNN, and @USAToday.

Tweet Sophistication Features. Our remaining three categories of variables did not appear in Chapter 3 but instead come from our inductive investigation of the data. The first of these categories, *Tweet Sophistication Features*, comprises 23 miscellaneous variables that roughly proxy for the sophistication with which the user uses Twitter. In particular, these variables indicate tweet geocoding; the "source," or specific tool or application from which the tweet was sent; the tagging of places (such as a city, tourist site, restaurant); and the inclusion of symbols. As far as we are aware, such variables have not been examined in studies of public reactions and no literature exists that can be tapped to generate deductive insights. Instead, our insights are inductive. We argue it is plausible that, for instance, geocoding a tweet, tagging a "place," or using symbols signals a more sophisticated tweet and/or Twitter user, and that "sophisticated" users and messages could be more likely to generate attention. We similarly believe it plausible that some of the "sources" could signal greater sophistication. Our feature selection analyses will show whether these assumptions are valid.

Account-Level Variables. Because recent evidence suggests that *who* sends a message is an important determinant of public reactions (e.g., Saxton et al. 2019; Xu and Saxton 2019), we next examine 34 account-level variables. All are derived from data in the *user* object returned by the Twitter API. First, as in Chapter 3, *Number of Likes* is a count of the cumulative number of tweets to date the organization has "liked"; it reflects the overall level of activity and is a rough proxy for the level of sophistication of the organization's social media use. Using similar logic, we operationalize variables that reflect how long the organization has had a Twitter account, the length of its profile description, and whether the description included hashtags or user mentions. The latter two variables are developed in response to novel behaviors we have seen in our analyses of the organizations' Twitter profiles. Inductive reasoning also leads us to measure whether the organization changed its Twitter screen name since 2013; we saw a number of organizations that made changes to their Twitter handles, and we thought a name change could cause a change in the level of public attention an account receives. The remaining 28 variables derive directly from the *user* API object and indicate such things as whether the organization set a location or used customized profile images. These 28 objects are all included based on the intuition that account sophistication is a likely driver of attention.

Admittedly, here we come closest to "data fishing." We analyze all 28 features because we do not know which of these features best captures sophistication, nor are we certain account-level sophistication is in fact an important factor in driving attention. Despite the uncertainties, the potential payoff is increased understanding of our phenomenon of interest. Indeed, one of the core benefits of our method is the capacity to explore a great many more hunches and intuitive and inductive insights in our model-building efforts. In the end, if the new variables are not important, they will be dropped during the feature selection stage and we will have lost only some analytical and data-generating effort.

Organizational Characteristics. Finally, we consider 37 "offline" organizational variables. Our reasoning is similar to that outlined for account-level characteristics: that *who* is talking has a bearing on how much attention is paid to what is said. The difference is that these 37 features reflect non–social media characteristics that have been found to be important in the nonprofit literature. Starting with the age and revenue controls included in Chapter 3, we first add two alternative measures of size: total assets and expenses. We then include two variables common in the nonprofit financial literature (e.g., Gordon, Knock, and Neely 2009; Khumawala, Neely, and Gordon 2010; Saxton, Neely, and Guo 2014; Weisbrod and Dominguez 1986): the program spending ratio, which reflects the proportion of spending devoted to programs rather than fundraising or administration; and the amount of spending on fundraising. We argue more efficient organizations could be more likely to garner public attention, and organizations that spend more on fundraising could be more oriented toward boosting their public profile and level of public attention. We next measure the presence of "donor advisories" given by the third-party ratings agency *Charity Navigator.* Donor advisories indicate potential organizational mismanagement (Saxton and Neely 2019), which could affect other organizational activities such as social media usage. A series of nine binary variables, based on the NTEE "major groups" categories (http://nccs.urban.org/classification/national-taxonomy-exempt-entities), then indicate the industry or subsector in which the organization is operating. Finally, state is commonly included in nonprofit organizational studies as a control (e.g., Harris, Petrovits, and Yetman 2017; Saxton and Neely 2019); we include it to tap potentially different levels of social media usage patterns across states, which might in turn affect levels of public attention. We thus include 21 state (as well as the District of Columbia) dummy variables indicating the state in which the organization is located. The District of Columbia is the most frequently represented, followed by New York and Virginia. Given the advocacy focus of our organizations it is not surprising to see a high concentration located near the federal capital.

Feature Selection

Guided by existing theory and available data, in the previous stage we generated 133 variables for potential inclusion in our theoretical model. In the second stage, feature selection, we seek to identify the variables with the greatest explanatory and/or predictive power, while removing those that are unnecessary, irrelevant, or redundant. In line with our methodological approach outlined earlier, feature selection proceeds in three main steps: (1) univariate, (2) bivariate, and (3) multivariate. As in the preceding section, in the main text we present only the most important details for each step—the methodological appendix contains a more detailed presentation of the univariate, bivariate, and multivariate feature selection steps.

Univariate Feature Selection

The first step is to conduct univariate feature selection. In machine learning terminology, univariate techniques focus on characteristics of each explanatory variable in isolation. It is thus analogous to what is found in typical social scientific terminology with, for instance, univariate statistics such as the mean and standard deviation. Our focus here is on an initial "filtering" (Blum and Langley 1997; Guyon and Elisseeff 2003; John, Kohavi, and Pfleger 1994) of the features by removing zero-variance and low-variance features. First, we apply the *VarianceThreshold* class found in Python's *scikit-learn* package. We find 19 account-level and tweet-level variables that have zero variation, and all are omitted at this stage (see methodological appendix Table A.2 for a detailed list). We also use the *VarianceThreshold* class to identify six variables with extremely low variation. In sum, 25 variables are omitted in the univariate stage, leaving 108 variables for bivariate feature selection.

Bivariate Feature Selection

We now take our 108 remaining variables and conduct two types of bivariate[5] feature selection techniques (see Guyon and Elisseeff 2003), or techniques where we consider the statistical relationship between the dependent variable *Retweeted* (which indicates whether the organization's message received one or more retweets) and each individual explanatory feature. First, we conduct a series of bivariate "feature importance" tests, which are helpful for screening variables for *relevance* (Yu and Liu 2004). As discussed in the methodological appendix, we select five data-appropriate feature importance classifiers and triangulate the results. We find nine features have scores of 0 on all five feature selection algorithms and thus drop all nine of these low-relevance features. While we could be more stringent at this stage, we opt to remove only the least relevant features during this stage, for the multivariate techniques are better suited to selecting features taking the interactions among variables into account.

Second, we examine correlation matrices to help identify *redundancy* (Guyon and Elisseeff 2003, 1173) among pairs of explanatory features. Specifically, we use the above-mentioned relevance tests in conjunction with correlation tests in order to identify the more relevant of each redundant pair of features. In effect, we use correlation matrices to identify the redundant features and then (referring back to the rank orderings of relevance) omit the less relevant feature in each pair of redundant features. For instance, three features related to organizational size—*Revenue, Assets,* and *Total Functional Expenses*—are highly correlated, and because *Revenue* is the most relevant of the three as indicated by our feature relevance tests, it is retained and the two redundant variables are dropped. We thus identified a total of 10 redundant variables (to learn more about how the redundancies were identified, please refer to the methodological appendix). To summarize, we began our bivariate analyses with 108 variables and removed nine due to relevance and 10 due to redundancy, leaving us with 89 variables for the multivariate stage.

Multivariate Feature Selection

In the multivariate stage we undertake a more rigorous pruning of the set of features that will go into our final theoretical model. Specifically, we employ four types of multivariate feature selection methods on the remaining 89 variables: recursive feature elimination (RFE), linear support vector classification with L_1 penalty, linear support vector classification with L_2 penalty, and a stochastic gradient descent *support vector machine* (SVM) classifier with *elasticnet* penalty (for a complete discussion of these algorithms see the methodological appendix).

For each of the 24 of 89 variables that were selected for our final model, Table 4.1 shows the relevance/importance scores on our four multivariate feature selection algorithms (see the methodological appendix Table A.4 for scores on all 89 variables). We normalize scores on the four algorithms, generate a mean score for each variable, and then the variables are ranked from most to least relevant based on this mean score. As before, the *Number of Lists* feature is most relevant. In the next section we elaborate on the process for determining the cutoff point of 24 variables.

Model Selection

Our final feature selection method is a comprehensive model selection algorithm. Here, information from the triangulated results (the *MEAN* algorithm scores shown in Table 4.1 and appendix Table A.4) for all 89 variables is used in a custom feature-selection algorithm to find the ideal number of variables to include in our final model. Specifically, we employ a custom *forward-selection* algorithm to find the "elbow" (e.g., Ketchen and Shook 1996) at which the inclusion of additional variables results in diminishing returns in model accuracy. As described in greater detail below, we find this point of diminishing returns occurs at around 20 variables, and thus use this as the cutoff point for our final model, while also adding four theoretically chosen variables based on findings from Chapter 3.

If we were to rely on only a single multivariate method we would not need to take this final comprehensive step, for each of the four methods provides its own "feature selection" outcome. For instance, RFE yields a score of 1 for 44 of the 89 variables, effectively considering those 44 features to comprise the "best" model. Similarly, the L1 and elasticnet penalties will make some coefficients equal to zero; those variables could be considered to be "unselected" features. The L2 norm will push certain coefficients toward zero; the researcher can use those results to find some meaningful cutoff in the number of features selected.

Yet our approach here is not to rely on a single algorithm. Instead, in line with our overall methodology, we aim for an approach based on multiple methods and researcher judgment. Namely, our final model selection is based on multiple methods insofar as the relevance of the 89 variables is not based on any single multivariate algorithm but on the mean score across four different algorithms. Researcher judgment comes into play, meanwhile, in allowing some flexibility in the variable selection cutoff point based on theory and domain knowledge.

We should note that, with any of the four multivariate feature selection methods, a key next step would be to refine and validate the model in order to

TABLE 4.1   24 chosen variables, ordered by mean score on four multivariate feature selection techniques

Variable	Rank (out of 89)	MEAN	RFE	LinearSVC (L1 penalty)	LinearSVC (L2 penalty)	SGDC (elasticnet penalty)
No. of Lists	1	0.980	1	1	1	0.92
@ Message	2	**0.808**	**1**	**0.65**	**0.58**	**1**
Alabama	3	0.743	1	0.55	0.53	0.89
Source—HubSpot	4	0.723	1	0.51	0.5	0.88
Description	5	0.675	1	0.09	0.69	0.92
NTEE—Environment and Animals	6	0.590	1	0.51	0.5	0.35
Program Expense %	7	0.575	1	0.36	0.35	0.59
No. of Friends	8	0.540	1	0.34	0.35	0.47
Display URL	9	0.440	1	0.2	0.15	0.41
Cumulative No. of Messages Sent	**10**	**0.418**	**1**	**0.32**	**0.26**	**0.09**
Revenue	**11**	**0.403**	**1**	**0.27**	**0.23**	**0.11**
No. of Mentions	**12**	**0.375**	**1**	**0.15**	**0.14**	**0.21**
Michigan	13	0.375	1	0.24	0.18	0.08
Age	**14**	**0.373**	**1**	**0.13**	**0.14**	**0.22**
Source—Facebook	15	0.370	1	0.2	0.21	0.07
No. of Followers	**16**	**0.368**	**1**	**0.12**	**0.19**	**0.16**
No. of Likes	17	0.363	1	0.14	0.12	0.19
No. of URLs	**18**	**0.353**	**1**	**0.15**	**0.14**	**0.12**
Default Profile	19	0.353	1	0.2	0.14	0.07
Place Type—Admin	20	0.350	1	0.17	0.16	0.07
Video	**35**	**0.290**	**1**	**0.05**	**0.06**	**0.05**
Photo	**48**	**0.255**	**0.8**	**0.06**	**0.05**	**0.11**
No. of Hashtags	**55**	**0.233**	**0.71**	**0.07**	**0.1**	**0.05**
Value Framing	**58**	**0.195**	**0.69**	**0.03**	**0.03**	**0.03**

NOTE: This table shows only the 24 variables chosen for the final theoretical model. Complete results for all 89 variables are in the methodological appendix. Variables in bold are those that were included in the organizational-level analyses in Chapter 3. "MEAN" indicates average score on the four feature selection techniques shown in the table. RFE, recursive feature elimination; linear SVC, linear support vector classification; SGDC, stochastic gradient descent classifier.

find the optimal number of features for our final model (Guyon and Elisseeff 2003). We effectively do the same, but with a custom algorithm that can both incorporate researcher domain knowledge and the findings from multiple techniques for feature selection. Specifically, we use a type of *forward stepwise selection*: "Forward stepwise selection begins with a model containing no predictors, and then adds predictors to the model, one-at-a-time, until all of the predictors are in the model. In particular, at each step the variable that gives the greatest additional improvement to the fit is added to the model" (James et al. 2013, 207).[6] Our particular forward-selection algorithm begins by adding the most relevant variable from Table 4.1, *Number of Lists,* and calculates the predictive accuracy of the model—where predictive accuracy is assessed as the ability for the independent variable(s) to accurately predict whether the message is retweeted or not. It then adds the second most relevant variable, *@ Message,* and again calculates predictive model accuracy. The forward-selection algorithm continues until all 89 variables are included, calculating model accuracy at each stage.

We then use the "elbow curve" method (e.g., Ketchen and Shook 1996) to select the top 20 variables shown in Table 4.1. The elbow method relies on visual and/or statistical examination of change in the accuracy score. Figure 4.1 plots the number of features included by model accuracy. As the number of features increases from 1 to 8, the increase in accuracy with each new feature is relatively large. An upward trend generally continues until the number of features reaches around 20. At this point a classifier using 20 variables will achieve slightly over 86.5% accuracy. After this point, there are substantially diminishing returns in the level of increased accuracy with each additional feature added. As highlighted by the oval added to the figure, the "elbow" thus occurs around 20 features, and this is the chosen cutoff for our feature selection.

Our final model thus includes the top 20 variables shown in Table 4.1. We also use researcher judgment and add four variables (*Photo, Video, Number of Hashtags,* and *Value Framing*) below the cutoff that were found to be important at the organization/month level in Chapter 3. Not only does this incorporate additional deductive reasoning into the feature selection process, but it allows us to make more comprehensive comparisons to the organization/month model posited in the previous chapter.

Final Proposed Theoretical Model

Table 4.2 summarizes the 24 variables along with the expected direction of the relationship as inferred from the bivariate logits and chi-squared tests (see the methodological appendix to the book) along with nonnormalized scores on the feature selection tests. We should point out that 11 of the variables (as indicated by bold font in Table 4.1) come from the "deductive" element insofar as they were found in prior tests (Chapter 3 and/or Guo and Saxton 2018). The

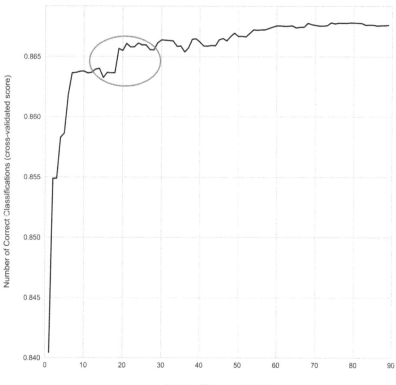

Number of Features Selected

FIGURE 4.1   Cross-validated accuracy scores by number of features

NOTE: Figure shows cross-validated accuracy scores (the proportion of tweets correctly classified as retweeted or not) for models containing from one through 89 variables. Accuracy scores are calculated using *k*-fold cross-validation using *scikit-learn*'s *cross_validate* function. *K*-fold cross-validation involves splitting the data up into *k* subsets, training and testing the model *k* times, and then averaging the model accuracy scores from the *k* rounds. We ran *five-fold* cross-validation; this means that, for each number of variables from one through 89, the accuracy scores shown are the average of five rounds of accuracy tests. In each round, a different *fold*, or subset, is chosen as a hold-out sample used to test model accuracy, while the remaining *k*-1 folds are used as the training sample to fit the prediction model. Differently put, each of the 89 accuracy scores plotted in the figure is the average of five rounds of model testing; in each of the five rounds the prediction model is trained and fitted using *k-1* folds and the fold left out is the test data used for testing the prediction accuracy of the fitted model.

remaining 13 variables come from chiefly inductive reasoning (e.g., *Source— HubSpot*) or a mix of inductive and deductive logic (e.g., *Program Expense Percentage, Number of Friends*).

However, we do not wish to merely present a set of variables. In line with our methodological approach, the addition of new variables should be paired with a refining of an existing model and/or reconceptualization of the existing

▮LE 4.2 Descriptive statistics for final model variables, with expected direction of relationship ▯ attention

▮ategory *and Variable*	Expected *Direction*	*Count*	*Mean*	*SD*	*Min.*	*Max.*
▮tention Proxy						
▮essage Is Retweeted		52,226	.845	.362	0	1
▮etwork Characteristics						
▮o. of Lists	+	52,226	1,756	2,569	5	14,101
▮o. of Friends	+	52,226	8,128	23,958	3	167,788
▮o. of Followers	+	52,226	103,376	207,077	46	1,428,059
▮argeting and Connecting						
Message	-	52,226	.061	.239	0	1
▮o. of Mentions	-	52,226	.532	.878	0	10
▮o. of URLs	+	52,226	.879	.402	0	4
▮o. of Hashtags	+	52,226	.727	.938	0	14
▮iming and Pacing						
▮umulative No. of Messages Sent	+	52,226	19,340	10,500	241	83,406
▮ontent Variables						
▮hoto	+	52,226	.109	.312	0	1
▮ideo	+	52,226	.004	.062	0	1
▮alue Framing	+	52,226	.197	.398	0	1
▮weet Sophistication Variables						
▮ource—HubSpot	-	52,226	.0152	.122	0	1
▮ource—Facebook	-	52,226	.0107	.103	0	1
▮lace Type—Admin	-	52,226	.0019	.044	0	1
▮ccount Variables						
▮escription (0,1)	+	52,226	.998	.016	0	1
▮isplay URL (0,1)	+	52,226	.998	.012	0	1
▮efault Profile (0,1)	-	52,226	.018	.133	0	1
▮o. of Likes	+	52,226	3,863.03	4,592	1	29,881
▮rganizational Characteristics						
▮ge	+	52,226	35.50	14.25	11	93
▮evenue (dollars)	+	52,226	14,811,069	20,088,801	237,098	158,694,033
▮rogram Expense %	+	52,226	77.1	9.55	13.3	94
▮labama	+	52,226	.021	.142	0	1
▮ichigan	-	52,226	.017	.131	0	1
▮TEE—Environment & Animals	-	52,226	.021	.144	0	1

▮TE: This table shows descriptive statistics for the dependent variable plus the independent variables chosen during the feature ▮ction process (see Table 4.1). The *N* of 52,226 reflects the 20% "hold-out" sample that, in line with machine learning con-▮ition, is used for the model testing portion. Note that in our regressions we include binary variables for all state and NTEE ▮le categories; we show *Alabama, Michigan,* and *NTEE—Environment & Animals* here for illustrative purposes. SD, standard ▮viation.

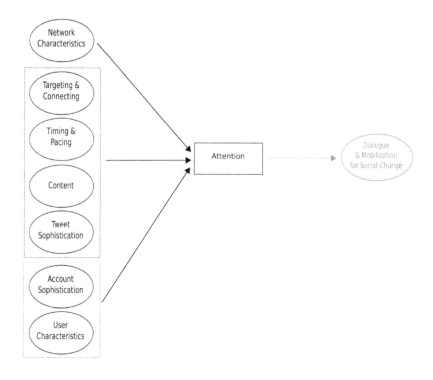

F I G U R E   4 . 2   Proposed theoretical model

relationships in a way that deepens our understanding of the core nonprofit organizational context. Accordingly, after completing the feature selection process we then cycle back and forth between the data, existing models (Chapter 3) and literature, our domain knowledge, and the proposed set of 24 variables in order to "'lift' the data to a conceptual level" (Suddaby 2006, 636) and thus build theory. And theory, in our view, is related to relationships among *concepts* rather than variables.

Figure 4.2 shows our updated theoretical model. Three new conceptual categories are visible: *Tweet Sophistication, Account Sophistication,* and *User Characteristics.* All three represent the outcome of our efforts to inductively examine the data and conceptualize the newly found empirical relationships. On the basis of this process we consider seven of our new variables to reflect the sophistication of the organization's tweets and of its Twitter profile. Using chiefly inductive reasoning, we now posit that more sophisticated tweets and more sophisticated organizational users will be more likely to generate audience attention on social media. Similarly, we propose that "offline" user characteristics (as represented by four new variables in conjunction with two prior variables, *Age* and *Revenue*) are a driving force of audience attention.

For three of our user characteristics variables, we likewise recognize that we are not interested in the variables *Michigan, Alabama,* and *NTEE—Environment and Animals,* but rather the more general concepts of state and industry. Accordingly, and in line with standard statistical practice, our conceptual model replaces the first two variables with the variable *State* and the last variable with the variable *NTEE category.*

Two of our new variables *(Number of Lists* and *Number of Friends),* meanwhile, fit within the existing conceptual category of *Network Characteristics.* To reiterate, our goal is *not* to multiply the number of variables included in a set of regressions. Rather, our goal is to increase our understanding of what drives attention, and it is our firm belief that understanding is driven by improvements at the conceptual level. Adding new variables to the network characteristics category can help refine, or make more precise, the nature of the relationship between network characteristics and audience attention.

To recap where we have come so far in this chapter, in the first stage of our analysis—feature engineering—we have inductively identified and analyzed a large range of potentially interesting variables. Our second stage—feature selection—served to help us reduce the set of 133 engineered features down to the 24 most relevant, nonredundant features. Examining the 24 variables through a theoretical lens, we then propose a theoretical model organized into the seven core conceptual categories shown in Figure 4.2: network characteristics, targeting and connecting, timing and pacing, content, tweet sophistication, account sophistication, and organizational characteristics. We now have an expanded theoretical model featuring seven core conceptual categories. In our final stage we test the model we have built. It is to this task that we now turn.

Model Testing

In the previous section we undertook model selection. Now we proceed to model testing. This stage is what is seen in the typical quantitative study published in, for instance, *Nonprofit and Voluntary Sector Quarterly, The Accounting Review,* or the *Academy of Management Journal.* We take the usual approach seen in these journals and test our model with a series of regressions.

Model Testing in Machine Learning Versus the Social Sciences:
Prediction versus Understanding

We should note that machine learning and the social sciences typically diverge in how model testing is approached. This is largely due to a distinction in the use of the term "model." In a data science approach, the term "model" refers not only to (1) the set of features but to (2) a specific machine learning algorithm, such as SVM, along with (3) a specific set of algorithm *hyperparameters*, or fine-tuning parameters that were shown to optimize the accuracy of the SVM algorithm in the testing phase. Using our case as an example, a data scientist might refer to the model as the 24 chosen features run with an SVM algorithm using an "rbf" *kernel*, a *gamma* value of 0.1, and a *C* value of 1 (the hyperparameters). This tuned SVM algorithm run with 24 features—that is, the model—would then be used to predict which of a given set of tweets will garner attention. We would be less interested in the effects of individual variables than in the performance (i.e., accuracy) of the entire model. Such approaches are highly useful for generating predictive models, especially models that can be run quickly on real-time data to generate a prediction for the outcome variable of interest.

In a typical social science approach, however, we would likely test the model with a logit or probit regression (given our binary dependent variable), and the "model" would refer solely to the core concepts and variables. More specifically, we would consider the model shown in Figure 4.2 to represent the "theoretical model" (or "conceptual model"), while we would actually test an "empirical model" that comprises the specific set of variables used to operationalize the theoretical model. In either case, the statistical method is kept separate from "the model." The key reason for this separation is alluded to above: in a social scientific approach we are not interested in prediction as much as understanding.

In the predictive approach, in contrast, we do not need to see nor examine the effect size or interactions among the various features, nor do we need some keen conceptual insight driving the inclusion of a particular variable; so long as a new variable increases the accuracy of the prediction, it will be added to the model. For the same reason, the machine learning approach is not so interested in the performance of individual variables but rather the performance of the set of variables as a whole.

In our current social scientific approach, however, we are only partially interested in the performance of the model as a whole as reflected in, for example, the F statistic returned by an ordinary least squares (OLS) regression. We are instead more interested in three things: (1) whether the individual variables are significant, (2) the direction of the relationship (positive or negative), and (3) the effect size of the variables (or how much of an effect an individual variable has on the dependent variable). Moreover, after the regressions are run and analyses interpreted, we will cycle back to our theoretical model and again seek to lift the data to the conceptual level and then revise our theory accordingly. In brief, it is our aim for theoretical understanding over atheoretical prediction that pushes us to employ a social scientific approach to model testing.

Data and Descriptive Statistics

In either the machine learning or social scientific approaches, best practices would require that the model be tested on a different set of data than that which was used for model development. We therefore run our regressions on the 20% "hold-out" sample described earlier. Specifically, we run logistic regressions where *retweeted* is the (binary) dependent variable on 52,226 tweets. Of the 167 organizations, 166 are represented in these tweets.

Table 4.2 shows descriptive statistics for all independent variables plus the dependent variable *Retweeted*. To facilitate understanding, Table 4.3 contains variable descriptions for each of the variables.

Starting with the dependent variable, the mean value of 0.845 indicates 84.5% of tweets sent received one or more retweets. Most organizational tweets are getting at least some attention. Our model will help us understand what separates these tweets from the 15.5% of tweets that receive no attention from the intended audience.

Turning to the network characteristics variables, the average for *Number of Lists* is 1,756 with a range from 5 up to 14,101. The average *Number of Friends* is 8,128, indicating the number of other Twitter users followed by the message sender. As with *Number of Lists,* the range is vast, from a low of 3 to a high of 167,788. *Number of Followers,* which indicates the number of other Twitter users who follow the organization, has a mean value of 103,376 and a range of 46 to 1,428,059.

Next are four targeting and connecting variables: the binary variable @ *Message* has a mean value of 0.061, *Number of Mentions* has a mean of 0.532 and a range of 0 to 10, *Number of URLs* a mean of 0.879 and a range of 0 to 4, and *Number of Hashtags* a mean of 0.727 and a range of 0 to 14.

TABLE 4.3 Variable descriptions, final model variables

Category/*Variable*	Source/Description
Attention Proxy	
Retweeted	Tweet receives one or more retweets (0,1).
Network Characteristics	
No. of Followers	Number of other Twitter users who follow the nonprofit. *Source:* Twitter *user* API
No. of Friends	Number of other Twitter users followed by the nonprofit. *Source:* Twitter *user* API
No. of Lists	Number of public Twitter "lists" on which the nonprofit appears. *Source:* Twitter *user* API
Targeting and Connecting	
@ Message	Tweet begins with "@" or ".@". Based on tweet characteristics
No. of Hashtags	Number of hashtags included in the tweet. Based on tweet *entities* object
No. of URLs	Number of hyperlinks included in the tweet. Based on tweet *entities* object
No. of Mentions	Number of @USER mentions included in the tweet. Based on tweet *entities* object
Timing and Pacing	
Cumulative No. of Messages Sent	Cumulative number of tweets sent by the nonprofit to date. *Source:* Twitter *user* API
Content	
Photo	Tweet contains a photo (0,1). Based on tweet *media* object.
Video	Tweet contains a video (0,1). Based on tweet *media* object.
Value Framing	Tweet contains one or more words in Harvard IV *RcEthic* dictionary (0,1).
Tweet Sophistication Features	
Place Type—Admin	Tweet tagged with an "admin" place (e.g., county, state). Based on *place* object
Source—Facebook	Tweet sent from Facebook application. Based on tweet *source* object
Source—HubSpot	Tweet sent from HubSpot application. Based on tweet *source* object
Account-level Variables	
No. of Likes	Number of tweets the nonprofit has "liked" to date. *Source:* Twitter *user* API
Description (0,1)	Profile page contains a written description. *Source:* Twitter *user* API
Default Profile (0,1)	Organization uses default Twitter profile. *Source:* Twitter *user* API
Display URL (0,1)	Organization displays a URL in its profile. *Source:* Twitter *user* API
Organizational Characteristics	
Revenue	Total revenues. *Source:* Charity Navigator
Age	No. of years nonprofit has held IRS recognition. *Source:* IRS Business Master File (BMF)
Program Expense %	Program expense ratio. *Source:* Charity Navigator
NTEE	NTEE 10 industry code. *Source:* IRS BMF
State	State in which organization is located. *Source:* IRS BMF

NOTE: This table shows variable descriptions for dependent variable plus the independent variables chosen for the final model (see Table 4.2). Note that for NTEE code and state we include binary variables for all state and NTEE code categories.

As in Chapter 3, there is a single timing and pacing variable: *Cumulative Number of Messages Sent.* This variable indicates the total number of tweets the organization has sent as of January 1, 2017, and has a mean value of 19,340 and ranges from 241 to 83,406.

There are then three binary content variables. The mean values shown in Table 4.2 indicate that roughly 11% of tweets contain a *Photo,* 0.4% contain a *Video,* and just under 20% contain a *Value Framing* word.

Next, there are three binary variables in one of our new conceptual categories—tweet sophistication. The first two, *Source—HubSpot* and *Source—Facebook,* indicate the application from which the tweet was sent. Only 1.5% of tweets were sent from HubSpot and 1.1% from Facebook. The other variable, *Place Type—Admin,* reflects sophistication insofar as the user has geotagged the tweet as coming from a geographic location. The "Admin" tag is how Twitter classifies a location above the neighborhood and city levels and below the country level, meaning a tweet with a *Place Type—Admin* value of 1 (0.2% of tweets) could indicate a county, state, or province, etc. As shown in Table 4.2, we expect a negative relationship between this variable and retweetability. Compared to other place types (such as a city, or a restaurant or a coffee shop), the Admin tag is likely too broad to generate significant attention.

Another new conceptual category (compared to Chapter 3) is account sophistication, and our feature selection analyses identified four relevant variables. First, *Description* is a binary variable that indicates whether the sending account includes a written profile description. The mean value of 0.99 indicates the vast majority of the organizations include a written description. The same percentage of organizations include a *Display URL* in their written profile. Organizations that do neither are sending a signal that they are not sophisticated users of Twitter. Not only could this make audiences see the organization's messages as less credible or worthy of retweeting, but it could increase the likelihood the organization's account is a nonvalid, "spam" account. The same problems are presented by *Default Profile,* which indicates the 1.8% of tweets sent from accounts that still use the default profile page. Finally, *Number of Likes* captures the cumulative number of tweets the organization has "liked"; as indicated in Table 4.2, the average is 3,863 tweets and ranges from 1 to 29,881.

Our final conceptual category, also new, is organizational characteristics. Rather than representing a single coherent concept, the variables in this category reflect our intuitive understanding—corroborated by the analyses undertaken in this chapter—that *who* sends a message is a key determinant of

TABLE 4.4 Regression results with four dependent variables: retweeted (0,1) and counts of retweets, likes, and replies

	DV = Retweeted (0,1)		DV = Number of Retweets		DV = Number of Likes		DV = Number of Replies	
Network Characteristics								
Log(No. of Lists)	0.17	(0.20)	-0.20	(0.19)	-0.50*	(0.21)	-0.32	(0.59)
Log(No. of Friends)	-0.08	(0.09)	-0.18*	(0.07)	-0.11	(0.08)	-0.57*	(0.23)
Log(No. of Followers)	0.86**	(0.16)	1.12**	(0.14)	1.43**	(0.15)	1.09**	(0.39)
Targeting and Connecting								
@ Message	-3.30**	(0.25)	-1.73**	(0.22)	-1.49**	(0.19)	-0.84*	(0.36)
No. of Mentions	0.04	(0.04)	-0.11**	(0.03)	-0.04	(0.03)	-0.08	(0.07)
No. of URLs	0.29**	(0.10)	-0.14	(0.09)	-0.37**	(0.09)	-0.24+	(0.13)
No. of Hashtags	-0.03	(0.04)	-0.08**	(0.03)	-0.10**	(0.03)	-0.20**	(0.07)
Timing and Pacing								
Log(Cumulative No. of Messages Sent)	-0.43**	(0.15)	-0.35*	(0.16)	-0.52**	(0.18)	1.37	(0.84)
Content Variables								
Photo	0.09	(0.10)	0.15	(0.13)	0.24+	(0.14)	0.11	(0.22)
Video	0.32	(0.33)	0.79*	(0.31)	0.50+	(0.29)	0.78*	(0.36)
Value Framing	0.31**	(0.06)	0.24**	(0.04)	0.22**	(0.04)	0.35**	(0.11)
Tweet Sophistication Features								
Source—HubSpot	-0.78*	(0.34)	-1.24**	(0.32)	-1.14**	(0.38)	-1.96+	(1.01)
Source—Facebook	-1.32**	(0.29)	-1.05**	(0.34)	-0.68*	(0.28)	0.14	(0.76)
Place Type—Admin	-0.37	(0.27)	0.09	(0.38)	0.18	(0.43)	-0.76	(0.53)

	Model 1		Model 2		Model 3		Model 4	
Account Variables								
Description (0,1)	−0.53	(0.64)	−0.40	(0.53)	−0.22	(0.55)	−7.88**	(2.88)
Display URL (0,1)	−1.40+	(0.75)	−1.57*	(0.70)	−2.54**	(0.64)	−0.90	(3.11)
Default Profile (0,1)	−0.004	(0.34)	−0.13	(0.26)	0.08	(0.24)	−0.71	(1.11)
Log(No. of Likes)	0.04	(0.07)	0.10+	(0.06)	0.16**	(0.06)	0.30+	(0.17)
Organizational Characteristics								
Log(Age)	0.23	(0.23)	−0.03	(0.20)	−0.11	(0.21)	−0.37	(0.54)
Log(Revenue)	0.10	(0.09)	0.10	(0.08)	0.10	(0.08)	0.29+	(0.17)
Program Expense %	0.01	(0.01)	0.01	(0.01)	0.01	(0.01)	−0.03	(0.03)
Constant	−2.18	(1.53)	−2.81+	(1.49)	−1.85	(1.52)	−11.06*	(4.58)
STATE FIXED EFFECTS	YES		YES		YES		YES	
NTEE FIXED EFFECTS	YES		YES		YES		YES	
STD. ERRORS CLUSTERED ON ORG	YES		YES		YES		YES	
N	52,226		52,226		52,226		51,553	
Pseudo R^2	0.29		0.12		0.13		0.08	
Model Sig. (χ^2)	13,167.2**		52248.18**		58096.36**		7,714.23**	
Log likelihood	−15,982.99		−184,870.60		−199,447.35		−43,058.83	

NOTES: Standard errors in parentheses; R^2 shown is McFadden's pseudo-R^2. Model 1 (retweeted) estimated with logit regression and Models 2–4 (number of retweets, number of likes, and number of replies, respectively) estimated with negative binomial regression. DV, dependent variable.

+ $p < 0.10$
* $p < 0.05$
** $p < 0.01$

whether the message receives attention. The six variables included in this category represent "offline" characteristics that were shown to be relevant features in driving audience attention. First, the average *Age* of the organizations is 35.5 years and ranges from 11 to 93. Average *Revenue* is \$14,811,069 and ranges from \$237,098 to \$158,694,033. The well-known *Program Expense Percentage,* which captures the ratio of program spending to total spending, is 77% and ranges from a very low 13.3% up to 94%. The next two variables are binary indicators of the state in which the organization is located; just over 2% of tweets are sent from Alabama and 1.7% are sent from Michigan. Finally, 2.1% of tweets are sent by organizations in the NTEE major category Environment and Animals. As mentioned earlier, while the feature selection process identified the three latter variables, in our regressions we conform with standard practice and include a full suite of state and NTEE code dummy variables.

Results

Table 4.4 shows the series of four logit and negative binomial regressions used to test our model. Specifically, Model 1 provides the direct test of our model, while Models 2 through 4 extend the analyses by replacing the binary *Retweeted* dependent variable with, respectively, *Number of Retweets, Number of Likes,* and *Number of Replies.* By containing tweet-level versions of the organization/month-level dependent variables from Chapter 3, these latter three regressions allow for a valuable set of comparisons with Chapter 3. Not only will these three models tie in with and build on Chapter 3 in a more meaningful way, but they will allow us to see how well our message-level model, driven by machine learning, extends to the other three dependent variables.

Testing the Model. We first present results for Model 1. Because this model uses the same dependent variable as in the feature selection stage (*Retweeted*) on new data, it represents a direct test of the model we have built.[7] Given that *Retweeted* is a binary dependent variable, we estimate a logit regression. In line with standard research practice, we run a full complement of state fixed effects (state dummy variables; for an example see Harris, Petrovits, and Yetman 2017) instead of only *Alabama* and *Michigan* along with a full complement of NTEE fixed effects (NTEE 10 classification dummy variables, as in Saxton and Neely 2019) instead of only *NTEE—Environment and Animals.* We also cluster standard errors on organization.

We discuss results by conceptual category. Among the network characteristics, we see that only *Number of Followers* obtains a significant positive association with the dependent variable *Retweeted; Number of Lists* and *Number of Friends* both fail to achieve statistical significance.

Of the targeting and connecting variables, two variables (@ *Message* and *Number of URLs*) obtain significance, with the former being negatively associated with retweets and the latter being positively associated. The other two variables (*Number of Mentions* and *Number of Hashtags*) are not significantly associated with *Retweeted*.

The timing and pacing variable, *Cumulative Number of Messages Sent*, obtains a significant negative association. Apparently, the more tweets an organization has sent, the less likely each additional tweet is to receive audience attention.

Of the three content variables (*Photo, Video,* and *Value Framing*), only *Value Framing* obtains a significant relationship, being positively related to retweeting. Surprisingly, while *Photo* and *Video* are positively associated with the dependent variable, they both fail to achieve significance.

Two of the three tweet sophistication variables, *Source—HubSpot* and *Source—Facebook*, obtain a significant (negative) relationship with retweets. *Place Type—Admin* is not significantly related to retweets.

Next we turn to the account-level variables. The first three reflect characteristics of the account profile. The first variable, *Description,* fails to achieve significance; so too do *Default Profile* and *Number of Likes. Display URL,* in contrast, obtains a significant, negative association.

The final category is "offline" organizational characteristics. Interestingly, and unlike what occurs in many studies of offline phenomena, *Age, Revenue,* and *Program Expense Percentage* are all not significantly associated with audience attention. Overall, older organizations with larger revenues and higher program spending ratios are no more likely to generate audience attention than are younger, smaller, and less efficient organizations.

Extensions: Number of Retweets, Number of Likes, and Number of Replies.
We now turn to the results in Models 2 through 4, which cover, respectively, determinants of the *Number of Retweets, Number of Likes,* and *Number of Replies.* Because all three are count variables, we estimate the models using negative binomial regression.

Looking at network characteristics, we see that, as in Model 1, the *Number of Followers* obtains a strong positive association with audience retweeting in Model 2, with audience liking in Model 3, and with audience replying in Model 4. Comparing these findings with Chapter 3, we see that results are consistent with the follower count: the number of followers is significantly positively associated with attention in all models. The other two variables, *Number of Lists* and *Number of Friends*, are negatively related to attention in Models 2 through 4, though they only reach significance half of the time. We believe there are two reasons for these findings. First, referring back to Chapter 2, there is a power law distribution for the follower count—where the "rich get richer"—and this variable seems to be overpowering the effects of the listed count, which is an alternative measure of influence. Second, the number of "friends," or other Twitter users followed by the organization, does not seem, other things being equal, to be an important determinant of attention. In effect, it is not important how many people you follow; what matters is how many people follow you.

Of the four targeting and connecting variables, we see some differences in Models 2–4 compared to Model 1. To start, *@ Message* sees results consistent with Model 1: it obtains a significant negative association with the dependent variable in Models 2, 3, and 4. *Number of Mentions* and *Number of URLs*, in contrast, see the sign switch from positive in Model 1 to negative in the remaining models (though they are not significant in all models). Ostensibly, the more user mentions and URLs that are added to a message, the lower the amount of attention received. We find the same thing with *Number of Hashtags*, which is negatively related to attention in all four models. Our interpretation of these findings is that, first, user mentions provide a way of targeting and interacting with a focused user or a small subset of users; while this allows for a more intense interaction with the targeted user(s), it is not necessarily the best way to garner widespread attention. Differently put, there appears to be a trade-off between strengthening ties to specific users and gaining attention. Organizations should thus have a clear purpose of the goal of each tweet.

Our timing and pacing variable, *Cumulative Number of Messages Sent*, is, as in Model 1, significantly negative in Models 2 and 3 and is not significant in Model 4. What we take from these results is that organizations are not gaining more attention with volume.

Turning to our three content variables, *Photo, Video,* and *Value Framing* are positively related to attention throughout all of our regressions. However,

Photo only obtains significance in its relationship in Model 3, which has likes as the dependent variable; this is similar to the organizational-level findings in Chapter 3, where *Photo* obtained a significant positive relationship with liking but not retweeting or replying. *Video,* in turn, is not significant in Model 1 but is significant in Models 2 through 4. In effect, while the inclusion of a video does not seem to be related to *whether* a tweet receives attention, as indicated by Model 1, it does appear to be strongly related to the *amount* of attention a tweet receives. The most stable results with respect to content are seen with our *Value Framing* variable; it is consistently a strong predictor of whether a tweet receives attention as well as the amount of attention received. Comparing these findings with Chapter 3, we see that results are consistent with our measure of value framing: the use of ethical and values-based words is significantly positively associated with attention in all models.

We next look at our three tweet sophistication variables. None are positively, significantly related to attention in Models 2 through 4. Yet the coefficients still provide us relevant information about the nature of attention, at least with respect to the two variables for source. Namely, we find that compared to the baseline category, tweets being sent from HubSpot—a "customer relationship management" application/email marketing tool—and from Facebook are less likely to receive attention. Regarding HubSpot, our interpretation is that something about tweets sent from email marketing tools—or the organizations that choose to use them—does not seem appealing to the organizations' audiences. Regarding Facebook, in turn, tweets sent from Facebook are essentially being recycled for Twitter and are thus not original. It is therefore plausible that audiences are seeing through these actions.

Turning to our four account variables, we do not find meaningful positive relationships with *Description, Display URL,* or *Default Profile.* However, the results are notable for *Number of Likes,* which obtains a significant positive association in Models 2 through 4. This variable is an indicator of the organization's level of activity on Twitter—specifically, how engaged it is with other users' tweets—and it appears this activity is related to the amount of attention the organization receives in return.

Finally, we examine the three "offline" organizational characteristics of *Age, Revenue,* and the *Program Expense Percentage.* We find that *Age* is insignificant in all four models, as is the *Program Expense Percentage,* our proxy for efficiency. *Revenue,* meanwhile, is positively related to attention in all four models but only obtains significance in Model 4, which has the *Number of*

Replies as the dependent variable. Our takeaway from these findings is that, while stakeholders (especially donors) may care about the age, size, and level of efficiency of organizations in the offline context, particularly with regard to financial matters (e.g., Gordon, Knock, and Neely 2009; Khumawala, Neely, and Gordon 2009; Weisbrod and Dominguez 1986), such organizational characteristics are less relevant to the social media audience.

Discussion

In this final section we summarize our main empirical findings, discuss limitations and future research, discuss the contribution made by our novel methodological approach, and cover the practical implications of our study before proceeding to a brief set of conclusions.

Summary of Empirical Findings

Examining 261,127 tweets sent in 2017 by 167 diverse advocacy organizations, in this chapter we built and then tested a model of attention to organizational messages. What have we learned here about message-level attention?

For one, the organizational-level model from Chapter 3 "scales down" to the message level fairly reliably. Some of the variables needed a different measurement technique, while others (e.g., the cumulative number of tweets the organization has retweeted) made less sense at the message level and were thus left out of the model used in this chapter.

The model we tested had seven main conceptual categories—network characteristics, targeting and connecting, timing and pacing, content, tweet sophistication, account features, and organizational characteristics. In each of these categories we found one or more variables to be significant. This lends support to the overall theoretical model.

We have identified a number of new variables that appear to drive public attention. For instance, network characteristics appear to play a more prominent role than previously thought. Conversely, we found the indicators of tweet-level and account-level "sophistication" to be less powerful than our feature selection algorithms suggested. While they are significantly related to attention, this does not appear to be the most important category of behaviors.

In addition, organizational-level characteristics—covering network features, timing and pacing, and account-level features—seem to play a more prominent role than previously considered. Overall, *who* is doing the speaking appears to play a crucial role in determining the level of attention an advocacy organization's message receives.

We also need to recognize that not all of the variables that were selected in the model-building phase proved to be significant. Namely, *Place Type— Admin, Default Profile, Age,* and *Program Expense Percentage* failed to obtain significance in any of the regression models. This highlights the importance of separating feature selection and model building from model testing. The reason the four variables were nonsignificant is likely a combination of two factors. First, the model testing is done on a different sample of data—the 20% "hold-out" sample. Second, the feature selection algorithms are—by design—not identical to the statistical technique (logit regression) employed in model testing.

That said, in light of the above findings, a more parsimonious empirical model could likely be created that operationalizes our seven-factor conceptual model. Not counting the state and NTEE code fixed-effects variables, our regressions included 21 independent variables; a half dozen fewer variables could likely work just as well in future research. Beyond dropping several nonsignificant variables, one way to do this could be to combine related variables into indices; for instance, given the large number of features that tap account sophistication and tweet sophistication, creating index variables for these two concepts would be a reasonable approach.

Limitations and Future Research

One promising, and largely untapped, area, concerns the examination of textual content. In our 2018 article we began the focus on "content," although we limited the examination to visual content, and we found images were related to retweetability. In Chapter 3 we then extended the idea of content to include examination of ethical and values-based words in tweets. In this chapter we brought this textual examination down to the tweet level, and our measure of *Value Framing* was one of the most important new variables we added to the model. Yet we have only scratched the surface of the array of textual content that could be examined. Future studies could build on this research.

We have also purposefully focused on attention as our outcome of interest. Our core argument is that attention is a key *prerequisite* on social media. Before building other resources—economic capital, human capital, intellectual capital, or social media capital, etc.—advocacy organizations must capture the audience's attention. Attention is, however, merely a means to an end.

This begs the question: What precisely can and should organizations do after gaining attention? Indeed, studies are now needed that shift "attention" to the other side of the regression equation and make it the independent variable. How can organizations leverage message-based attention to acquire volunteers, to increase donations, to mobilize protest, or to influence legislation and public opinion? These are the types of studies that have yet to be done.

Of course, scholars should also examine whether our model transfers to organizations that are smaller, that are not focused on advocacy, and that are found in different geographic locations. Similarly, research could be done at different levels. In Chapters 3 and 4 we have collectively examined the organizational level and the message level. The most promising remaining level of research is the network level. Social media have, for instance, facilitated the development of new forms of advocacy-relevant *issue networks*. An issue network (Heclo 1978) is a relatively broad, loose community of actors interested in a particular policy issue such as the environment, child welfare, corruption, or government regulation, and who are connected by the transmission of information or resources (Kleinman and Hossain 2009; Ryan 1999). We could see each of the 167 tweeting organizations in our study as belonging to one or more issue networks. Studies could then build on our research by examining what drives attention to some issue networks and not others. Here other methods would be helpful, particularly social network analysis tools, which are becoming more common in nonprofit and public administration research (e.g., Doerfel, Atouba, and Harris 2016; Lecy, Mergel, and Schmitz 2014; Taylor and Doerfel 2011; Xu and Saxton 2019).

Finally, future research could continue to refine, extend, and challenge our set of seven core concepts. Such extensions could be achieved through traditional qualitative analysis or traditional quantitative deductive analysis. We have offered another alternative here: a quantitative inductive approach driven by machine learning. Differently put, one of our contributions in this chapter is the development of a novel method for building social scientific theory. We now turn to a discussion of this contribution and how it could help future research.

Summary of a Novel Theory-Building Algorithm and Comparison to Other Approaches

We argued earlier that previous data analytic/data science/machine learning approaches are too atheoretical to be applied directly to more theory-driven

TABLE 4.5 Seven-stage algorithm for building and testing conceptual models using inductive machine learning methods

---

Throughout these 7 stages, use feature selection based on quantitative machine learning, along with inductive reasoning, to "'lift' the data to a conceptual level" (Suddaby, 2006, 636) and thus build your theoretical model:

---

1. Engineer a large number of relevant features
   • Leverage prior theory/literature (deduction), domain expertise, and inductive analyses of the data
2. Univariate feature selection
   • Remove features with no variation
3. Run various bivariate feature selection techniques
   • Triangulate results and remove features that are not relevant
   • Triangulate results and remove features that are redundant
4. Conduct multivariate feature selection
   • Triangulate different feature selection techniques
5. Comprehensive "forward selection" feature selection
   • Find optimal number of variables to include in model
6. Conceptualize your model/push the theory
   • "Lift" your data and variables to a conceptual level
7. Test your model with an appropriate multivariate statistical technique, then revise theory accordingly

---

social scientific problems such as ours, while existing qualitative inductive and quantitative deductive approaches are not as well suited to developing models in new areas involving Big Data. Our technique combines tools and best practices from all three approaches to develop an innovative, data analytics–based approach that we use to extend our theoretical model.

In effect, in this chapter we have developed a novel methodological approach that can serve as a template for scholars similarly interested in expanding existing explanatory models through the melding of Big Data, data analytics, and social science. In that light, Table 4.5 summarizes the seven key sequential steps involved in the algorithm employed in this chapter.

While the approach is *largely* inductive, the first stage, *feature engineering,* involves a mix of deductive and inductive logic; the list of 133 potential variables identified during this feature selection stage was not made in a vacuum. We deliberately created message-level "translations" of all the organization/ month variables tested in Chapter 3. We also included variables that our knowledge of the social media, advocacy, and nonprofit domains suggested might be relevant to our dependent variable (attention). At the same time, we included variables on a purely inductive basis—they are available and *potentially relevant,* so we examine them. Yet even here we do not have a "data fishing" expedition; instead, we use the logic of the qualitative inductive theorist to develop and refine the list of variables.

Stages 2 through 4 cover, respectively, univariate, bivariate, and multivariate feature selection. Here the goals are to remove variables that have insufficient variation, that are redundant, and that are highly nonrelevant, and to provide a baseline of relevance for further tests of the remaining variables. In both the bivariate (step 3) and multivariate (step 4) stages we believe triangulation is key; just as a nonprofit manager would not want to have only one performance measure for each core outcome, we do not want to rely too heavily on a single feature selection algorithm. In part, this is because these techniques are so new; while we have a general sense of which techniques are appropriate for certain types of variables and questions, this knowledge is not yet precise enough to rely on a single algorithm, for we are not yet certain which techniques are best suited to all social science problems.

The fifth stage is where much of the culling takes place. At this point you will have a good idea of the relative order of your remaining variables in terms of relevance. What the fifth stage will tell you is where you are getting diminishing returns in model performance. In our case, that was at around 20 variables, which was the closest to the "elbow" point that indicated diminishing returns. Depending on how much parsimony is desired, we could have scaled this down to as few as 8 variables or up to as many as 30.

You will then have your final slate of model variables. These variables collectively represent the independent variables of your *empirical model.* We argue it is important to take time in the sixth stage to conceptualize further what those variables mean. Concretely, we would urge the researcher to present a *conceptual model* that theorizes the key relationships among the concepts represented by your chosen variables.

Finally, in the seventh stage the researcher tests the empirical model that has been built. Once complete, the researcher should revisit the conceptual model and make appropriate revisions to the model. Throughout the seven stages, the key is to continually *conceptualize,* for it is concepts (and not variables) that are the building blocks of theory. We believe this represents a potentially valuable, novel approach that reflects how typically atheoretical, prediction-focused machine learning techniques can be "translated" to explanation-focused social scientific questions.

Practical Implications

This study carries a number of practical implications. To start, we found that the "offline" user characteristics, such as age, revenue, and the program efficiency ratio, collectively have a very weak relationship to audience attention. Yet a number of other user characteristics are important and "programmable" by the advocacy organization. These other variables all reflect decisions the organization makes on Twitter. We found only weak support for our argument that profile characteristics—having a written description, displaying a URL, and moving away from the default profile—have a bearing on the amount of attention the organizations' tweets will have. In effect, the static profile elements appear to be the least important factor. Instead, it is that large collection of dynamic elements—the decisions of who to follow, whose tweets to like, and what to include inside each tweet—that truly matter.

Starting with the non-message-based factors, we tested five organizational-level network, account, and timing and pacing characteristics. Three of these variables (*Number of Likes, Number of Friends,* and *Cumulative Number of Messages*) represent actions the organization takes—and these were the least powerful of the four, with the number of messages even being negatively related to retweets. The other two factors (*Number of Followers* and *Number of Lists*) represents audience actions that affect the organization—and this is where the real power lies. Differently put, the number of public lists that other Twitter users place the organization on and the number of Twitter users that follow the organization are both indicators of the organization's reputation and influence on Twitter (Bakshy et al. 2011). As we have argued elsewhere (e.g., Saxton and Guo 2014; Saxton and Guo in press), they both also reflect the amount of *social media capital* the organization has accrued on Twitter, and this represents a resource the organization can leverage to mobilize followers to act, engage, discuss, resist, or donate.

Before acquiring such social media capital, the organization must first gain the audience's *attention.* Determining what drives attention to some messages and not others is what has motivated this chapter. The greatest dynamic, day-to-day choices the organization can make concern the nature of the messages the organization chooses to send. Our model has three categories with message-level factors, covering content, tweet sophistication, and targeting and connecting. Regarding content, our findings suggest organizations should strive to use visual content (specifically, photos) wherever appropriate. Organizations should also be explicit in their use of values-based and ethical words; this conforms with the mission of a large proportion of nonprofit organizations. Our findings for tweet sophistication, meanwhile, suggest that too much cross-platform integration—such as automatically posting Facebook messages to Twitter—may turn off audience members. Beyond that, the practical implications of tweet sophistication are in need of further research.

The final message element that social media managers can control is the *targeting and connecting* aspect of tweets—the hyperlinks (URLs), direct messages (@ messages), hashtags, and user mentions. To start, we found that retweetability had a positive relationship to the use of user mentions and hyperlinks—but only in certain situations. Ostensibly, connecting the organization's message to external sources (through the use of hyperlinks) and other Twitter users (through the use of user mentions) make tweets more credible and/or engaging (de Vries, Gensler, and Leeflang 2012; Saxton and Waters 2014). But we issue the caveat that URLs and mentions obtain negative relationships in some models.

The use of hashtags, in turn, helps not only to categorize a tweet but, more importantly, to connect the message to existing conversations. Our finding of a negative relationship between the number of hashtags employed and retweetability suggests organizations should refrain from simply adding more hashtags to their messages. Instead, hashtags should be chosen with care and used sparingly—one or two at most. Similarly, direct messages (@ messages) are negatively related to retweetability. The likely reason is that such messages explicitly target a single audience member rather than a broad audience. We do not, however, believe organizations should refrain from using @ messages; instead, organizations should recognize that direct messages serve to help strengthen ties to a single user rather than garner attention from a wide audience. Understanding the difference between the two types of messages is important.

Conclusions

In this chapter, we leverage our understanding of deductive quantitative social science, qualitative inductive theory building, and machine learning and data science/data analytics to develop a novel multimethod approach to developing and expanding theoretical models. The approach we have outlined improves on typical machine learning–driven approaches in being decidedly theoretical; our goal is not merely to predict but rather to deepen our understanding of what drives attention. At the same time, our approach improves on traditional theory building that uses qualitative inductive methods by dramatically increasing the number of cases and number of variables that can be analyzed and added to our theoretical model. In effect, our new approach constitutes a way to leverage Big Data to expand and develop theoretical models while still conforming to our theoretical/understanding-driven social scientific norms.

Using our novel methodology, we aimed in this chapter to bring the model presented in Chapter 3 down to the message level, and to expand the number of variables. Moreover, we seek to do so in a new way—a way that incorporates machine learning/data science/data analytic methods into the social scientific enterprise. In so doing, a secondary goal is to provide a template for scholars similarly interested in using data science methods to expanding existing models.

More importantly, we have used this method to bring insights to bear on what drives attention to individual organizational messages. Applying insights from data science and inductive analyses of fresh data, our study has sought to push forward research on attention in the social media age. Using "Big Data" from 167 Twitter accounts managed by 188 nonprofit advocacy organizations, this chapter has provided evidence, as in the prior chapter, that the composition of the tweet—including its content, targeting and connecting tactics, and use of sophisticated tools—influence the amount of attention the public will pay to a given message. Our findings further support the idea that aggregate organizational actions covering network features and account usage—the liking and following activity along with the extent to which other users follow the nonprofit and place it on "lists"—can also drive attention to individual messages. To a lesser extent, so too can more sophisticated account profiles as well as a suite of "offline" organizational characteristics. These additions to our theoretical model corroborates our intuition that *who* sends a message is a key driver of audience attention.

CHAPTER 5

BEYOND CLICKTIVISM

From Attention to Impact

In the previous two chapters, we set some parameters—at both the organizational and message levels—for understanding the attention-garnering strategies of nonprofit advocacy organizations. Nevertheless, one crucial question remains unaddressed: Is the attention gained by the organization leading to any tangible or intangible organizational outcomes? Above all, for advocacy and social movement organizations, the ultimate long-term goal is not attention but instead spreading awareness, building coalitions, and mobilizing supporters in order to achieve some broader societal or policy goals. In other words, it is good if an organization's voice is being heard on social media, but can this attention help create any meaningful change?

Indeed, some have raised doubts about the effectiveness of advocacy campaigns carried out on online forums or organized through social media. In the eyes of skeptics, such practices are not really engagement but rather "clicktivism" or "slacktivism": they are turning advocacy work into "a button-pressing game analogous to channel flipping with the TV remote or point-and-click adventures on video-game consoles" (Guo and Saxton 2018, 23). In that case, the critics would argue, the audience's reactions to social media messages—such as likes or retweets or replies—are not much different from a spontaneous response of the body to a stimulus, and they would contribute little to the cause that the organization is serving.

In this chapter, we counter this skepticism by arguing that attention represents a crucial first step toward meaningful advocacy actions and outcomes.

More specifically, we suggest three possible pathways by which organizations can turn attention into more substantive and tangible strategic outcomes.

A first pathway is to *accelerate attention* through boundary spanning and coalition building. So far in this book, we have treated each organization as an independent actor, as if they are working in silos, despite the fact that coalition building is one of the key advocacy tactics adopted by nonprofit organizations. However, the networked nature of social media platforms makes them a natural tool as an organization joins forces with others across organizational and sector boundaries to engage in advocacy work. In Chapter 3, our organizational-level analysis has provided some evidence that a connecting strategy (e.g., retweeting others' tweets, making user mentions, using hashtags) leads to increased attention to a focal organization on social media. Hashtags in particular have demonstrated a tremendous potential for connecting an organization to a wide range of stakeholders who otherwise would not even be aware of the organization's work.[1] By attaching the message to a particular issue, movement, or cause-based community through hashtags, the organization signifies its position and willingness to engage in the discussion, participate in the movement, or join the community.

A second pathway is to *transform attention* by turning it into a new, novel, and highly valuable social media–based organizational resource. Labeled as "social media capital," this new resource is a special form of social capital that is accumulated through an organization's formal online social media network. Organizations generate this key immediate resource through their activities on social media. Nonprofits cannot expect to get donations, find volunteers, or mobilize constituents for advocacy action simply by having a presence on social media; rather, they must first build their stock of social media capital by growing and nurturing their networks of social media followers. They cannot grow and nurture their networks of social media followers, in turn, without obtaining and sustaining the attention of followers.

A third pathway, which is the focus of this chapter, is to *leverage attention* by creating online-offline synergy in advocacy work. With the understanding that any organization has at its disposal an "advocacy mix"—a mixture of online and offline advocacy tools—we examine the different ways in which nonprofit advocacy organizations combine the use of online and social media tools with traditional offline advocacy tactics to influence public policy. Through in-depth interviews with key informants from three nonprofit advocacy organizations (which, to maintain anonymity, we refer to as *Alpha, Beta,* and *Gamma*) and analysis of Twitter data from the same organizations, we reveal how social media tools complement traditional offline advocacy work with their strong capacity for reaching out to and soliciting real-time feedback from a wide variety of stakeholders. We also explore the various scenarios wherein social media advocacy replaces some elements of traditional offline advocacy work and wherein it enters some uncharted waters that have never been touched by traditional methods.

In the remainder of this chapter, we first briefly discuss the first two pathways: (1) spanning boundaries and building coalitions, and (2) generating social media capital. Then we turn to the third pathway, wherein an organization works to achieve a desired outcome by creating online-offline synergy. We take a deeper dive into the interview and Twitter data to understand the patterns and trends in the social media advocacy work of organizations Alpha, Beta, and Gamma. We conclude the chapter with a discussion of case study findings and implications for research and practice.

Accelerating and Transforming Attention

Spanning Boundaries and Building Coalitions

The first pathway concerns how social media has engendered new forms of communication that greatly facilitate boundary spanning and coalition building. One of the most innovative tools is the hashtag. Since Twitter employee Chris Messina invented it and sent the very first tweet containing a hashtag (#sandiegofire) in 2007, hashtags have become popular and spread to other social media platforms. Hashtags, made up of short words or phrases that follow the hash or pound sign (#), such as *#BlackLivesMatter* and *#MeToo*, are used on social media platforms to brand advocacy movements, archive messages for the movement, and allow those not personally connected to a user to see and comment on messages that use the hashtag (Bruns and Burgess 2011; Saxton et al. 2015). Using hashtags in online advocacy efforts allows movements to spread organically to like-minded individuals and organizations while spreading virally to other users of the social media platform.

In a prior study (Saxton et al. 2015), we investigated the use of hashtags on Twitter by 105 organizational members of the National Health Council (NHC), a large US-based patient advocacy coalition that works with diverse stakeholders across the public, nonprofit, and business sectors. Members of the NHC include three types of organizations: patient advocacy nonprofits, professional interest organizations, and business interest organizations. We collected data from each organization's Twitter account for an eight-month period spanning January through August 2014. We found that hashtags were widely used among these organizations. The 75,934 tweets collectively contained 9,934 unique hashtags. The mean number of times hashtags were used was 853 (standard deviation [SD] = 969) and ranged from 0 to 4,720. The number of unique hashtags employed was fewer: an average organization employed 202 unique hashtags (SD = 189.8) in its tweets over the eight-month period, with a range of 0 to 770 unique hashtags. We also found that the frequency with which the various hashtags were employed followed a power law distribution (Shirky 2003): a small number of hashtags received extremely heavy usage while the great majority of them were used only sparingly.

Using inductive coding of data, we classified the hashtags into eight categories. The most prevalent category is *Public Education*, which includes three types (medical condition, knowledge base, and policy) and accounts for half of the hashtags (50.4%). The second type of hashtag is *Event* (19.3%), which often reflects fundraising and awareness-raising events. The third type of hashtag (3.2%) is *Call-to-Action*. These hashtags can be used to mobilize audiences for collective action, whether to engage in direct online or offline action or simply to assist in further disseminating public education messages. A fourth category is *Values and Goals* (9.0% of hashtags), which helps the organization differentiate itself from others in a way that serves to strengthen the organization's mission through tags that reflect its mission, values, and goals. The fifth category is *Branding* (7.2% of hashtags), which refers to tags that employ some variation of the organization's name, programs, or slogans. The sixth category, *Dialogue* (5.0% of hashtags), refers to tags that foster dialogue with audience members. The majority of these hashtags are chat-focused ones that serve as the focus for regularly scheduled chats with constituents. Others either target audience members or ask questions to produce responses. The final two types of hashtags are more descriptive: *Time and Place* hashtags (3.3%) serve to denote a time or place of importance to the tweet and organization, whereas *Business* hashtags (2.2%) are those that pertain to business issues, specific sectors of the economy, or particular stocks.

This study also compared the different ways in which organizations can use hashtags to accelerate attention (as measured by the number of retweets each message receives). The first strategy simply involves increasing the number of hashtags in a single tweet. The second strategy involves finding common ground with partners across sectors by identifying and including sector-spanning hashtags (i.e., tweets that are not limited to use by just one sector or category of organization) in a tweet. A third strategy focuses on the selective use of certain hashtag types. For example, an organization might choose to include particular types of hashtags (e.g., call-to-action hashtags) believed to be more noticeable. Regression analyses showed that these strategies had significant and positive effects on attention when tested separately, offering evidence that each of the hashtag strategies helps to increase the level of audience engagement. When tested together, the significance of the hashtag count variable disappears; however, the sector-spanning variable and several hashtag type variables (i.e., public education, values and goals, branding, call-to-action, and chat and dialogue) were significant.

Generating Social Media Capital

The second pathway concerns how organizations can transform attention into a new and highly valuable organizational resource based on social media. We label this resource "social media capital," a special form of social capital that organizations can accumulate through their formal online social media network (Saxton and Guo 2014; Saxton and Guo in press; Xu and Saxton 2019). It is discernible along a number of structural and cognitive dimensions. Possible measures include the size of the organization's audience network, the organization's position within the audience network, the length and/or number of interactions the organization has with each audience member, and the norms and values developed in the organization's network.

Social media capital can be acquired using two main tools on social media platforms: making connections and sending messages. Making connections can be thought of as relationship building because it solidifies a connection or tie to another user. Connecting tools include the organization's friending and following of other users. Connecting actions are designed to make, build, foster, or maintain ties to a specific member (a particular individual or organization) within an organization's ideal (strategically defined) network. Messages take various forms, such as videos on YouTube, photos on Instagram, pins on Pinterest, messages on LinkedIn, tweets on Twitter, and status updates on Facebook. These messages are designed to provide value-added content to the audience. They can also be used for targeting or connecting purposes, and they may take the form of replying and commenting, liking, sharing, making user mentions, and using hyperlinks and hashtags.

What is the relationship between attention and social media capital, then? Does more attention lead to more social media capital, or vice versa? To answer these questions requires an understanding of the nature of each construct. Both attention and social media capital are social media–based resources, and both are acquired using two main tools: making connections and sending messages. Thus the difference between the two is subtle: as social media–based resources, attention is more temporary and dwindling, while social media capital is more permanent and stable. As such, the relationship between attention and social media capital is analogous to that between the internal storage (or RAM) and external storage (or hard disk drive) of a computer. Accordingly, transforming attention essentially involves turning a short-term, temporary resource into a more permanent and stable resource (i.e., social media capital).

As a preliminary check of the connection between the two, in Guo and Saxton (2018) we analyzed the relationship between the total amount of attention an organization received over the course of 2013 (as indicated by the total number of retweets and likes) and its total amount of social media capital (measured by the total number of new followers gained by the organization) over the same time period via its social media efforts. The results show a clear positive association between attention and growth in networks of followers. For the present book, we replicated the analysis using the 2017 data, adding the total number of replies as another measure of attention. More specifically, we analyzed the relationship between the total amount of attention an organization received over the course of 2017 (as indicated by the total number of retweets, likes, and replies) and its total amount of social media capital (measured by the total number of new followers gained by the organization) over the same time period via its social media efforts. The results have demonstrated similar patterns. Figure 5.1 presents scatter plots (with regression line and 95% confidence intervals) for the increase in followers for retweets and likes, respectively.

What Figure 5.1 shows is a clear positive association between attention and growth in the follower networks. An increase in attention, it appears, leads to an increase in social media capital.

Taken together, our results indicate that an increase in attention leads to an increase in social media capital. We further argue that, once accumulated, social media capital becomes a potentially robust resource that an organization can leverage to grow its base of supporters, attract donations and other

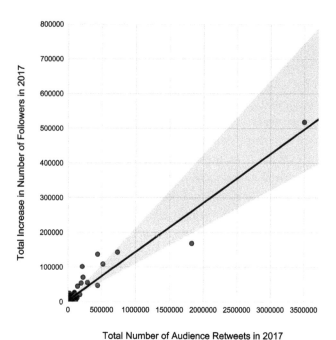

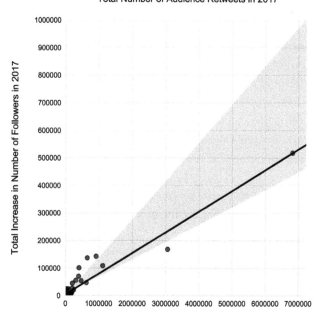

FIGURE 5.1 Total audience reactions (retweets and likes) in 2017 vs. total gain in # of followers over 2017

social support, develop collaborations, and achieve other strategically motivated objectives.

Leveraging Attention

The third pathway—leveraging attention by creating online-offline synergy in
an organization's advocacy work—is based on the observation that new forms
of advocacy are emerging on the Internet and social media and that they can
synergize with traditional offline advocacy activities. Proponents argue that
social media, which delivers the ability to spread messages to and receive
immediate feedback from larger audiences, can create new opportunities
for individuals and organizations to access information, cooperate with one
another, and participate in advocacy activities (Deschamps and McNutt 2014;
McNutt and Menon 2008). As such, social media advocacy work may supplement traditional offline advocacy.

Opponents, on the other hand, argue that social media advocacy efforts may
in fact have an adverse effect on engagement with offline activities. That is, social media advocacy may be promoting a form of "clicktivism" or "slacktivism,"
a false sense that online participation (e.g., signing an online petition or sharing
an organization's tweet) in itself will produce definitive social change (Brady,
Young, and McLeod 2015; Karpf 2010). Owing to this false belief, advocacy efforts on social media may demotivate potential supporters from taking further
action, reducing commitment and participation in offline advocacy activities.

Although scholars recognize the importance of having an advocacy mix in
the development of social media advocacy beyond traditional offline strategies
(Guo and Saxton 2014b; McNutt and Menon 2008), much of the emerging literature on social media advocacy has focused on what is happening on social
media, while paying virtually no attention to how organizations combine social media tools with more traditional offline activities. In fact, we know very
little about what extra value social media advocacy brings to the table.

To address this gap in research, we employed a multiple case study approach.
We conducted in-depth interviews with six key informants from three advocacy
organizations. In order to cover common material and gather reliable information, we recruited organizations that actively used social media platforms for advocacy purposes and selected interviewees whose job criteria included advocacy
and/or social media operation (e.g., advocacy director and social media manager). We conducted the interviews either in person or via video conferencing.

Each interview lasted approximately 40 to 50 minutes. For confidentiality purposes, the names of the organizations and individuals have been changed.

A Twitter Tale of Three Advocacy Organizations

Founded in the mid-1930s, Alpha Union (Alpha hereafter) is a US-based non-profit organization that engages in product testing, investigative journalism, and consumer advocacy. It publishes a magazine that provides reviews and comparisons of consumer products and services as well as purchasing guides. Currently, the magazine has over six million subscribing members. In addition to in-house product testing and consumer research, the organization has been engaged in extensive consumer advocacy work.

Alpha has a strong social media presence: As of January 2019, it is on Twitter, Facebook, YouTube, Instagram, and Pinterest. Alpha has an official Twitter account (@Alpha) for its advocacy functions; active since July 2008, @Alpha has 15,600 followers and 18,100 tweets. Alpha also has a Facebook page that currently has 962,000 followers.

Beta Project (Beta hereafter) is a Philadelphia-based public charity that provides housing, employment opportunities, medical care, and education to homeless and low-income people. Although Beta's primary focus is on providing housing and supportive services, advocacy has been an indispensable part of its work since the very beginning. During its opening years, for example, Beta received national media exposure for its four-year political and legal battle to establish a residence for formerly homeless individuals at a particular location. Despite the fact that it had secured the property's zoning permit in 1990, the development process was delayed as Beta was challenged in court by neighborhood associations that wanted to overturn the building permit. After a lengthy appeal process and a series of advocacy activities such as community petitions and a vigil outside the mayor's office, Beta finally won the case in 1994.

Beta has been on Facebook and Twitter since August 2009 and on YouTube since March 2010. Its Facebook page has 8,332 followers; its Twitter account (@Beta) has 8,920 followers and 9,102 tweets. Its YouTube channel has 203 subscribers and 61,100 views in total. Beta also runs a blog and an email newsletter. The organization maintains a high level of activity on social media: it uploads one to three YouTube videos per month and posts multiple tweets per day. Facebook updates are less frequent, but they are usually longer.

In 1985, a group of housing advocates founded Alliance Gamma (Gamma hereafter) in response to the burgeoning homelessness crisis in the state of

Pennsylvania. In the early 2000s, the organization renewed its strategic focus to establish a broader base of support while continuing its commitment to low-income people. As a statewide coalition, Gamma's mission is to "provide leadership and a common voice for policies, practices and resources to ensure that all Pennsylvanians, especially those with low incomes, have access to safe, decent and affordable homes." It achieves this mission through information sharing, education, training and technical assistance, coalition building, research, and advocacy work.

Compared to Alpha and Beta, Gamma does not have a very strong social media presence. Its Facebook page has 1,471 followers; its Twitter handle has 2,339 followers and 4,603 tweets in total. Gamma has also experimented with other social media platforms such as LinkedIn and blogging in the past, but it is not currently active in either.

To compare the Twitter activities of the three organizations, we have conducted further analysis of their Twitter data.[2] Our summary statistics show some interesting results (see Table 5.1).

Alpha was the most active on Twitter among the three groups, posting about 5.4 tweets per day; in contrast, Beta and Gamma posted 1.4 and 0.9 tweets, respectively. All three organizations were about equally likely to mention another user or include hashtags in their tweets: The mean number of mentions per tweet is 0.5, 0.4, and 0.2, respectively, while the mean number of hashtags per tweet is around 0.6 for all three organizations. However, the level of attention they received on Twitter (measured by retweets and likes) varied significantly, with Gamma lagging behind. On average, Alpha received 3.5 retweets and 4.1 likes per tweet sent, Beta received 2.3 retweets and 3.7 likes per tweet sent, and Gamma received merely 0.6 retweets and 0.7 likes per tweet sent. We should note, however, that the level of attention each organization received is more or less proportional to the number of followers.

Spikes of Activity and Attention

Alpha

We collected data on Alpha's original tweets (excluding the organization's retweeting of other users' content) sent between December 1, 2017, and December 13, 2018 (a one-year time frame). With this data, we observed several spikes of Alpha's Twitter activities in terms of the number of original tweets sent daily. Below are some of the highlights:

TABLE 5.1 Interorganizational comparison of Twitter activities

Number of Tweets Sent per Day		
	Alpha	Beta	Gamma
Mean	5.4	1.4	0.9
Min	0	0	0
Max	40	33	23

Number of Retweets Received per Day		
	Alpha	Beta	Gamma
Mean	18.8	3.2	0.5
Min	0	0	0
Max	254	264	19

Number of Likes Received per Day		
	Alpha	Beta	Gamma
Mean	22.1	5.2	0.6
Min	0	0	0
Max	576	844	24

Number of Mentions Used per Day		
	Alpha	Beta	Gamma
Mean	2.5	0.6	0.2
Min	0	0	0
Max	29	61	28

Number of Hashtags Used per Day		
	Alpha	Beta	Gamma
Mean	3.3	0.8	0.5
Min	0	0	0
Max	51	34	27

NOTE: The above summary tables report the Twitter activities of Alpha between 12/1/2017 and 12/13/2018 (within which Alpha was active on Twitter for 262 days); the Twitter activities of Beta between 12/9/2015 and 12/12/2018 (within which Beta was active on Twitter for 538 days); and, the Twitter activities of Gamma between 12/10/2014 and 12/11/2018 (within which Gamma was active on Twitter for 653 days). The mean measure of activities is calculated by the total count of the respective activities divided by the total number of days within the timeframe.

- On December 5, 2017, Alpha produced the highest number of tweets ($n =$ 40), many of which focused on its Electric Vehicle campaign and event, using hashtags such as #EVchat and #EV.
- On February 27, 2018, Alpha posted 17 tweets centering on #NetNeutrality and the #OneMoreVote event to mobilize public support to persuade local lawmakers.
- On March 20, 2018, Alpha posted 17 tweets on issues of net neutrality and affordable care, including #TeamInternet, #ACA, and #ProtectOurCare.
- On May 9, 2018, Alpha posted 21 tweets, continuing to advocate for #NetNeutrality.
- On May 11, 2018, Alpha sent 24 tweets discussing #NetNeutrality and #MenuLabeling.
- On June 13, 2018, Alpha sent out 28 tweets advocating for #NetNeutrality, soliciting feedback on peer-to-peer payment experience and ending robocalls.
- On December 4, 2018, Alpha produced 24 tweets, discussing multiple issues related to #Selfdriving, #StopAVSTARTAct, and #privacylaw.

As these highlights indicate, net neutrality was a key focus area of Alpha's advocacy work during the 12-month period. Net neutrality has been a fiercely contested public policy issue in the United States for some time. In 2015, the Obama administration promulgated the net neutrality policy that requires Internet service providers to offer equal access to all web content. After the Trump administration assumed office, the Federal Communications Commission (FCC) planned to repeal the net neutrality policy. On November 21, 2017, the FCC released a draft policy document indicating its plan for repealing the rules. On December 14, the FCC approved the repeal with a 3-2 party-line vote. On January 4, 2018, the FCC released an official policy document on the net neutrality repeal order. On June 11, the FCC's repeal of net neutrality rules took effect. The repeal allowed Internet service providers to charge more for certain content or give preferential treatment to certain websites; it also made it possible for service providers to censor online content or charge additional fees for better service—bad news for small companies.

To better analyze Alpha's advocacy activities promoting net neutrality, we made a data subset for tweets that are related to net neutrality only ($n = 266$). We then created a plot that reports Alpha's advocacy activities for net neutrality on Twitter—namely, on a given day, how many times Alpha sent original tweets, and received retweets and likes, supporting net neutrality and/or opposing the FCC's repeal. The plot is presented in Figure 5.2. The data indicate that Alpha has participated actively to advocate against the repeal, swaying congressional opinion all over the country and encouraging Twitter users to call or submit comments to congressional representatives.

As we can observe in Figure 5.2, Alpha tweeted on the topics of open Internet and net neutrality on several dates when the messages went viral. A closer look at the "viral" dates and all of the tweets sent on those dates reveals that these activities correspond well with the timeline of significant events associated with the debate over net neutrality. For example, the first viral date occurred on December 12, 2017, two days prior to the FCC's vote to approve the repeal of the net neutrality policy. On this day, Alpha sent 15 original tweets during working hours. It is worth noting that 87% of the tweets (13 out of 15) were call-to-action, grassroots lobbying tweets, asking people to call their members of Congress and urge them to stop the FCC from repealing the net neutrality policy.

The second viral date occurred on February 27, 2018, which was the date for Operation #OneMoreVote, an Internet-wide day of action launched by a coalition of major websites and advocacy groups. According to the press release, "On this day, internet users, small businesses, online communities, public-interest groups and popular websites will harness their reach to flood lawmakers with calls, emails and tweets aimed at securing the final vote in the Senate needed to pass a Congressional Review Act (CRA) resolution of disapproval overturning the FCC's unpopular repeal of Net Neutrality protections. The groups will also hold constituent meetings with key lawmakers." On this day, Alpha sent 10 original tweets during working hours. Similar to the previous viral date, 90% of the tweets (9 out of 10) were call-to-action, grassroots lobbying tweets asking people to contact their members of Congress; the remaining tweet is an informational public education message.

The third viral date occurred on May 15, 2018, the day before the US Senate met to vote on the CRA resolution. On this day, Alpha sent 7 original tweets within six hours, including 5 call-to-action tweets, 1 media advocacy tweet, and 1 public education tweet, although the total number of tweets is smaller than those from the two preceding viral dates.

The next viral date, June 11, 2018, marks the day when the US House of Representatives failed to act under the CRA and the FCC's repeal of net

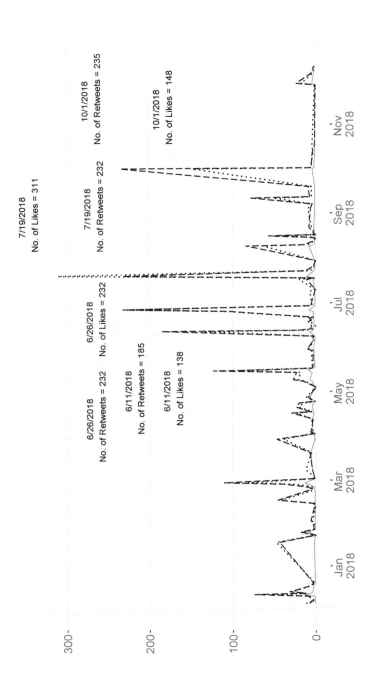

FIGURE 5.2 Alpha's advocacy for net neutrality on Twitter over time (12/1/2017–12/13/2018)

neutrality rules took effect. In response, Alpha and allies participated in an Internet-wide day of action to drive emails to members of Congress in support of reviving net neutrality. Within five hours, Alpha had sent 7 original tweets, all of which are call-to-action, grassroots lobbying messages asking people to email their representatives.

Then on June 26, 2018, Alpha and allies organized another campaign called Net Neutrality Advocacy Day at the Capitol Building in Washington, DC. The day started with an advocacy training session, followed by group visits to the representatives' offices so that activists could tell their representatives in person how much they value net neutrality and ask their representatives to support the CRA resolution; the day concluded with a reception. On this day, Alpha sent 8 original tweets. This set of tweets differed from those posted on the previous viral dates in that it provided highlights of the offline event and contained images of a congressional representative and many activists. In addition, the number of call-to-action messages decreased to 2 (25%).

On July 19, 2018, Alpha and allies organized another campaign called Thursday Call-In Day for Net Neutrality before the lawmakers returned home for the August recess. Once again, the coalition encouraged activists to call their representatives and demand that Congress restore net neutrality. On this day, Alpha sent 11 original tweets, all of which were call-to-action messages. Among these call-to-action messages, 10 were grassroots lobbying messages and 1 was a direct lobbying message.

The last viral event occurred on October 1, 2018, when California Governor Jerry Brown signed California SB 822 into law, officially restoring net neutrality protections that had been repealed by the FCC. On this day, Alpha sent 4 original tweets, 3 of which related to what had happened in California. In contrast to most of the tweets sent on previous peak days, the 3 tweets sent on this day took a more celebratory tone; the content of the messages is information- and community-oriented rather than action-oriented.

VICTORY: @JerryBrownGov Signs Law Restoring #NetNeutrality https://t .co/pVFFybolIW

Gov. Jerry Brown signed #SB822, officially restoring #NetNeutrality protections that were repealed by the FCC last year. This marks a huge victory, not only for Californians but for the future of the internet. Thank you to everyone who took action and made this victory possible! https://t.co/ NLEBBhTfRd

California won #NetNeutrality and will defend the new law in court. Read our quote on this historic victory in . . . https://t.co/8DfxadLM9A

Beta

We collected data on @Beta's original tweets (excluding the organization's retweeting of other users' content) sent between 12/9/2015 and 12/12/2018 (a three-year time frame). We then created a plot that reports Beta's activities on Twitter—namely, on a given day, how many times Beta sent original tweets as well as received retweets and likes. This plot is presented in Figure 5.3.

In Figure 5.3, we see several spikes of Beta's Twitter activities in terms of the number of original tweets sent daily; below are some of the highlights:

- On January 12, 2017, Beta sent out 30 tweets, most of which related to #CarsonHearing, #EndHomelessness, and #Congress. Note that #CarsonHearing is a hashtag intended to draw attention to the Senate confirmation hearing for Dr. Ben Carson to become the seventeenth Secretary of the Department of Housing and Urban Development (HUD).
- On May 19, 2017, Beta posted 22 tweets, most of which targeted lawmakers.
- On October 30, 2017, 29 tweets were sent out to support the #TheseCutsHurt Day of Action campaign. #TheseCutsHurt is a call-to-action hashtag created by a participatory advocacy project called Witnesses to Hunger. The project used this hashtag to draw attention to how the federal government's proposed 2018 budget cuts would negatively affect hunger, housing, and healthcare programs, including Temporary Assistance for Needy Families (TANF), Supplemental Nutrition Assistance Program (SNAP), Medicaid, Children's Health Insurance Program (CHIP), and Social Security Disability Insurance.
- On November 1, 2018, Beta produced 25 tweets sharing information about the Hub of Hope project and acknowledging their supporters and funders. The Hub of Hope is a homeless engagement center located in Philadelphia's Center City subway concourse. According to Beta's website, this project "offers a safe place where people can enjoy a warm cup of coffee, take a shower and wash laundry, and speak to peers or case managers to begin the process of finding a permanent home."

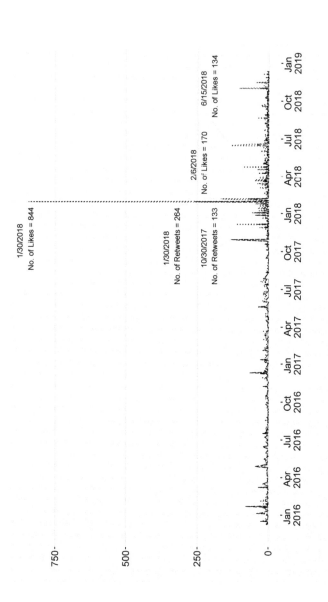

FIGURE 5.3 Beta's activities on Twitter over time (12/9/2015–12/12/2018)

- On November 15, 2018, Beta sent out 33 tweets (the highest number of tweets in its social media history) to promote Raise the Roof, a fundraiser for the capital campaign for its Gloria Casarez Residence.

Similar to the case of Alpha, Beta's "viral" dates and all the tweets sent on those dates reveal that these activities correspond well with the timeline of significant offline events. Unlike the case of Alpha, however, Beta's viral dates (i.e., dates with more attention received) do not seem to closely align with its "busy" dates (i.e., dates when it sent more original tweets).

For example, on January 12, 2017, the Senate held the confirmation hearing for Dr. Ben Carson to become the secretary of HUD. Beta live-broadcasted the event on Twitter, sending out 30 tweets; however, these tweets did not go viral. Similarly, on November 15, 2018, Beta hosted Raise the Roof, a fundraising and awareness-building event, as part of the capital campaign for its Gloria Casarez Residence, the very first LGBTQ-friendly permanent supportive housing for young adults in Pennsylvania. This housing project is named after the late LGBTQ activist Gloria Casarez, who served as the first director of the Mayor's Office of LGBT Affairs in the City of Philadelphia. On this day, Beta sent out 33 tweets to live-broadcast the event; again, none of the tweets went viral.

In both instances, the numerous tweets that Beta sent are information-oriented rather than action-oriented, which might explain why these messages did not make much noise: people seem to pay more attention to action-oriented messages than informational messages. It is also possible that people did read the tweets but did not share or like them because Beta had made no explicit call for action. This lack of attention on Twitter (in the form of shares and likes) does not necessarily suggest that the offline event itself was not successful. In the case of the Raise the Roof fundraiser, supporters ended up giving more than $350,000 to LGBTQ-friendly young adult housing, tripling the organization's original fundraising goal.

Gamma

Given Gamma's less frequent tweeting, we gathered this organization's Twitter data over a longer time period. We collected data on @Gamma's original tweets (excluding the organization's retweeting of other users' content) sent between December 10, 2014, and December 11, 2018 (a four-year time frame). Similar to the cases of Alpha and Beta, we created a plot that reports Gamma's activities on Twitter—namely, how many times on a given day Gamma sent original tweets as well as received retweets and likes. The plot is presented in Figure 5.4.

In general, as shown in Figure 5.4, Gamma did not receive as much attention as the other two organizations—a huge amount less than Alpha and noticeably less than Beta. The number of tweets per day and proxies for the attention from those tweets were much lower, all below 30. The relatively more popular tweets were those sent during the first three years, not those sent in 2018. We observed several spikes in the number of tweets sent, as well as corresponding attention as shown in the retweet count and likes count. Following are some of the highlights:

- On June 23 and June 29, 2015, Gamma sent out 16 and 29 tweets, respectively. The tweets sent on June 23 received 19 likes, while the tweets sent on June 29 received only 3 likes. Most of the tweets targeted senators, thanking them for supporting Pennsylvania Senate Bill 566 and the Pennsylvania Housing Affordability and Rehabilitation Enhancement Fund (PHARE). Also known as the state housing trust fund, PHARE provides funding opportunities for local housing programs in Pennsylvania.
- On November 17, 2015, Gamma sent out 21 tweets to promote its Homes Within Reach conference, an annual event that convenes service providers, housing professionals, community builders, and other stakeholders to discuss housing-related issues.
- On November 23 and December 4, 2015, Gamma sent out 12 and 16 tweets, respectively, as it participated in the Stand for Pennsylvanians Day, an advocacy campaign that Gamma co-organized to push for passing a budget for the Commonwealth of Pennsylvania. On November 23, 2015, over 100 public and nonprofit sector organizations came together to speak with a unified voice on the issue of budget impasse, and to mobilize people and communities to support the bipartisan efforts to pass the budget.
- Gamma held an event called Home Matters Day on June 15, 2016; this annual educational and advocacy event was intended to increase state resources for affordable housing programs. Most of the tweets sent on June 14 and 15 presented event highlights.
- On December 4 and 5, 2017, Gamma sent 17 and 23 tweets, respectively. Most of these tweets were event highlights of its annual Homes Within Reach conference.

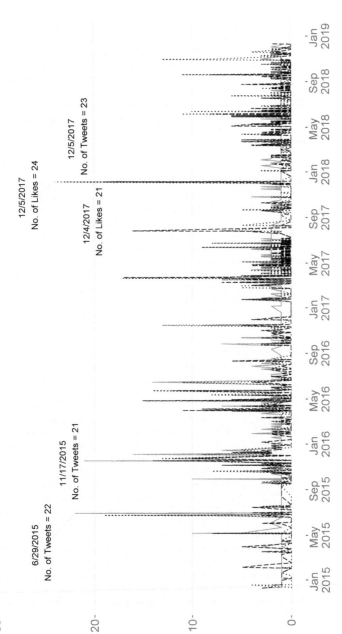

FIGURE 5.4 Gamma's activities on Twitter over time (12/10/2014—12/11/2018)

Strategies and Practices for Online-Offline Synchronization

A close inspection of the Twitter data in these three case studies reveals several interesting strategies and practices associated with the three organizations' synchronization of online and offline activities.

Live Broadcast of Offline Events

This is one of the popular practices seen in each organization's social media work. With a live broadcast, the organization generally provides rolling Twitter coverage of an ongoing event in real time. The following five tweets, showing Alpha's coverage of the Net Neutrality Advocacy Day on June 26, 2018, collectively present an excellent example of a live broadcast:

> CU joins consumers from across the U.S. on Capitol Hill today to urge members of Congress to restore open internet protections. Net neutrality may be repealed but our voices won't be silenced! Follow the action with #NetNeutrality and #AdvocacyDay https://t.co/jNbntlGFiA

> @USRepMikeDoyle kicks off #NetNeutrality #AdvocacyDay. RT to cheer on the advocates speaking out for the open Internet today! https://t.co/2RJH6tWBoZ

> Andrea Figueroa from TX, fighting for internet freedom for her students to learn and organize! #NetNeutrality #AdvocacyDay https://t.co/7EJKToosPv

> Representing Louisiana, Colorado, South Carolina, Arizona consumer and small business voices for #NetNeutrality! #AdvocacyDay https://t.co/5aQfVStyzs

> Tell your lawmakers to keep the internet fair! We're in DC today with our #NetNeutrality advocacy partners and constituents from across the U.S., but you can take action right now here: http://ms.spr.ly/6011rNCiR #AdvocacyDay https://t.co/AiJ6HTtfCu

Beta's coverage of the Ben Carson hearing on January 12, 2017, offers another example. To illustrate, here are some excerpts of tweets from that live broadcast:

> Dr. Ben Carson's hearing on his nom as next Housing and Urban Development Sec. begins at 10 AM. Live stream: here: https://t.co/FkFraHjlLr

> We will be watching today's #CarsonHearing for @HUDgov Sec sharing thoughts throughout the day. Live stream: https://t.co/FkFraHjlLr

#CarsonHearing getting underway now. Stream: https://t.co/FkFraHjlLr

There are some subtle differences in the two examples: Beta's coverage of the Ben Carson hearing is a more typical live broadcast in that it follows the event chronologically each step of the way; Alpha's coverage of the Net Neutrality Advocacy Day, in turn, looks more like highlights of the event, although it does follow the event chronologically.

Balancing Action and Information

When a deadline is around the corner, it is natural to strive to mobilize supporters to take action. Even under such circumstances, we observe that an organization can manage to strike an appropriate balance between call-to-action and informational messages. Take Alpha's Twitter campaign on December 12, 2017, as an example: Alpha sent 15 tweets, 13 of which are call-to-action, grassroots lobbying tweets, such as the following two:

> The FCC is about to vote to end #NetNeutrality—so today we join with others to #BreakTheInternet to #SaveNetNeutrality and #StopTheFCC. Join in: http://ms.spr.ly/6019rIUZd https://t.co/Xk22xXogq2

> #SaveNetNeutrality: Tell Congress to #StopTheFCC from repealing #NetNeutrality. Call Congress now by clicking here: . . . https://t.co/W7NFYH6m7C

Even amid the urgent call for action, Alpha was careful to post the following two tweets that are information-oriented, public education messages:

> HERE'S HOW THE END OF NET NEUTRALITY WILL CHANGE THE INTERNET via @WIRED #SaveNetNeutrality #BreakTheInternet . . . https://t .co/oJJMdzIjyM

> The FCC's plan to undo #NetNeutrality is built on a false narrative. Read our new @washingtonpost op-ed by . . . https://t.co/WCyDmiQg3z

Signaling a Sense of Urgency

With a deadline looming, an organization may enhance the power of its call-to-action messages by signaling a sense of urgency to its followers and supporters. It does so by using significantly stronger language in its messages, like the following messages from Alpha:

> We have less than 24 hrs to save #NetNeutrality Call your Senators again! https://t.co/xxL8nUJxOr

> Stop everything you're doing and tell your Senators to vote YES on the reso-
> lution to save #NetNeutrality and keep o . . . https://t.co/qBwNCHmJgU

Strong language aside, the organization may also double down on its effort by including multiple advocacy tactics in a single message. For example, the following tweet contains two advocacy tactics in the same message: direct lobbying (urging the senator to vote for the resolution) and grassroots lobbying (asking the senator's constituents to call their senator). In addition, it represents the first direct lobbying message sent by Alpha in the context of net neutrality. It is also the first targeted message (indicated by the use of the "@USER-NAME" convention at the start of the message) sent by Alpha in the context of net neutrality. Such unusual behaviors (for Alpha) also indicate that Alpha saw the need for its supporters to feel a sense of urgency as time was running out.

> @lisamurkowski please be an Internet hero and vote for the resolution to
> restore #NetNeutrality. #Alaska businesses and Internet users are counting
> on you to do the right thing. If you live in AK, call Sen Murkowski before she
> votes tomorrow: https://BattleForTheNet.com https://t.co/QAvSpX4E9Y

Sometimes a sense of urgency might be triggered by unexpected, nonroutine events, such as the Code Blue emergency spurring the following tweets from Beta:

> Outreach Coordination Center is #OpenInPHL. Call the hotline at 215-232-
> 1984 to help someone w/o shelter. #codeblue https://t.co/KZ7FSLZc1c

> A #CodeBlue has been issued until Monday. If you see someone in need of
> shelter from the cold, call please the Outr . . . https://t.co/BCichACFIw[3]

All three tweets listed above were posted by Beta in response to its city's extreme-cold weather alert. These tweets received a relatively high level of attention, with a total of 140 retweets and 56 likes. The inclusion of the #CodeBlue hashtag signaled a great sense of urgency, which the group reinforced with a call to action that explicitly asked people to call the hotline to help someone without shelter.

Intense Direct Lobbying

In our prior research (Guo and Saxton 2014b), we have observed the presence of direct lobbying messages that targeted a policymaker, but only occasionally. In the current study, however, it is somewhat surprising to see this type of message popping up so frequently. Direct lobbying messages are prevalent in the Twitter activities of all three organizations; on certain occasions, direct lobbying was all the organization was doing on Twitter. For example, on May 19, 2017, Beta posted 22 tweets. A closer look at the tweets reveals that 91% (20 out of 22) were direct lobbying messages: They were addressed to politicians (particularly from the US House of Representatives), urging them to answer Sister Mary Scullion's call for a "revolution of tenderness" and support a humane budget that protects housing and essential services. In her commencement address to Georgetown College (part of Georgetown University) that day, Sister Mary asked the graduates to pursue a "revolution of tenderness" and work together to "forge a new path to economic inclusivity."

> @RepJohnFaso as alum, will you join @SMaryPhilly's call to @Georgetown-Coll grads for a #RevolutionOfTenderness? https://t.co/5uJwPVEsZy

> @RepGallagher as alum, will you join @SMaryPhilly's call to @Georgetown-Coll grads for a #RevolutionOfTenderness? https://t.co/5uJwPVEsZy

Because these tweets targeted less than two dozen lawmakers who were alumni of Georgetown University, the broader audience likely did not feel the need to respond or take any action, which might explain why Beta's Twitter activity that day received very little public attention in the form of retweets and likes.

Targeted Public Recognition

The direct lobbying tweets discussed above represent one form of targeted message. A more popular form of targeted message can be found in the numerous public recognition messages sent by organizations. The following message sent by Alpha offers a good example:

> Great piece from @ChadAaronMarlow about how the fight for internet freedom is far from over . . . https://t.co/BrFj8E6sWP

This tweet did not receive much attention in the form of shares and likes, probably because the message targeted just one individual (a senior advocacy and policy counsel with the ACLU).

Celebrity Poking

Although an organization can send a public recognition tweet to any user, a message that publicly praises (or criticizes) a celebrity tends to attract more attention on Twitter. This practice of publicly recognizing a celebrity is sometimes referred to as "celebrity poking" or "celebrity fishing" (Guo and Saxton 2014b). Because celebrities have tremendous networks, a tweet directed at a celebrity can reach an audience of hundreds of thousands, even millions, of followers. Thus, a targeted message to a celebrity might serve to exponentially increase the diffusion of an organizational message or call to action. These two tweets from Beta provide good examples:

> We are so thankful to @JBJSoulFound & @JonBonJovi for their continued leadership and their commitment to ending homelessness #HubofHope https://t.co/tmrwoSboVI

> Thank you @SenBobCasey for taking a stand to #fixthecliff. Health Center patients and staff can't wait any longer and we are in a state of #RedAlert-4CHCs. Lives and jobs are at stake! https://t.co/Idm8biSt9J

As the tweet content shows, the former viral tweet, which was retweeted 143 times and received 603 likes, was a thank-you note to Jon Bon Jovi, an American singer-songwriter and philanthropist, for his support to Beta to establish the Hub of Hope. While Beta didn't seem to catch much attention on social media in general, this tweet showcases that having a celebrity like Jon Bon Jovi as a supporter (and targeting him on social media) immediately increased Beta's visibility, particularly since celebrities such as Jon Bon Jovi are usually seen as opinion leaders and connected to many followers. Similarly, the latter tweet was a thank-you note to Senator Bob Casey from Pennsylvania, which attracted 61 likes and was retweeted 22 times.

Likewise, a targeted message to an organization with a large social media following can have a similar effect. For example, Gamma posted the following tweet on July 26, 2017, to promote a public dialogue hosted by the National Low Income Housing Coalition (NLIHC), a nonprofit research and advocacy organization that operates nationwide:

> Join @NLIHC twitterstorm today at 2:00 pm ET! Use the #OurHomesOur-Voices along with your tweet! https://t.co/tcOLaLv8gV

This tweet received a relatively high level of attention. Similarly, two of the tweets that Gamma sent on March 23, 2017, shared research findings released by the NLIHC. Those two tweets also received a relatively high level of attention. Considering the NLIHC's strong presence and large following on Twitter (over 14,000 followers and over 27,000 tweets sent), it is possible that mentioning @NLIHC attracted a higher influx of attention to Gamma's tweets.

What Is the Added Value of Social Media Advocacy?

In addition to the analysis of the Twitter data, we also conducted in-depth interviews with the key informants from Alpha, Beta, and Gamma to learn how social media advocacy work is organized and managed in an established organization, and to further examine the extent to which the use of social media adds value to and transforms how policy advocacy is done. Six themes emerged from the interviews. The first two themes relate to the structure and process for online-offline synchronization and coordination among multiple online/social media platforms; the remaining four themes provide additional insight into the unique or critical contributions of social media advocacy: enhancing citizen engagement, increasing bargaining power, establishing open and direct channels to policymakers, and contributing to coalition building.

Online-Offline Synchronization

Our analysis of Twitter data in the previous section demonstrated that, across all three organizations, what has happened on social media—particularly the spikes in activity and attention—corresponds strongly with the timeline of significant offline events. Echoing this finding, our interviews further indicated that the routinization of activity and attention on social media is shaped, at least in part, by the development of standard operating procedures for online-offline synchronization.

During the net neutrality campaign, for example, a small social media team was formed within Alpha to facilitate Alpha's overall work on net neutrality. The team comprised Alpha's social media manager, who served as the point person for the team, a staff member specializing in social media mobilization and playing the role of organizer or campaign manager, a policy lead who works on the legislation and understands the bill and relevant lawmakers, and a content person who has written several articles about the net neutrality debate. The team met once a week to go over the status of the bill and discuss the next steps. The following recollection from Charlotte, Alpha's social media manager and point-person of the net neutrality team, illustrates the degree of online-offline synchronization that took place on a day-to-day basis:

[W]e meet and talk about what things we can do . . . to mobilize people, especially in advance of what's happening with the legislation, and any grassroots support we need to build . . . to move key lawmakers. It is really combined efforts between what we are going to do offline, what we are going to do online, and how we are going to coordinate everything. So, if we knew in advance we're going to make a press release around a vote, then I would know ahead of time like "hey, I'm gonna have to tweet that as soon as it's published so that we can make sure reporters and our coalition partner know where Alpha stands on it." If we have an article around net neutrality that Alpha published, I would know in advance like, "hey, this is going out and I'm gonna schedule that for myself." And then . . . our campaign manager would work very closely with our coalition partners for net neutrality [to coordinate the efforts]. (Charlotte, Advocacy Social Media Manager at Alpha, May 14, 2019)

Charlotte also noted that the frequency of tweets that the organization sent on a daily basis was essentially based on how much content Alpha had for the day—whether it had any media mentions (i.e., stories quoting Alpha), Alpha press releases, new Alpha articles about their advocacy efforts, or new graphics to use. Generally, her team tried to tweet or post Facebook updates at least three to five times a day, but they did more if there was something urgent.

Similarly, Gamma has a staff meeting at the beginning of each week where people bring up topics based on organizational priorities. Gamma's advocacy director David observed,

[There are] things that we care about that we want to move through the legislature. So if there's ever any news about that, that's going to rise to the top of the list. Then of course [there] are things that are just happening in the world that might be relevant to our work that we feel like people should know about that we would discuss. And then sometimes there's upcoming events and things that we want people to know about. So that's sort of the three main areas. And we have a staff meeting every week on Monday, and we go over those things and that's how we decide what we're going to talk about that week. And then the newsletter always goes out on Wednesdays. . . . Social media posts are going to go out based on what we put in the newsletter following. So from Thursday to the next Tuesday or Monday, depending on how many different posts there are until Wednesday rolls around again. So we kind of have a system in place. (David, Advocacy Director at Gamma, October 25, 2018)

During our conversation about online-offline synchronization, David raised an interesting point about a potential downside of getting too much attention on social media: If something gets national attention and becomes a polarized left-right issue, it could potentially become harder for a state- or local-level nonprofit organization to do its work:

> *[We] work a lot in sort of a bipartisan way at the state level and at the local level. Like we're very nonpartisan and we can work with Democrats and Republicans very easily. . . . [Sometimes] we can bring people to the table quietly and . . . find common ground and move forward, which is harder to do when you got the national spotlight.* (David, Advocacy Director at Gamma, October 25, 2018)

Coordination Among Multiple Online/Social Media Platforms

The coordination and synchronization are not limited to balancing online and offline activities; they are also reflected in how the organization manages its various platforms of online advocacy work. David from Gamma explained,

> *[We] actually have our social media link closely to our email outreach strategy. So every week we have a curated newsletter that includes clips that, you know, just articles that we think are of importance that people should read related to our work. It includes upcoming events and it includes action alerts on things where people should either call their member of Congress or call their state representatives and, you know, express a position. So every week we curate the content for the newsletter. And then the social media content comes from that. So we'll have four to five clips in every newsletter and then in the four to five days following the newsletter . . . clips all go up on social media. And then any action that we take in the newsletter will also go up on social media.* (David, Advocacy Director at Gamma, October 25, 2018)

At Beta, different social media platforms are utilized in different ways: Twitter and Instagram for posts during an event, Facebook for recaps. Overall, social media plays a minor, supportive role in organizational strategy. Michael, Beta's social media specialist in the development department, commented,

> *While social media is a useful part of our strategy, we value our websites and email tools much more strongly as both fundraising tools and messaging platforms.* (Michael, Social Media Specialist in Development Department at Beta, May 22, 2019)

Enhancing Citizen Engagement

The third theme that emerged from the interviews is that social media enhances citizen engagement in an organization's advocacy work by allowing citizens to become message disseminators, content generators, and influencers. Considering their highly interactive framework, social media platforms provide new channels for advocacy organizations to better convene, communicate with, and mobilize their stakeholders. The number of platforms employed (e.g., Facebook, Twitter) and the number of accounts and users involved in sending messages on social media can dramatically increase the number of "voices" involved in communicating with the public. Our interviews indicate that advocacy organizations are taking advantage of this possibility. Adam, the advocacy program director at Alpha, commented,

> *[The] online community aspect of social media has been helpful for some causes to find their voice and be able to get organized online in ways that have been a lot harder if you were just doing it in the old days, in your bricks and mortar organizations, having a meeting in the basement of a church, you know; you would not find this many people that have kind of a focused approach to that particular issue.* (Adam, Advocacy Program Director at Alpha, December 20, 2018)

One typical type of constituent engagement on social media is to serve as *message disseminators* by helping broadcast messages produced by the focal organization. For instance, not only an organization's audience size (e.g., Twitter followers or Facebook friends) but also the networks of its followers or friends (e.g., Twitter followers of the followers of an organization) are pivotal to effective dissemination of information. The network structure of social media can help advocacy organizations bring in new supporters in response to their call to take action. David from Gamma noted:

> *Somebody does it because they care about Gamma, but maybe they also are doing it because their friends told them, "Hey, I saw this thing on Facebook."* (David, Advocacy Director at Gamma, October 25, 2018)

As we can see, by disseminating information through its network of social media followers and getting attention from the followers of its followers, the organization increases its stock of social media capital.

In addition to playing roles as message disseminators, social media platforms also allow citizens to become active *content generators* in social media–

based nonprofit advocacy. They are no longer "consumers and passive spectators," but rather active contributors (Benkler 2006, 272). In the context of nonprofit advocacy, an organization's social media page provides a public sphere where citizens are encouraged to discuss certain policy issues. Alpha often asks people to share their own stories and opinions about advocacy issues on its Facebook public page. Charlotte from Alpha told us,

> *We just had in the past . . . It was just people who got our email and consumed it. No one ever saw what was going on. But now we have this public space where we want people to interact, and it's all there for everyone to see.* (Charlotte, Advocacy Social Media Manager at Alpha, December 14, 2018)

Social media also enables an organization to identify and target *influencers*. An influencer is a platform user "with several crucial capacities in information dissemination and impact upon other users' opinions" (Bodrunova, Litvinenko, and Blekanov 2016, 212; Grenny et al. 2013). Network scholars have found that influencers serve as key structural elements of power and that they affect distribution on social media (Bodrunova, Litvinenko, and Blekanov 2016). Advocacy organizations may leverage the power of influencers to attract public attention and interest in their causes. Gamma's work offers an interesting example of using the power of influencers, as David describes:

> *Liz Gilbert, who wrote the book* Eat, Pray, Love, *wrote us a card and made a donation for one of our new buildings helping especially LGBT young adults. . . . Like, "I made a donation, will you?" And we shared her card on our (Facebook) page (and received) almost 100 likes or something. She shared it on her page about us and it had—last night when I looked—3,900 likes and a really big conversation.* (David, Advocacy Director at Gamma, October 25, 2018)

Increasing Bargaining Power

The fourth theme concerns the Internet and social media's potential to enhance the bargaining power of an organization in its effort to advocate for policy change. Most interviewees believed that social media not only had increased the visibility of their organizations but had also made their connection with supporters visible. For instance, Alpha has almost one million Facebook followers and over 15,000 Twitter followers, which indicates that a sizable audience is listening to what Alpha says and can likely be mobilized to engage in its policy advocacy work. Adam acknowledged,

In the old days we used to just write letters to a state legislator and say, "You have to believe us because, uh, we're a trusted organization." Our influence was based more on just what the name and the brand were and a reputation. . . . I get more respect when I enter that office; you know, they feel like, "Oh, here's a guy that has some kind of connections to people in New Jersey. We have to take that seriously and listen to him a little more." (Adam, Advocacy Program Director at Alpha, December 20, 2018)

One of the opportunities that social media creates for nonprofit advocacy is public attention for an organizational message. Over the past decade, we have witnessed a number of successful social media–based nonprofit campaigns that have garnered tremendous public attention. For instance, the Ice Bucket Challenge for ALS produced more than 2.4 million videos circulating on Facebook, leading to $115 million in donations in 2014. When it comes to nonprofit advocacy, public attention on social media can increase the bargaining power of an organization. This opportunity can be particularly attractive to smaller nonprofits that have limited access to media and policymakers. As Jenny, a deputy director at Beta, pointed out,

Senator [Anonymous] in Pennsylvania has never met with any of our staff in person and he's not going to because he doesn't care about homelessness or affordable housing. That's the dynamic, but I could imagine a scenario in which us getting national attention would give us an opening to call their office and say, "You know, Senator [Anonymous] should really weigh in on this. Would you like us to comment? Brief him?" Yeah. And he might actually say yes, if we had that level of, you know, attention on us. (Jenny, Deputy Director at Beta, January 9, 2019)

Establishing Open and Direct Channels to Policymakers

Advocacy organizations have used multiple means, including letters, phone calls, and emails, to speak to policymakers about policy issues they would like to address. Social media platforms establish another mechanism by which citizens can interact with and influence their representatives. The direct message functions on social media, such as Twitter's Direct Message and Facebook Messenger, allow organizations to directly communicate with policymakers in real time and at a low cost. Combined with offline efforts, social media advocacy has the potential to lead to tangible outcomes. David made the following observation:

One way that you can have another touchpoint with [traditional press or policymakers] beyond calls, emails and in-person visits is on social media. So when

we are advocating for an issue, we will often tweet or . . . direct Facebook mes-
sages directly to members of the legislature or members of Congress and make sure
that they hear about it in that way as well. I wouldn't say that we believe that
(social media message) in itself would ever influence their decisions, but that in
conjunction with other touchpoints like calls and in-person meetings and letters
and emails, we think it does make a difference. (David, Advocacy Director at
Gamma, October 25, 2018)

Jenny at Beta explained in a similar vein:

We might ask them to like or retweet something that tags the legislators so that
they get multiple content touchpoints there. Or we would include a link in a social
media post that gives a person another way to contact their legislator, which is
usually going to be a phone call or an email. (Jenny, Deputy Director at Beta,
January 9, 2019)

From a different angle, Adam commented on how social media allows
people to reach policymakers or reporters in a timely manner:

[If] we're working on something and we're tweeting, the reporters who are cover-
ing that issue find us more quickly. So it kind of cements a connection between
the advocacy organization and the media and probably also to some degree
with the policymakers. (Adam, Advocacy Program Director at Alpha, December 20, 2018)

Unlike other advocacy channels, social media offers an open channel in
which anyone can observe and join a conversation unless users change pri-
vacy settings to private. This openness of social media provides a new opportunity to influence policymakers on policy issues. For instance, if a nonprofit
tweeted about what a lawmaker had done regarding a specific policy issue and
mentioned (@) his or her name in the tweet, the lawmaker would be immediately informed about the tweet and able to track public reactions (liking or
retweets) to it. The power of social media as an open channel is well described
in the following statement from Jenny:

Senator [Confidential], he is a Republican and very good on our issues. . . . So we
tweeted immediately congratulations to him because we want to publicly praise
him. We privately praised him as well, but we want to be public about the fact
that this is a good thing and that he is a champion and, and we want him to feel
compelled to continue to do that. The other way that the public nature of social

media works is to shame them into doing something. (Jenny, Deputy Director at Beta, January 9, 2019)

Contributing to Coalition Building

Adam shared an illustrative story about Alpha's involvement in coalition building with various organizations, including the Natural Resources Defense Council, the Environmental Defense Fund, and Food and Water Watch, in a campaign to pass a bill in New York labeling food that contains genetically modified organisms (GMOs):

> *So all of our groups we would coordinate doing email together. And so when we were trying to get more sponsors for the bill, so we're using the full suite of tools for advocacy, you know, we're going door to door with the legislators, we're telling them that we have a big coalition, we're having news conferences, but we are also on the same month. We all go out to our lists and say we have got thousands of people to write to their legislator. We then pulled together all those names and we did a petition drop. We printed out the names, like I had maybe 5,000 names from our list—I can't remember the exact number, but we put them all together and we had about 50,000 names and we, you know, we've had a news conference in Albany, and say we have all these people that agree with this position. I think that that is potentially powerful when . . . you're layering on several organizations that are aggregating their lists and it looks like you're speaking for lots and lots of people and it becomes sort of an irresistible force for the legislators. [The legislators] don't want to be against you on something that they see as wildly popular.* (Adam, Advocacy Program Director at Alpha, December 20, 2018)

In terms of the outcome of the GMO campaign, the coalition was close to winning but eventually fell short of passing the bill out of the assembly, as the policymakers were hit hard on the other side by lobbyists for the companies that make the GMO seeds and pesticides, like Monsanto, as well as retailers and grocery manufacturers. Despite the fact that the bill did not pass, the campaign was successful to some degree. First, the coalition managed to change the position of some legislators as soon as they had the opportunity to meet and have an evidence-based conversation. Second, not only did the legislators change their position, but some members of the opposing camp also changed their opinion after the campaign. Adam asserts:

> *[Some of the big companies] changed in the marketplace because they were also feeling pressured directly from customers to them. [For] example, during the*

campaign . . . I think it was Campbell's Soup and General Mills just said, screw it, we're just gonna label our products anyway. And over time a number of the leading companies actually resigned from the big trade group, the Grocery Manufacturers of America. They divided over this issue because they said, even if the customers are wrong about the science, it's their right to decide what they want to put in their body. . . . And so the mainstream companies sort of shifted their position. (Adam, Advocacy Program Director at Alpha, December 20, 2018)

Discussion

In this chapter, we first identified three possible pathways by which organizations can move beyond attention to action and impact: *accelerating attention* through boundary spanning and coalition building; *transforming attention* by generating social media capital; and *leveraging attention* by creating online-offline synergy in their advocacy work. With a focus on the third pathway, we then conducted three case studies to examine how social media advocacy work is organized and managed in established organizations, and the extent to which the use of social media has added value to and transformed how policy advocacy is done. Our Twitter data analysis reveals six interesting strategies and practices associated with the synchronization of online and offline activities in the three organizations. They include: (1) live broadcast of offline events; (2) balancing action and information; (3) signaling a sense of urgency by using strong language, adopting multiple advocacy tactics, and taking advantage of unexpected, nonroutine events; (4) intense direct lobbying; (5) targeted public recognition; and (6) celebrity poking. Furthermore, six themes emerged from the interviews that provide fresh insight into the various ways in which social media contribute to the advocacy work of an established organization: (1) online-offline synchronization; (2) coordination among multiple online/social media platforms; (3) enhancing citizen engagement; (4) increasing bargaining power; (5) establishing open and direct channels to policymakers, and (6) contributing to coalition building.

Collectively, these findings have enhanced our understanding of how the three pathways we discussed work in real life. In particular, our interview findings provide valuable details on how the organization can create online-offline synergy and enhance coordination among multiple online/social media platforms. The findings illuminate how the organization can accumulate its stock of social media capital by engaging its followers in advocacy work, and how it can leverage its social media capital to increase bargaining power. The findings also shed light on how the organization contributes to coalition building through coordinated programs and activities, and how it reaches out to and influences policymakers through direct and open social media channels.

In our earlier work (Guo and Saxton 2014b), we proposed a three-stage pyramid model of social media–based advocacy: reaching out to people, keeping the flame alive, and stepping up to action. This pyramid model aims to describe how the function of social media actually varies with the stage of the advocacy process. At stage one, the organization's priority is to grow its networks of supporters by reaching out to people and raising awareness of its cause. At stage two, the organization's priority becomes sustaining communities of interest and networks of supporters. At stage three, the organization focuses on mobilizing supporters to take certain actions such as signing a petition, calling representatives, or attending an event. Although it has not been explicitly discussed, the role of attention is deeply embedded in each stage of the model. An organization cannot persuade people to join its network of followers and supporters without first getting them to pay attention to its advocacy work. Further, because followers and supporters can choose to exit the network at any time without any hassle, organizations must find ways to keep their attention and interest in their work at a certain level so they do not leave the group for another organization or cause. Additionally, organizations must be able to pass the supporters' attention threshold before they will be willing to take any action on behalf of the organization or cause.

The findings of the current study do not contradict this pyramid model, but they add some interesting nuances and complexity to the model's broad strokes. First, our findings suggest that an organization manages its social media advocacy work by regulating its rhythm of activity and attention. More specifically, it stays active on a daily basis, posting a small number of messages but maintaining a relatively low level of activity—just enough to keep followers and supporters in the loop. This overall low level of activity and attention is routinely punctuated by large spikes (or cascades) of activities and attention, during which the organization significantly increases the intensity of its activities and demands the attention and action of its supporters. Second, the organization regulates its rhythm of activity and attention through online-offline synchronization. Its spikes (or cascades) of social media activities correspond well with the timeline of significant offline activities or events. Some of the offline activities or events are planned in advance, such as an advocacy campaign or a congressional hearing, while others are unplanned, such as a natural disaster or other crisis. Some of the offline activities or events occur routinely, such as an annual conference or workshop, while others occur sporadically. Our findings indicate that much of the social media advocacy work at the three studied organizations falls into two broad categories of Internet activism as identified by Earl and colleagues (2010): online facilitation of offline activism, and online participation.

Our earlier work (Guo and Saxton 2014b) took a first crack at understanding the advocacy mix that organizations employ in seeking to reach their public policy–related goals. We identified four advocacy tactics that were relatively common: public education, which took a commanding lead and accounted for 40% of all tweets sent; followed far behind by grassroots lobbying, public events and direct action, and voter registration and education. Our interpretation was that social media advocacy took a mass approach that favored indirect advocacy tactics (e.g., public education, grassroots lobbying) aimed at diffused publics, and that using social media for advocacy would work less well with direct lobbying.

In this chapter, our case studies of three well-established nonprofit advocacy organizations have revealed some emerging trends. While public education tweets remain most common, grassroots lobbying and direct lobbying have become increasingly popular. In the case of Alpha, grassroots lobbying as an advocacy tactic is extensively used on a regular basis, while direct lobbying tweets are occasionally sent to complement grassroots lobbying. Somewhat surprisingly, in the cases of Beta and Gamma, direct lobbying is used significantly more frequently; in fact, direct lobbying tweets dominate some social media campaigns. Why has this reshuffling of advocacy tactics occurred? One possible explanation is that the use of social media has become much more prevalent than before among citizens in general and policymakers in particular, which makes grassroots and direct lobbying more feasible and convenient for activists. Our findings suggest that a targeted approach is indeed feasible on social media.

CHAPTER 6

THE FUTURE OF NONPROFIT ADVOCACY IN A DATA-DRIVEN WORLD

In his seminal work, *The Good Society*, the late Robert Bellah, a prominent sociologist, and his coauthors wrote, "democracy is paying attention" (Bellah et al. 1991, 254). That is, in order to do their jobs, democratically minded policymakers and public administrators must pay attention to the public, and to do so effectively they must develop their capacities to listen to the voices of the citizenry (see Denhardt and Denhardt 2015; Stivers 1994). As a tribute and response to Bellah, we argue in this book that (to paraphrase Bellah) advocacy is *getting attention*. In order to voice citizens' concerns, change public opinion, and influence public policy, an organization must first develop its capacity to speak and to be heard. Its voice must be able to stand out above the noise, and its message must blaze a trail through the bushes and shrubs of this Big Data world in which we live today.

This book represents a systematic attempt to develop what we may call an attention-based theory of nonprofit advocacy. A key takeaway for the book is to highlight "attention" as a key intermediate goal and important resource for advocacy organizations. Yet we also acknowledge that attention is not the ultimate aim: in order to effectively promote their causes, not only must these organizations obtain and sustain public attention on social media, but they also must be able to turn that attention into action and impact. Accordingly, we have presented and examined a conceptual framework for understanding how advocacy organizations seek and sustain attention on social media and how they transform this attention into tangible and strategic organizational outcomes.

With an eye on the big picture, this chapter summarizes the preceding chapters while giving a broader overview of the theoretical, methodological, and practical challenges and opportunities implied by the research presented in this book. After summarizing important findings from each of the preceding chapters, we present a section where we seek to bring together our key findings in a way that both theoreticians and practitioners will find valuable. We do this through the heuristic device of a logic model (Suchman 1968). In the subsequent two sections, we then discuss our methodological innovations and future research directions, respectively. Brief concluding remarks end the chapter.

Summary of Chapters

In our first chapter we began by arguing that the dawn of the social media era has also engendered a new paradigm for nonprofit advocacy work, one where attention is an increasingly scarce resource. Social media has essentially altered the informational landscape. The challenge is that, while attention is critical to advocacy organizations, grabbing and holding audience attention is growing increasingly difficult. In Chapter 1, we discussed the *resource challenge* faced by contemporary nonprofit advocacy organizations as well as what we referred to as the *relevance challenge*, or the challenge these organizations have in seeking to remain influential in shaping the policy directions of our society. With these twin challenges in mind, we elaborated how attention fits into contemporary organizations' advocacy work and how it is central to understanding and tackling the resource and relevance challenges. We then presented an overview of the overarching conceptual framework guiding the research conducted for the book.

In our second chapter we presented evidence and frameworks designed to help the reader better understand the social media context. After presenting a historical background of the development of social media, we provided a definition of social media and presented up-to-date evidence of advocacy organizations' adoption rates of each of the major social media platforms. We then turned to material that laid out a means of conceptualizing the activities organizations undertake on social media in their quest for attention. Our focus here was on the two central tools available on all social media platforms: messages and connecting actions. This novel way of conceptualizing the affordances of social media was designed to help the reader both to better understand key elements of the conceptual framework presented in Chapter 1 and to gain a deeper appreciation of the commonalities across social media sites. Our third task in Chapter 2 was to discuss core features of social media. Here we focused on the key role social networks play in influencing audience attention and thus devoted space to elaborating on some of the unique aspects of the social networks that predominate on social media. We ended the chapter by paying attention to attention—highlighting the transparent, drama-focused, and unequally distributed nature of attention in the social media context.

We trust that the first two chapters provide important advances in the ways readers will conceptualize and theorize nonprofit organizations' advocacy work on social media. The goal is to push readers to view social media-related phenomena in a new theoretical light. In Chapter 3 we then sought to combine these theoretical insights with data and conduct empirical tests of what drives attention on social media. Elaborating and further specifying the conceptual model presented in Chapter 1, in this chapter we built and then tested an original explanatory model for understanding why some advocacy organizations get attention on social media while others do not. We specifically modeled the amount of attention an organization receives as a function of network characteristics and communication strategy. In colloquial terms, we argued that the extent to which an organization is "being heard" (i.e., the attention it receives) depends on the size of the audience, how much and how it speaks, and what it says. Using three proxies of attention—the number of retweets, likes, and replies received from audience members—we found attention was most closely associated with network size (number of followers), the frequency with which the organization tweeted, and the use of hashtags and values-based words. More generally, in each of the four main conceptual categories in our model—network characteristics, timing and pacing, targeting and connecting, and content—we found one or more variables to be significant. This lent support to the overall theoretical model.

In our fourth chapter we moved from organizations down to messages. Specifically, determining what drives attention to some messages and not others is what motivated this chapter. We sought to not simply test a "message-level" version of our conceptual model from Chapter 3, but rather we significantly expanded the range of factors considered using advanced data science and data analytics tools. Yet we argued previous data analytic approaches were too atheoretical to be applied directly to more theory-driven social scientific problems such as ours, while existing inductive-qualitative and deductive-quantitative approaches were not as well suited to developing models in new areas involving Big Data. We therefore devoted considerable efforts in Chapter 4 to developing a novel methodological approach to model building. Our machine learning–based approach combined with inductive analyses of the data and quantitative algorithms led us to expand our conceptual model to include three more factors: at the message level, *tweet sophistication;* and at the organization level, *account sophistication* and *user characteristics.* We then tested the expanded model and found that, while some static user characteristics were significant, it is the *dynamic* elements—the decisions of whom to follow, whose tweets to like, and what to include inside each tweet—that truly matter. We found particularly important associations with the use of values-based and ethical words; this is something that conforms with the mission of a large proportion of nonprofit organizations. Continuing a theme in our findings throughout this book, we also found that two key organizational-level "network" measures—the number of public "lists" that other Twitter users place the organization on and the number of Twitter users that follow the organization—proved to be highly associated with whether a message receives attention or is ignored. These are indicators of the organization's reputation and influence (Bakshy et al. 2011). They also reflect the amount of *social media capital* the organization has accrued (Saxton and Guo 2014; Saxton and Guo in press), which in turn represents a resource the organization can leverage to mobilize followers to act, engage, discuss, resist, or donate.

We extended this idea of mobilizing attention in Chapter 5. Bringing the importance of strategic outcomes to the forefront and building on evidence from Chapters 3 and 4, we identified three pathways to moving from attention to strategic outcomes: *accelerating attention, transforming attention,* and *leveraging attention.* The first pathway concerns specific facets of the organization's "boundary-spanning" communication strategy, the second focuses on developing the key intermediate resource we call *social media capital,* and the third involves intensive efforts at fostering online-offline synergies in communicative and advocacy efforts. Then, with a strong focus on the third pathway, we conducted case studies of three US nonprofit advocacy organizations operating at the national, state, and local levels, respectively. Combining both interview and social media data, we examined how advocacy organizations organize and manage their social media–based advocacy efforts as well as how the use of social media has added value to and transformed how organizations undertake policy advocacy.

Theoretical and Practical Takeaways

Elsewhere, we described the social media age for nonprofit organizations as the age of *attention philanthropy*. We define attention philanthropy as "the challenges, opportunities, and responses associated with the phenomenon in which all players in the philanthropic and charitable sector (e.g., donors, funders, supporters, nonprofits, etc.) are potentially overwhelmed by information overload and a dearth of attention" (Guo and Saxton 2014a, 44). For nonprofit organizations engaged in advocacy work, attention philanthropy is not "business as usual." It requires a specialized set of skills and new ways of thinking about advocacy work. Fortunately, we believe the research we have presented in this book carries valuable insights in this regard.

One of the overarching lessons from our research is that attention is an immediate effect of social media efforts that is both valuable to nonprofit advocacy organizations and necessary to help achieve organizational objectives. Organizations need to think strategically in order to maximize attention—the *right kind* of attention. Effort needs to be involved in setting long-term outcomes and then developing and implementing a communication plan that will help the organization achieve its intended outcomes.

Our research brings much to bear on these issues. Accordingly, below we bring together our theoretical and conceptual insights into a practice-oriented framework intended to help organizational managers see the connections between their day-to-day social media behaviors and strategic outcomes. In so doing, our aim is that this also proves useful for academics who are looking for new ways to theorize about social media, advocacy, and attention.

We present our framework in terms of a *logic model*. Logic models, which have a long history as program planning and evaluation tools in the government and nonprofit sectors (Suchman 1968), are documents that describe the hypothesized chain of causes and effects leading to a desired organizational outcome. A typical logic model includes a textual and/or visual depiction of the causal chain flowing from organization inputs to key activities/outputs to targeted organizational and/or societal outcomes. Logic models are especially useful in contexts where the mission and vision—and hence the outcomes—are nonfinancial, as is the norm in the nonprofit sector. Our context is particularly amenable to the logic model approach: an organization's social media efforts should, we argue, be approached as a specific "program," one where the hypothesized cause-and-effect relationships are clear; and given that attention is nonfinancial, the logic model approach is particularly well suited to organizational efforts aimed at acquiring it, as well as, in the long term, reaching advocacy-related outcomes. Figure 6.1 graphically summarizes our logic model.

Antecedent Conditions

The beginning point of the logic model is what we have labeled *Antecedent Conditions*. These are organizational and contextual factors that generally precede the decisions that are made regarding social media advocacy work. Our findings suggest that certain core organizational characteristics influence the level of attention the organization will achieve; this relationship is represented by the first arrow that goes from *Organizational Characteristics* directly to *Attention*. In line with this argument, our message-level analyses in Chapter 4 suggested that messages from older, larger, and more efficient organizations will be more likely to garner attention. Moreover, we found relationships for some location (state) variables as well as for certain industries (NTEE codes). While some of these characteristics are under the organization's control, all are "outside the (causal) loop"; none are manipulated for the purposes of leveraging social media to do advocacy work. Accordingly, we label these "antecedent conditions." These conditions are potentially related to attention but are either chiefly unchangeable or are not part of the "decision matrix" when it comes to advocacy-related (or at least attention-related) decisions.

The arrow from *Organizational Characteristics* to *Attention* is a recognition that there is not necessarily a level playing field in the market for attention: larger organizations, more efficient organizations, and organizations working in certain issue areas have a head start in the race for attention. The other two arrows that emanate from *Organizational Characteristics* in our logic model go to the two key inputs—*Resources* and *Strategy*. We now turn to a discussion of how organizational characteristics influence the inputs an organization devotes to its advocacy work on social media.

The Inputs: Resources and Strategy

The next section of the logic model is the inputs that support and guide the organization's social media efforts. Though social media platforms do not charge for basic use of their services, effective social media use nonetheless requires organizations to dedicate inputs (Schaupp and Bélanger 2013; Suddaby, Saxton, and Gunz 2015). Figure 6.1 highlights two elements to these inputs. The

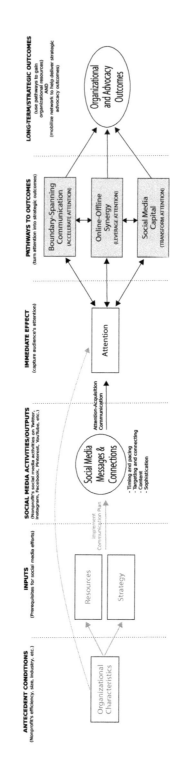

FIGURE 6.1 Logic model depicting social media efforts, attention, and the pathways to strategic outcomes

first element is straightforward: *resources*. It is not cost-free to get social media up and running for an organization: the successful adoption and use of social media require that organizations devote the necessary time, space, money, and staff to the endeavor. Thus the resources to be invested include tangible resources such as physical, financial, and human resources: Is the organization willing to devote some of its (often tight) budget, staff time, and office space to social media advocacy work? The resources also include intangible resources such as intellectual and reputational resources: Does the organization have the necessary technical expertise in the policy area? Is the organization willing to risk its reputation in extending its work into a new domain where it has relatively little control? Much is at stake, and yet such resource commitments are often sorely underestimated by the traditional "bricks-and-mortar" organization, with social media tasks passed off to a single staff member or intern as additional or secondary duties.

The other element is *strategy*. In a broad sense, a strategy is a plan for achieving an organization's mission, a plan "that integrates an organization's major goals, policies, and action sequences into a cohesive whole" (Quinn 1988, 3). For a nonprofit advocacy organization in particular, a strategy is a plan of action to help accomplish its policy goals and outcomes. In a narrow sense, a strategy is a road map that facilitates an organization's social media advocacy work, particularly regarding its communicative role and its target audience (Suddaby, Saxton, and Gunz 2015). It is not enough to simply *be* on social media. Instead, the organization needs to think strategically about what it wants to achieve through its presence. The starting point for this strategy should be the final elements in Figure 6.1—namely, the main outcomes it is hoping to achieve. With those outcomes in mind, the organization needs to backward map and lay out a social media communications plan for reaching that outcome.

At the heart of this plan is determining which specific audience(s)—stakeholders who can affect or can be affected by the organization's advocacy work—the organization wishes to target and the communicative role it will adopt to reach that audience. Here, the organization needs to do some research, preferably with the assistance of some stakeholder identification and analysis techniques: An environmental organization working to reduce water consumption at home, for instance, would consider as its stakeholders local lawmakers, coalition partners, opinion leaders such as journalists and educators, or current and future household owners (including teens and young adults). An LGBT-rights organization's stakeholders would include not only nonheterosexual individuals and their families, but also the government, media groups, and the general public. The point is that the organization should seek to cultivate a specific, well-defined audience through its social media communications.

The organization then needs to decide how it will engage with that audience and, more specifically, the role it will adopt to add value to its target audience's social media feeds (Guo and Saxton 2016). Each of the hypothetical audiences identified above requires a different communicative approach. Concretely, the organization might choose to become an expert or *thought leader* on a specific subject issue by crafting original content designed to inform, sway, or educate. Alternatively, it might seek to be a *curator* of information on that subject—becoming, in effect, a go-to source for the latest and most relevant information produced by others. Or, the organization might consider itself a *convener* or *community builder*, relying on social media activities designed to foster connections among stakeholders and thus build a more cohesive online community. Differently put, the organization needs to define its intended *strategic role* on social media. Does it wish to be an information source? An opinion leader? A market builder? A curator? A community builder? Each role potentially adds value to its audience's social media feeds. What the organization should seek to do is to match its own proclivities, interests, and resources with the audience's needs.

In brief, before even beginning to bring hand to keyboard, the organization needs to develop a plan that clearly lays out its desired outcomes, clearly indicates the target audience, and clearly lays out a broad strategic identity for the organization's communicative efforts. In so doing, the organization should develop something akin to a logic model that clearly lays out the intended outcomes of its social media program, the role of social media capital in meeting and obtaining these outcomes, and the resources it will devote to supporting the activities that will help achieve them. These resources will be tracked by the organization's information system, and the audience strategy— along with the entire logic model/causal chain model—should form part of the organization's integrated information systems. Both inputs are instrumental to the success of an organization's social media advocacy work: to use an analogy of driving a vehicle, resources provide the necessary fuel while strategy functions as the navigation system; both are needed to get us where we need to be.

Social Media Activities and Outputs

As described in Chapter 2, there are two main activities on social media: messages and connections. It is these dynamic actions that comprise the essential elements of advocacy organizations' day-to-day social media work, and it is these elements that are designed to garner attention from the organization's strategically defined audiences.

The central offering the organization makes to the social media attention market is its dynamic stream of social media messages. Our findings in Chapters 3 and 4 have documented a number of message factors associated with attention under the broad categories of timing and pacing, targeting and connecting, visual and textual content, and message sophistication. Valuable lessons can be generated from those findings for the organizational decision maker or social media manager wishing to engage with—and receive attention from—his or her intended audience.

At the broadest level, an organization's messages are designed to provide value-added content to the organization's strategically identified audience. The extent to which the organization can effectively develop and maintain a social media network depends on whether the messages are meeting and exceeding what the network wants from the organization. In addition to offering content to establish an organization's strategic role, messages can also be used for targeting or connecting purposes, and may include replying and commenting, liking, sharing, user mentions, hyperlinks, and hashtags. These actions form message ties that can be reciprocated, and over time the repeat use of message-based connecting also serves to develop ties with new users or strengthen ties with existing users.

The key here is to see the messages as the central micro-level efforts that can help the organization gain attention from its strategically identified audience. We would also like to stress that Figure 6.1 shows only one arrow emanating from social media activities—and that is to attention. In effect, there is no getting around attention; without gaining the audience's attention the organization's social media efforts achieve nothing.

Attention

The immediate effect of sending messages and making connections is capturing attention from the organization's strategically identified audience. For the purpose of this book, we define attention as the extent to which multiple audience members react to the messages sent by an organization on its social media platform(s). In Chapter 2, we discussed important aspects of the nature of attention in the social media context. We noted the centrality of the social network and covered several unique and/or salient features of social networks on social media. We further noted how attention on social media is eminently observable, has a preference for drama, and is regulated by the power law distribution.

Figure 6.1 highlights the key role of attention in the logic model. There is, in effect, no path to strategic outcomes that can be made in the absence of attention. It is for this very reason that our book title highlights "The Quest for Attention." Because of the novelty of this idea, we have purposefully focused on attention as our outcome of interest. Yet to be clear, our core argument is that attention is a crucial first step toward meaningful outcomes driven by social media. Attention is, in other words, simply a means to an ends, albeit an important one. Above all, for advocacy and social movement organizations, the ultimate long-term goal is not attention but instead spreading awareness, building coalitions, or mobilizing supporters in order to achieve some broader societal or policy outcomes.

Pathways to Outcomes

Before reaching important strategic outcomes, advocacy organizations must capture the audience's attention. Attention is, however, merely a means to an end. This begs the question: What precisely can and should organizations do after gaining attention? To answer this question, we need to shift attention to the other side of the equation and consider it to be the independent variable. In Chapter 5 of this book, we identified three pathways by which organizations can turn attention into more substantive and tangible strategic outcomes: *accelerating attention* through boundary spanning and coalition building; *transforming attention* by generating social media capital; and *leveraging attention* by creating online-offline synergy in their advocacy work.

Pathway 1: Accelerate Attention. Our first "pathway" to reaching strategic outcomes is to accelerate attention through boundary-spanning communication. Coalition building is a key advocacy tactic adopted by nonprofit organizations, and the networked nature of social media platforms makes them uniquely positioned to facilitate an organization's advocacy work as it joins forces with others across organizational and sector boundaries. Hashtags in particular offer a powerful tool that enables the organization to connect with a wide range of stakeholders who otherwise would not even be aware of the organization's work. In essence, this first pathway leans heavily on the organization's strategic communications plan. It also means the organization needs to incorporate considerations of potential boundary-spanning communication during the "Inputs" stage; the organization should have a clear plan of the specific "attention accelerators" (coalition partners) it wishes to target in its communication. In line with the decentralized and often ephemeral nature of groups and "ad hoc publics" (Bruns and Burgess 2011) on social media, the organization should ensure that its plans go beyond traditional "bricks-and-mortar" organizations and include a strategy for tapping into emerging discussions, events, and movements.

Pathway 2: Leverage Attention. Our second pathway involves leveraging attention through online-offline synergies. This pathway serves to recognize a fundamental fact: advocacy organizations cannot do everything online. For a traditional advocacy-focused charity, a sole reliance on social media could quickly decline into "clicktivism" and "slacktivism," increased attention that raises awareness but does not move on to meaningful social change. In effect, while the desire to leverage social media in order to bolster the organization's and/or the issue's political presence may usefully constitute a "wider purpose for digital advocacy strategies as it informs and shapes how, when and why actors engage in digital [advocacy work]" (Johansson and Scaramuzzino 2019, 1542), in order to be effective the organization needs to undertake a series of interconnected online and offline activities (Johansson and Scaramuzzino 2019). Our findings elaborate and shed light on processes examined in this and other studies (e.g., Bond et al. 2012; Petray 2011) that have concentrated on the online-offline interaction issue. Overall, our second pathway encapsulates our evidence regarding the different ways social media can complement and assist offline advocacy efforts.

Pathway 3: Transform Attention into Social Media Capital. Assuming the organization has gained the audience's attention, the next step in the causal model is an intermediate outcome that we refer to as *social media capital*. As discussed in Chapter 5, social media capital is a special form of social capital that is found on social media sites. It is a resource, and, given the critical role of social networks on social media, is a primary initial resource that can be developed on social media. The focus of social media capital is network resources, or the resources that flow from the network the organization has carefully built through its day-to-day dynamic messaging and connecting actions.

Moreover, a growing body of empirical research backs our proposition that social network–based resources are a *prerequisite* to successfully achieving organizational objectives on social media. For instance, looking purely at the social media arena—and social media objectives—an organization must have followers before any meaningful organizational engagement can take place (Lovejoy, Waters, and Saxton 2012). An organization will first see a new user follow the organization. Subsequently, the organization may begin to see the "digital footprints" of a budding organization-stakeholder relationship (Smith 2012) as reflected in a defined set of publicly visible behavioral indicators: (1) the user will archive/like, share/retweet, or upvote/downvote a social media message sent by the organization, or (2) a user will mention the organization in a social media message. Recent research has shown a strong relationship between the number of followers and these other, message-based outcomes indicators (Bakshy et al. 2011; Saxton and Waters 2014), and our findings in Chapters 3, 4, and 5 strongly corroborate this research.

With the caveat that measures of network size are only one component of social capital (and can be manipulated on some social media platforms), it is important to note that the simple size of an organization's network represents an important resource in and of itself. As Bourdieu argued, "The volume of social capital possessed by a given agent . . . depends on the size of the network of connections he can effectively mobilize" (2002, 286). Taking the case of Twitter, the number of followers indicates how many users will see an organization's messages. In a study of 150 public policy advocacy organizations on Twitter, Guo and Saxton (2014b) found the number of followers ranged from a low of 22 to a high of 188,655, with the average being 11,971. One of the most salient tactics of these advocacy organizations was public education, such that the number of times an organizational message is diffused by audience members—that is, the amount of attention audience members pay attention to the message—is a key metric. Common sense would dictate that an organization with 22 followers is practically incapable of effective message diffusion and would thus fail in a public education approach. Guo and Saxton's (2014b) data bear this out. The organization with 22 followers had precisely zero total retweets of its messages over the entire course of 2013. The same was true of the organization with 68 followers, as well as one with 319 followers. Contrast this with the 2013 retweet counts for the five organizations with more than

100,000 followers: all had more than 100,000 retweets, with a mean of 224,603 and a range from 100,773 to 567,778. In short, the size of an organization's network matters.

Our updated findings strongly support this previous research. More generally, this element of the logic model is substantially supported by findings throughout this book. In Chapter 2 we argued that social media is inherently network-based or, differently put, that behaviors on social media are mediated by networks of social relations. It is for this reason that, as argued in Chapters 3 and 4, the characteristics of the networks the organization has built are central determinants of the level of attention acquired by an organization and its messages. Specifically, the size of the network consistently proved to be one of the variables most strongly associated with attention.

We should stress that organizations should not be solely concerned with how many followers they have. More important is the quality and relevance of that network. It is through strategically building an "attention network" that an advocacy organization is able to not only acquire attention, but to acquire the right kind of attention from the right kind of (strategically determined) audience. The organization should strive to first identify and then build this *strategic attention network*.

The reader will also notice a causal arrow leading not only from *Attention* to *Social Media Capital* but also an arrow leading in the opposite direction. This second arrow is a recognition of our findings in Chapters 3 and 4 that network characteristics help determine the level of attention the organization will receive. The first arrow, meanwhile, reflects how attention is a prerequisite for building the organization's social media network.

Long-Term and Strategic Outcomes

A nonprofit organization's long-term and strategic outcomes cover a broad range. Such outcomes may include financial performance, operational performance, mission performance, and overall performance. For advocacy work in particular, such outcomes might include acquiring volunteers, increasing donations, mobilizing protest, influencing legislation, and changing public opinion. While the intended outcomes will vary across organizations, what does not vary is the need for each organization to have a plan for the long-term outcomes it wishes to achieve. Our logic model essentially presupposes that an organization knows what its ultimate ends are; for any organizations that are unsure of their course, then strategic planning should be considered a prerequisite to any further social media efforts. As Yogi Berra famously said, "If you don't know where you are going, you'll end up someplace else."

Methodological Innovations

In Chapter 4 we undertook a novel, inductively guided yet machine learning–assisted approach to expanding our theoretical model. We believe this novel approach carries benefits over existing paradigmatic methodological approaches. The benefits of our model-building algorithm become visible when compared to three other paradigmatic approaches: (1) traditional qualitative inductive theory building, (2) traditional deductive model building, and (3) machine learning–based model building.

To start, our approach differs from model building based on machine learning in being focused on understanding and explanation over prediction. While there are certainly plenty of cases where a purely predictive approach is helpful, in the social sciences we are generally much more interested in explanation. For this very reason we need an approach that is theory-driven, and that means focused on concepts rather than variables. It is our continual effort to "'lift' the data to a conceptual level" (Suddaby 2006, 636) that separates our approach from approaches based on computer science/machine learning. Without such effort, our approach would not be so helpful to social scientists interested in nonprofit advocacy.

Our approach improves upon traditional qualitative inductive theory-building approaches in facilitating a much larger number of variables as well as cases. Moreover, the qualitative inductive approach generally stops at theory building and leaves model testing to follow-up research; our approach, in contrast, conducts both model building and model testing. As seen in our findings, this final testing stage is important for assessing the strength of the model that has been built.

Our approach also carries benefits compared to the traditional quantitative deductive approach. Model testing is common across both approaches; where they differ is in terms of the number of variables added to the model. In the traditional deductive approach, a scholar might develop a hypothesis for an additional small set of variables (say, one to three) based on intuition, fundamental theory, or a related body of literature. The theory-building element is argument-based, based on deductive reasoning. The model-building portion of the study is somewhat implicit, however, and also brief; the focus of such papers is on the model testing. Moreover, the focus of the theory-building section is to convince the reader that the new variables are important in isolation; there is typically little to no explicit comparison with other variables that could be considered. In contrast, in our approach we can examine a much broader range of variables simultaneously and then add only those variables that prove to be more relevant than others.

In effect, we believe our approach could save numerous iterations of incremental research. Returning to our earlier example of the "economic model of giving" (Weisbrod and Dominguez 1986), a considerable body of literature has proceeded to add one or two variables at a time to the core three-variable model. This is the way the typical quantitative deductive approach works, and it is the paradigm in which we (the authors of this book) generally operate. In this chapter we have added 13 new variables to the model—in the process potentially saving several iterations of individual research studies. Moreover, we could have pushed further and added even more variables.

At the same time, it is important to add that our approach may be best suited to phenomena that are less well understood, such as the economic model of giving (Weisbrod and Dominguez 1986) in its initial iterations in the 1980s and 1990s. In any case, we urge future research that can help improve upon the seven-stage algorithm outlined in Chapter 4.

Implications for Future Research

In line with the theoretical and practical takeaways and methodological innovations, we identify three broad themes for future research: solving the puzzle of attention; determinants of attention; and attention-based advocacy processes.

Solving the Puzzle of Attention

Future research should further explore the conceptualization and operationalization of attention within the context of social media. More specifically, the following possible areas of research deserve further scholarly attention.

High Attention, Low Attention. For most of the book, we made our arguments based on an implicit assumption that higher levels of attention are always more desirable than lower levels of attention. However, this assumption needs to be considered more carefully. Not all the organizations are interested in garnering attention on social media. For example, an advocacy organization such as an environmental group tends to attract more like-minded followers than a home-less shelter; when this environmental group posts a message on its social media account, its primary aim may be progressing toward a particular strategic goal or disseminating policy-relevant ideas to frame the discussion. In either case, the goal is not necessarily to gain attention. Moreover, when a state- or local-level advocacy group gets the national spotlight and the issue becomes polar-ized, that could make it more difficult for the organization to get work done, as one of the respondents pointed out during an interview. Therefore, future research should consider documenting situations where the optimal level of attention is not high but rather in the low to mid range.

Good Attention, Bad Attention. Another related assumption on which our arguments were made is that attention is always a positive thing. While in most cases attention brings positive value to the organization, sometimes atten-tion hurts. The Susan G. Komen for the Cure Foundation offers an interesting example. In January 2012, the nation's leading breast cancer charity "quietly" decided to cut funding to Planned Parenthood, the nation's leading provider of health services to women. Yet Komen received unexpected attention on social media, when Planned Parenthood announced the "breaking" news on its Face-book page. Shocked and outraged, people poured their support into Planned Parenthood, not only in the forms of Facebook "likes" and Twitter followers, but also in the form of making donations; at the same time, they directed their criticism toward Komen on social media. This negative attention also led to heavy public scrutiny of Komen's own programs and finances (see Guo and Saxton 2014a, for a detailed discussion).

Secondhand Attention. Sometimes an organization can suffer from negative "secondhand" attention due to its affiliation with someone else who happens to be on the wrong side. The Livestrong Foundation (formerly known as the Lance Armstrong Foundation) offers a good example. During its early years after its founding by the world-famous cyclist Lance Armstrong in 1997, the foundation's success in fundraising and mission-related work had been closely associated with its celebrity founder and single largest donor. However, when the Lance Armstrong doping scandal broke in January 2013, not only did he receive tremendous negative publicity but the foundation also found itself in the spotlight due to its affiliation with Armstrong. As a result, the foundation's reputation risked suffering from this secondhand attention and had to develop a plan for damage control in response to its founder's scandal. Indeed, two months before Armstrong made his confession to Oprah Winfrey, the foundation changed its name to the Livestrong Foundation in November 2012 to distance itself from its founder.

Determinants of Attention

A core element in our conceptual framework that guides much of our organizational- and message-level analyses is network characteristics. We found that the amount of attention that an organization receives on social media depends on the size of the audience. While audience size is certainly a key network characteristic, future research should consider other characteristics as well. For example, the social media activity of an organization's *followers*, and the amount of followers those followers have, might in turn also affect the amount of attention the organization gets. In a recent study of social media use by homelessness nonprofits in their advocacy work, An (2019) used the frequency of being public-listed (which indicates the number of times an organization is included in other users' public Twitter lists) and the follower/following ratio as additional measures of network characteristics.

One interesting finding from our organizational-level analysis reported in Chapter 3 is that value framing—the inclusion of values-based words in Twitter messages—has a positive effect on attention in the forms of retweets and likes. The micro-practice of value framing has its theoretical foundation in the concept of *value representation* (Guo and Marietta 2015; Marietta 2010), which can be defined as a congruence of values between the organization and its supporters and followers. The fact that value representation leads to increased public attention suggests that advocacy organizations should not only "walk the walk" (i.e., promote agendas, policies, and activities on behalf of the expressed interests of their constituents) but also "talk the talk" (i.e., display shared values with their constituents) on social media. It is also likely that advocacy organizations are taking advantage of the interactivity of social media platforms to establish a participatory mechanism for eliciting the shared values of its constituents, which in turn can guide organizations in their forming of policy proposals and positions.

Future research on value framing and its effect on attention can also benefit from a deeper dive into the social movement literature, which has long highlighted the importance of framing processes to collective action (Benford and Snow 2000; Snow et al. 1986), particularly the importance of developing and strategically using frames that develop or tap into shared meanings and collective identities (King 2008). For instance, over the 1980s and 1990s, with notions of "welfare queens" and other stories, social conservatives in the United States were able to slowly change predominant frames and public opinion regarding the causes of poverty and the deservingness of the poor, with the frames—and the public policies—becoming increasingly anti-poor over time. Guetzkow (2010) shows how, over a four-decade span, US policymakers' changing frames about poverty and the poor shaped the nature of antipoverty policies that were adopted in each period.

Attention-Based Advocacy Processes

The findings from Chapter 5 put flesh on the bones of the pyramid model of social media–based advocacy (Guo and Saxton 2014b) from the lens of online-offline synchronization. We demonstrate six key strategies or practices that help organizations reach out to people, keep the flame alive, and result in people stepping up to act. These practices include (1) live broadcast of offline events, (2) balancing action and information, (3) signaling a sense of urgency, (4) intense direct lobbying, (5) targeted public recognition, and (6) celebrity poking; other practices may also work. While this chapter does not intend to offer a one-size-fits-all guide on how nonprofit leaders should capitalize on social media, the case analysis provides us with evidence that social media can complement and assist offline advocacy efforts in a number of important ways. And depending on each organization's goals and resources on advocacy and the nature of advocacy issues at hand, organizations might seek to reap the strategic value of social media through primarily relying on certain tactics or configuring attention-seeking tactics as needed.

Another lesson from findings reported in Chapter 5 is that an organization manages its social media advocacy work by self-regulating its rhythm of activity and attention. While attention is fluid and punctuated, nonprofit leaders may still play a proactive role in posting, targeting, and calling on stakeholders in order to capture a potential culmination of public attention that happens in the blink of an eye. Arguably, the spikes are perhaps the results of an attention function that has two parts: nonprofit efforts to get the messages out to the public (actionable) plus the vicissitudes of events that draw public attention (contingent). By taking the initiative to manage and seize the heat of the moment, attention will be less likely to slip through one's fingers.

Hence, what can be taken away from our findings is that nonprofit leaders should devise an action plan for being more intentional in using social media in general and being more purposeful in using some specific attention-seeking tactics based on the issues at hand and the overarching goals of advocacy. With such a plan, efforts on a busy day can be translated more effectively to tangible outcomes for the organization.

Twitter versus Other Social Media Platforms

Finally, we wish to discuss the limitations—and implications—of our focus on Twitter. To what extent are our findings generalizable to other Web 2.0 social media tools? To what extent does the conceptual framework (or logic model) apply to Web 1.0 tools such as organizational websites? What are the similarities and differences? Do these different tools serve different purposes in an organization's advocacy work? Prior research shows that each online and social media platform offers a unique communication experience (Pasek, More, and Romer 2009). For example, Facebook is shown to be better suited for bridging online and offline connections than Twitter and other social media platforms (Ellison, Steinfield, and Lampe 2007; Ellison et al. 2014). As a result, the range of factors that drive attention on Twitter as identified in our research may or may not be the same as those that drive attention on Facebook or Instagram or the website. In Chapter 2, we briefly compared the differences and commonalities of various social media platforms as well as the implications of such differences and commonalities. It is our hope that, by further exploring these questions, we can help stimulate future scholarly discussion pertaining to this exciting line of research.

Concluding Remarks

We hope this book has achieved several goals. One, we hope we have provided the reader with a new lens through which to see attention and, more importantly, advocacy organizations' efforts at grabbing the attention of social media audiences. Two, we hope our book has provided a standardized set of conceptual tools—a common language, so to speak—for thinking and talking about the day-to-day attention-building tools advocacy organizations can put to use on social media. Three, our aim has been to provide a conceptual framework that provides insights into why some organizations and some messages garner attention yet others do not. Our hope, in other words, is that the reader leaves this book with a better understanding of what drives attention. Just as importantly, we hope the reader will have gained a deeper, more intuitive appreciation of the main pathways through which an organization can move from attention to strategic, advocacy-related outcomes. In the end, we share this same goal: we did not wish to write a book merely about "attention"; instead, we sought to write a book that would help increase our understanding of how contemporary advocacy organizations can use attention as a tool to navigate the fast-paced, sometimes frustrating, and always fascinating social media environment—and in so doing, to once again overcome the pressing challenges to their resources and their relevance.

METHODOLOGICAL APPENDIX

TO CHAPTER 4

In Chapter 4 we used a number of complex machine learning procedures as part of a novel, data science–based approach to theory building. This methodological appendix includes additional details, background, and supporting tables related to these procedures. There are three main sections to this methodological appendix. The first section presents an overview of the analytical method and analysis plan, the second section contains additional information and tables related to the *feature engineering* stage, and the third section contains additional methodological details and supporting tables for the univariate, bivariate, and multivariate *feature selection* stages.

Analytical Method and Analysis Plan

Leveraging the opportunities presented by Big Data and the advent of an array of new data analytics and data science techniques, in Chapter 4 we developed and employed a novel theory-building approach. In this section we discuss the key features and stages of this approach.

An Inductive-Quantitative Approach

Our analyses in Chapter 4 comprise three stages: feature engineering, feature selection, and model testing. The first two stages are where our novel approach comes into play. As we describe in more detail below, these two stages are largely inductive and quantitative.

Primarily Inductive Logic

In order to develop insights into the relationship between characteristics of advocacy messages and the level of public attention those messages receive, we employ a mix of traditional qualitative inductive approaches (e.g., Miles and Huberman 1984) and "Big Data"–driven, machine learning approaches to theory building (e.g., Evans 2014). Yet these efforts are both, in contrast to Chapter 3, chiefly inductive. There is an important deductive component insofar as we look for and examine variables that are found in prior literature. It is inductive, however, in how we also consider variables and concepts that are not found in existing research but are nonetheless potentially relevant based on our investigation of the data.

Our goal in the first two stages of our analysis is to build a model—a theoretical explanation of what drives attention to social media messages—and this theory-building effort is largely inductive despite the mix of qualitative and quantitative techniques. Across the feature engineering and feature selection stages, in line with qualitative inductive methods espoused by Miles and Huberman (1984) and Strauss and Corbin (1998), the identification, coding, and selection of relevant variables involves a multistage, iterative process of cycling back and forth among data, literature, and emergent conceptual categories. Guided by extant theory, the goals are to identify and conceptualize relevant variables, to situate them within existing literature, and to theorize about the relationship of these concepts with our outcome variable audience attention. Inductive reasoning also comes into play in interpreting the results of quantitative feature selection algorithms.

Quantitative Feature Selection Analyses

Assisting this inductive model-building effort is a suite of quantitative machine learning techniques conducted in the Python programming language. *Machine learning* refers to a broad array of computer-assisted prediction, classification, and feature selection techniques that are well suited to generating fresh insights into social scientific phenomena (Parks 2014), and are an important subset of techniques in data science and data analytics. We employ what are known as *feature selection* techniques—techniques designed to help determine which of a large number of variables should be retained for a final empirical model (e.g., Verikas, Gelzinis, and Bacauskiene 2011). Such dimensionality-reduction methods are ideally suited to Big Data questions characterized by a large number of potential variables. The approach offers the potential for a more rigorous pruning of models than is offered by traditional inductive, or purely qualitative, approaches.

In effect, we argue our approach is chiefly inductive but also decidedly quantitative. The combination of inductive and quantitative may sound counterintuitive to many. Yet we argue the process is more analogous to typical qualitative inductive analysis than it is to purely deductive quantitative analysis. In fact, we maintain it would be best to characterize the process as inductive analysis *aided by* quantitative feature selection techniques.

For example, in one major paradigm of inductive qualitative research (Eisenhardt 1989), a typical scenario might be as follows. Let us assume the researcher is interested in what leads nonprofit organizations to "success." She is, in this paradigm, interested in building a theoretical explanation of nonprofit success. Using insights from prior literature, she might then find an appropriate sample of nonprofit organizations and collect data, such as a series of interviews with key personnel as well as data from archival materials (IRS 990 filings, newspaper articles, annual reports, social media, etc.). The researcher would then dig into the data, engaging in an iterative process of cycling back and forth among emergent conceptual categories, data, and the existing literature. In so doing, our hypothetical scholar would explore a wide variety of potential factors. Beginning with previously identified variables and concepts, qualitative variables would then be operationalized, refined, conceptualized, analyzed, and refined or dropped in an iterative process. Throughout the process, she would seek to "'lift' the data to a conceptual level" (Suddaby 2006, 636). In the end, she might boil her insights down into five major themes, or key relationships regarding what leads to success or failure. She might also derive a series of corollary propositions that could be tested in subsequent research. Ultimately, the research ends with a proposed parsimonious theoretical explanation of what drives nonprofit organizational success—a model that subsequent research could test in large-N statistical work.

Seen in a different light, this hypothetical researcher is engaged in a form of qualitative "feature selection" or "model selection" behavior. The research could not be considered model/theory *testing*, but is a solid example of model/ theory *building*—and this is precisely what we are doing here in our feature engineering and feature selection stages. The key difference is that, while our hypothetical researcher engages with qualitative data, here we are leveraging quantitative data, and doing so from a much larger set of both cases and

TABLE A.1   Research method by qualitative-quantitative and inductive-deductive dimensions

	Inductive	Deductive
Qualitative	Stereotypical "qualitative" research	Theory construction based on deductive reasoning and review of literature
Quantitative	Chapter 4	Chapter 3; stereotypical "quantitative" research

variables. The methodological skills (programming and statistical knowledge) are distinct but the mind-set, the need for domain knowledge, and the general processes are all the same: ask a question, look at the data, and use your domain expertise and knowledge of the literature to conceptualize the data (Suddaby 2006) to build theory. It is thus that a theoretical model is developed no matter the approach.

The flip side of this argument is that a statistical whiz or data scientist without domain knowledge would fail if she were to attempt theory-driven feature selection. So would a quantitative analyst without adequate inductive theory-building skills. To be successful, beyond domain expertise, there is a requirement for both quantitative skills and inductive skills—an admittedly uncommon pairing in most academic disciplines.

There are, in effect, two sets of choices: inductive versus deductive and qualitative versus quantitative. Table A.1 shows a 2×2 table capturing the two dimensions. While the typical researcher would tend to stay in one of the cells over his career—being either a deductive-quantitative or an inductive-qualitative researcher, there is no inherent reason a scholar could not stake a position in one of the other two quadrants. Moreover, many mixed-method and multimethod approaches cross the boundaries of one of the quadrants. For example, an article the second author wrote with Roy Suddaby and Sally Gunz (Suddaby, Saxton, and Gunz 2015) was a chiefly inductive paper that relied heavily on both qualitative analyses of interview data and quantitative analyses of website and social media data.

In effect, scholars rarely move out of the upper-left or bottom-right quadrant shown in Table A.1. To move into the bottom-left quadrant requires a particular set of statistical and programming skills along with a level of comfort with inductive theorizing. Moreover, to do this well requires significant domain expertise. A scholar without sufficient knowledge of nonprofit organizations, social media, and advocacy will simply not do well in this endeavor.

Analysis Stages

With the above in mind, we can now turn to a description of our specific methodological approach. There are three main stages to our analysis. In line with machine learning terminology, we call these three stages (1) feature engineering, (2) feature selection, and (3) model testing.

Stage One: Feature Engineering

Our first stage, *feature engineering*, is where we generate the "features," or what we in the social sciences would typically refer to as "variables," for inclusion in our analyses (Dong and Liu 2018). In the social sciences we might therefore simply call this the *variable generation* or *variable creation* stage. In data analytics/data science terminology, in turn, we might refer to it as *data wrangling, data manipulation,* or *data munging.* Whatever label we use, the key is to recognize that this stage involves two things: deciding what concepts or variables to examine and then operationalizing them.

Feature engineering might involve anything from whether to *stem* or *lemmatize* words (e.g., Forman 2003), render a variable binary instead of continuous (e.g., Forman 2003), create a series of dummy variables from a categorical variable, or run a logarithmic transformation on a continuous variable. The difference from traditional generation of social science data is chiefly in the scope of the number of variables generated along with the specific tools used to gather the data and create and transform the variables. One such set of tools often required for the gathering of Big Data is familiarity with each data source's idiosyncratic application programming interface (API) as well as how to access and use the API through a chosen programming language such as Python. A second tool set for working with many Big Data APIs is an understanding of unique data formats such as JSON or XML. Twitter, for instance, returns an extensive array of data through its *tweet* and *user* APIs. These data come in the form of nested *variable:value* "dictionaries" in JSON format. In the feature engineering stage, the researcher might first wish to generate numeric or categorical variables from these JSON data. Third, Big Data has facilitated the use of novel data creation tools. Notably, the widespread availability of textual data has led to the creation of numerous specialized text mining and text processing tools. Similarly, the connectedness of social media has led to the proliferation of social network analysis tools. Collectively, the above innovations are what allow us to pursue an approach at a scale much greater than seen in the typical variable creation stage in social science. Relying on such tools, at this stage we download the data, transform those data, and gen-erate new measures. As described in detail later, we engineer 133 variables for further consideration.

Stage Two: Three-Part Feature Selection
(Univariate, Bivariate, and Multivariate)

One of the opportunities and challenges with Big Data (e.g., Parks 2014; Vasar-helyi, Kogan, and Tuttle 2015) is the sheer number of possible variables that can be identified. In order to develop a more parsimonious theoretical model, we thus employ data analytic techniques designed to help select the most relevant features of the data. In the machine learning literature this process is known as *feature selection* (see Saeys, Inza, and Larrañaga 2007). Feature selection com-prises various dimensionality-reduction techniques designed to help determine which of a large number of variables should be retained for a final empirical model (Verikas, Gelzinis, and Bacauskiene 2011). In offering the potential for a more rigorous pruning of models than is offered by traditional inductive (or purely qualitative) approaches, dimensionality-reduction techniques are ideally suited to Big Data projects.

Accordingly, in the feature selection stage a number of primarily quantita-tive feature selection techniques are used to analyze the data and reduce the number of features from the beginning set of 133. The goal with feature selec-tion is to separate the more important identified variables from the less im-portant ones, which can be removed from the model. In line with the feature selection literature (e.g., Saeys, Inza, and Larrañaga 2007), a number of differ-ent techniques are employed to help triangulate the results. In particular, we begin the process of culling the 133 potential variables by employing *univariate* feature selection, discarding 25 variables with little to no relevant variation.

To further prune the model, we then incorporate two forms of *bivariate* feature selection techniques (see Guyon and Elisseeff 2003), specifically look-ing at (1) bivariate correlations, which are useful for helping identify *redun-dancy* in the nascent theoretical model (Yu and Liu 2004), and (2) a series of different bivariate feature importance tests, which are helpful for screening variables for *relevance* (Yu and Liu 2004) to our outcome variable *attention*.

In our third stage we then employ four types of *multivariate* feature selec-tion methods on the 89 variables that remain after the univariate and bivariate feature selection stages. Triangulating scores on these four methods provides an overall ranking of the multivariate relevance of each feature. Using this

information, the final feature selection method is a comprehensive model selection algorithm that indicates diminishing returns to model accuracy above
24 variables; our final theoretical model thus includes the 24 most relevant of
our 89 remaining variables.

The ultimate goal of the above feature selection processes is to retain only
those variables that are most useful for predicting values of the dependent
variable or, conversely, removing those variables that are not helpful. In line
with our aim to lift the data to a conceptual level, we end the feature selection
section (see Chapter 4) with the presentation of a theoretical model comprising seven conceptual categories based on the 24 variables.

Stage Three: Model Testing

The final stage is testing the model we have developed. This stage is familiar
to the typical quantitative researcher, who first develops a model and then
tests it through (for instance) a multiple regression technique. We do the same
in Chapter 4 in running logistic and negative binomial regressions on our
24-variable model.

In our analyses we implemented the three stages described above and
summarized the key details in Chapter 4. In the remaining sections of the appendix we provide additional details, background, and supporting tables for
the feature engineering and feature selection stages. Given that the third stage,
model testing, involves typical quantitative social scientific research, this stage
is not discussed in the appendix and is instead covered in detail in Chapter 4.

Feature Engineering

In machine learning, a "feature" is simply what we in the social sciences would
typically refer to as a "variable" or, even more generally, as an "attribute." For
our purposes we can thus consider the terms "feature" and "variable" to be synonymous. In our first analysis stage we undertake *feature engineering* (Dong
and Liu 2018). This is where we generate all of the variables for analysis. In
machine learning, *feature engineering* involves the processes of feature generation, transformation, and extraction (Dong and Liu 2018).[1]

Theory-Driven Feature Selection, not "Data Mining"

Guided by existing theory and available data, in the feature engineering stage
we generated 133 variables for potential inclusion in the final model. In this

stage there is a mix of deductive and inductive logic. Notably, the list of potential variables is not made in a vacuum. To start, we use deduction in deliberately creating message-level "translations" of all the organization/month variables tested in Chapter 3. We also use deductive reasoning to include variables that our knowledge of the social media, advocacy, and nonprofit domains suggested might be relevant to our dependent variable (attention). On the other hand, we also include variables on a purely inductive basis—they are available and potentially relevant, so we examine them. Yet even here we do not have a "data fishing" expedition; instead, we use the logic of the qualitative inductive theorist to develop and refine the list of variables.

The goal of the first two stages of the analysis is to develop a theoretical model of the determinants of public attention to organizations' social media messages. It is a mixed-methods approach that integrates data mining and machine learning techniques into the inductive theorizing process. Yet the term *data mining* may carry a negative connotation as being essentially atheoretical, which it often but not always is.[2] Our use of these techniques lies instead on the theoretical side. We leverage data mining techniques to help identify emergent conceptual themes and categories. Above all, we are interested here in concepts, or conceptual development, rather than the identification of variables per se. Concretely, this means that, for instance, as recommended by Eisenhardt (1989), the research process is initially guided by the identification of variables from the existing literature. Starting with the identification of variables, the qualitative and quantitative techniques combined are leveraged to "'lift' the data to a conceptual level" (Suddaby 2006, 636). Differently put, beginning with previously identified variables and concepts, variables are operationalized, refined, conceptualized, analyzed, and refined or dropped in an iterative process. The analytical process involves data mining, but it is guided by existing theory within a broad conceptual framework and is thus more akin to qualitative inductive theory building than atheoretical "data fishing."

Generating 133 Variables Across 7 Categories

Below we provide details on each of the 133 variables generated in the feature engineering stage for potential inclusion in the final model. To provide a useful reference, Table A.2 contains a comprehensive list of the 133 variables, the data source for each variable, and a description of where in the feature selection process the variable is dropped (or, alternatively, retained in the final model). As in Chapter 3, the variables are organized into the categories of *network characteristics*,

TABLE A.2 133 variables created in feature engineering stage by conceptual category, with source and stage dropped (if not in final model)

Category/Variable	Redundant/Low Relevance/Retained	Data Source
Network Characteristics		
No. of Followers	IN FINAL MODEL	Twitter *user* API
No. of Friends	IN FINAL MODEL	Twitter *user* API
No. of Lists	IN FINAL MODEL	Twitter *user* API
Targeting and Connecting		
@ Message	IN FINAL MODEL	Based on tweet characteristics
.@ Message	dropped final stage	Based on tweet characteristics
@/.@ Message	dropped—redundant	Based on tweet characteristics
PDR	dropped—redundant	Based on tweet characteristics
PDM	dropped—redundant	Based on tweet characteristics
URL	dropped—redundant	Based on tweet *entities* object
Hashtag	dropped—redundant	Based on tweet *entities* object
User Mention	dropped—redundant	Based on tweet *entities* object
No. of Hashtags	IN FINAL MODEL	Based on tweet *entities* object
No. of URLs	IN FINAL MODEL	Based on tweet *entities* object
No. of Mentions	IN FINAL MODEL	Based on tweet *entities* object
Quote Status	dropped final stage	Based on tweet *quote status* object
Timing and Pacing		
Cumulative No. of Messages Sent	IN FINAL MODEL	Twitter *user* API
Business Hours	dropped final stage	Based on tweet *created at* object
Business Day EST	dropped final stage	Based on tweet *created at* object
Business Hours/Business Day EST	dropped—redundant	Based on tweet *created_at* object
Content		
Photo	IN FINAL MODEL	Based on tweet *media* object
Video	IN FINAL MODEL	Based on tweet *media* object
Virtue	dropped final stage	Harvard IV dictionary content coding
Vice	dropped final stage	Harvard IV dictionary content coding
Value Framing	IN FINAL MODEL	Harvard IV dictionary content coding
Means	dropped final stage	Harvard IV dictionary content coding
POLIT	dropped final stage	Harvard IV dictionary content coding
Our	dropped final stage	Harvard IV dictionary content coding
You	dropped final stage	Harvard IV dictionary content coding
Yes	dropped final stage	Harvard IV dictionary content coding
No	dropped final stage	Harvard IV dictionary content coding
Negate	dropped final stage	Harvard IV dictionary content coding
Intrj	dropped final stage	Harvard IV dictionary content coding
Ovrst	dropped final stage	Harvard IV dictionary content coding
Undrst	dropped final stage	Harvard IV dictionary content coding
Ought	dropped final stage	Harvard IV dictionary content coding

(*continued*)

Category/Variable	Redundant/Low Relevance/Retained	Data Source
Truncated	dropped final stage	Tweet API
Possibly Sensitive	dropped—low variance	Tweet API
Chat Tag	dropped final stage	Derived from tweet content
Celebrity Fishing	dropped final stage	Derived from tweet content
Advanced Tweet Features		
Geo	dropped—low variance	Tweet API
Coordinates	dropped—low variance	Tweet API
Withheld in Countries	dropped—no variation	Tweet API
Symbol	dropped—no variation	Based on tweet *entities* object
No. of Symbols	dropped—no variation	Based on tweet *entities* object
Place	dropped—redundant	Based on tweet *place* object
Place Type—Admin	IN FINAL MODEL	Based on tweet *place* object
Place Type—City	dropped final stage	Based on tweet *place* object
Place Type—Country	dropped—low variance	Based on tweet *place* object
Place Type—Neighborhood	dropped—low variance	Based on tweet *place* object
Place Type—POI	dropped—low relevance	Based on tweet *place* object
Source—Buffer	dropped final stage	Based on tweet *source* object
Source—Facebook	IN FINAL MODEL	Based on tweet *source* object
Source—Hootsuite	dropped final stage	Based on tweet *source* object
Source—HubSpot	IN FINAL MODEL	Based on tweet *source* object
Source—Other	dropped final stage	Based on tweet *source* object
Source—Sprout Social	dropped final stage	Based on tweet *source* object
Source—Thingie	dropped final stage	Based on tweet *source* object
Source—TweetDeck	dropped final stage	Based on tweet *source* object
Source—Twitter Ads	dropped final stage	Based on tweet *source* object
Source—Twitter Web Client	dropped final stage	Based on tweet *source* object
Source—Twitter for Android	dropped final stage	Based on tweet *source* object
Source—Twitter for iPhone	dropped final stage	Based on tweet *source* object
Account-Level Variables		
No. of Likes	IN FINAL MODEL	Twitter *user* API
Time on Twitter in Days	dropped final stage	Based on Twitter *user* API
Location	dropped final stage	Twitter *user* API
Description Length	dropped final stage	Based on Twitter *user* API
Description	IN FINAL MODEL	Twitter *user* API
Description Hashtags	dropped final stage	Based on Twitter *user* API
Description @	dropped final stage	Based on Twitter *user* API
Default Profile	IN FINAL MODEL	Twitter *user* API
Default Profile Image	dropped—no variation`	Twitter *user* API
Geo Enabled	dropped final stage	Twitter *user* API
Extended Profile	dropped final stage	Twitter *user* API

Category/Variable	Redundant/Low Relevance/Retained	Data Source
Translation Enabled	dropped final stage	Twitter *user* API
Profile Background Tile	dropped final stage	Twitter *user* API
Profile Use Background Image	dropped final stage	Twitter *user* API
Verified	dropped final stage	Twitter *user* API
Profile Banner URL	dropped final stage	Twitter *user* API
Display URL	IN FINAL MODEL	Twitter *user* API
EST	dropped final stage	Based on Twitter *user* API
Screen Name Change	dropped final stage	Based on Twitter *user* API
Contributors Enabled	dropped—no variation	Twitter user API
Translator	dropped—no variation	Twitter user API
Protected	dropped—no variation	Twitter user API
Notifications	dropped—no variation	Twitter user API
Profile Background Color	dropped—no variation	Twitter user API
Profile Background Image URL	dropped—no variation	Twitter user API
Profile Background Image URL HTTPS	dropped—no variation	Twitter user API
Profile Image URL	dropped—no variation	Twitter user API
Profile Image URL HTTPS	dropped—no variation	Twitter user API
Profile Link Color	dropped—no variation	Twitter user API
Profile Sidebar Border Color	dropped—no variation	Twitter user API
Profile Sidebar Fill Color	dropped—no variation	Twitter user API
Profile Text Color	dropped—no variation	Twitter user API
Translator Type	dropped—no variation	Twitter user API
Contributors	dropped—no variation	Twitter user API
Organizational Characteristics		
Assets	dropped—redundant	Charity Navigator
Revenue	IN FINAL MODEL	Charity Navigator
Age	IN FINAL MODEL	IRS Business Master Files
Program Expense %	IN FINAL MODEL	Charity Navigator
Fundraising Expenses	dropped final stage	Charity Navigator
Total Functional Expenses	dropped—redundant	Charity Navigator
Advisory	dropped—low relevance	Charity Navigator
NTEE—Arts, Culture and Humanities	dropped final stage	IRS Business Master Files
NTEE—Education	dropped final stage	IRS Business Master Files
NTEE—Environment and Animals	IN FINAL MODEL	IRS Business Master Files
NTEE—Health	dropped final stage	IRS Business Master Files
NTEE—Human Services	dropped final stage	IRS Business Master Files
NTEE—International, Foreign Affairs	dropped final stage	IRS Business Master Files

Category/Variable	Redundant/Low Relevance/Retained	Data Source
NTEE—Public, Societal Benefit	dropped final stage	IRS Business Master Files
NTEE—Religion Related	dropped final stage	IRS Business Master Files
NTEE—Unknown, Unclassified	dropped final stage	IRS Business Master Files
AL	IN FINAL MODEL	IRS Business Master Files
AZ	dropped—low relevance	IRS Business Master Files
CA	dropped final stage	IRS Business Master Files
CO	dropped final stage	IRS Business Master Files
CT	dropped—low variance	IRS Business Master Files
DC	dropped final stage	IRS Business Master Files
FL	dropped—low relevance	IRS Business Master Files
GA	dropped—low relevance	IRS Business Master Files
IL	dropped final stage	IRS Business Master Files
MA	dropped final stage	IRS Business Master Files
MD	dropped final stage	IRS Business Master Files
MI	IN FINAL MODEL	IRS Business Master Files
MN	dropped—low relevance	IRS Business Master Files
MS	dropped final stage	IRS Business Master Files
MT	dropped—low relevance	IRS Business Master Files
NY	dropped final stage	IRS Business Master Files
PA	dropped—low relevance	IRS Business Master Files
TX	dropped final stage	IRS Business Master Files
VA	dropped final stage	IRS Business Master Files
WA	dropped—low relevance	IRS Business Master Files
WI	dropped final stage	IRS Business Master Files

NOTE: This table shows the 133 variables that were generated during the feature engineering stage. There are only nine *NTEE 10* categories given that there are no organizations in our sample in the "Mutual/Membership Benefit" category (NTEE code "Y"). There are only 21 "state" dummies (e.g., 'AL' for Alabama, 'MI' for Michigan) because none of the 188 organizations reside in 29 of the 50 US states. For additional details on variables taken from the Twitter API, please see https://developer.twitter.com/en/docs/api-reference-index.

targeting and connecting, timing and pacing, and *content.* On the basis of our Chapter 4 update to the model, there are also new categories for *advanced tweet features, account-level variables,* and *organizational characteristics.*

Network Characteristics

Our first category is network characteristics. For this category we operationalized three variables: *Number of Followers, Number of Friends,* and *Number of Lists.* As shown in Table A.2, all were grabbed directly from the *user* object facet of the Twitter API.[3]

Communication Strategy: Targeting and Connecting

We next examined 12 *targeting and connecting* variables. Five of the variables (*@ Message, .@ Message, @/.@ Message, PDR,* and *PDM*) overlap to some extent yet reflect different aspects of *whom* the organization is targeting in its tweets. Specifically, they tap diverse facets of the use of the "@[USER]" convention found in social media messages. All are binary variables. *@ Message* indicates tweets that begin with @[USER], which is used when a message is intended to be directed at a specific Twitter user; *.@ Message,* meanwhile, indicates tweets that begin with a "dot" before @[USER], a convention on Twitter that attempts to make the former types of targeted messages seen by a wider audience. *@/.@ Message,* in turn, indicates either of the two previous message types. *PDM* indicates a "public direct message," or a message that is, as indicated by the Twitter API, directed at a specific Twitter user; the message need not begin with @[USER]. *PDR,* finally, indicates a "public direct reply," or a tweet that is a reply to another user's tweet, as indicated by the Twitter API. Prior research has generally found such targeted messages to be associated with public reactions (e.g., Saxton and Waters 2014; Swani, Milne, and Brown 2013). We then code a binary variable from the tweet API, *Quote Status,* to reflect "quote tweets," which are effectively retweets to which a message is added by a second user, thereby making the tweet that user's own message (retweets, in contrast, are still linked to the original sender). Finally, using data found in the *entities* object of the tweet API, we generate a suite of three binary variables (*URL, Hashtag, User Mention*) and three continuous variables (*Number of Hashtags, Number of URLs,* and *Number of Mentions*) tapping the existence of URLs, hashtags, and user mentions in each tweet. Such variables are commonly included in tests of message effectiveness (Saxton et al. 2015; Saxton and Waters 2014; Swani, Milne, and Brown 2013), including Chapter 3 of this book and our 2018 *NVSQ* article (Guo and Saxton 2018).

Communication Strategy: Timing and Pacing

We examined four *timing and pacing* variables. The cumulative number of messages has been shown to be positively associated with the number of retweets (Saxton et al. 2015). The other three variables are binary variables based on the tweets' *created_at* object indicating the time the tweet was sent. For all three variables, the time stamp was changed from GMT/UTC (Coordinated Universal Time) to Eastern Standard Time (EST). The variable *Business Hours* then indicates tweets sent between 8 a.m. and 6 p.m., *Business Day EST* indicates tweets sent Monday through Friday, and *Business Hours/Business Day EST* indicates tweets sent during business hours Monday–Friday. The logic is that tweets may be more likely to receive a response during business hours, at least in the organizational context (Saxton 2016).

Communication Strategy: Content

There were 20 potential content variables. To start, analogous to Chapter 3, two binary visual content variables, *Photo* and *Video*, are included. Next, 14 word count variables are generated. Here we take a "dictionary-based" approach that has become increasingly common in management, finance, and accounting research (e.g., Suddaby, Saxton, and Gunz 2015; Tetlock 2007; Tetlock, Saar-Tsechansky, and Macskassy 2008). As in this prior research, we employ Harvard IV/General Inquirer dictionaries (http://www.wjh.harvard.edu/~inquirer/homecat.htm). The General Inquirer dictionaries contain dozens of prevalidated dictionaries, or collections of words, across multiple categories. Most commonly used in finance and accounting research is the *Negativ* dictionary, a list of 2,291 words of negative outlook and which is often used to measure sentiment (Tetlock 2007; Tetlock, Saar-Tsechansky, and Macskassy 2008). In Chapter 3 we argued that, in the nonprofit context, ethical appeals would be most likely to generate attention and thus generated a variable (*Value Framing*) based on the RcEthic dictionary; we found this variable to be positively related to audience attention. Building on these findings, we expand the analysis to additional word count variables; specifically, our 14 "dictionary" variables (*Value Framing, Virtue, Vice, Means, POLIT, Our, You, Yes, No, Negate, Intrj, Ovrst, Undrst, Ought*) indicate tweets that contain one or more words in, respectively, the RcEthic, Virtue, Vice, Means, POLIT, Our, You, Yes, No, Negate, Intrj, Ovrst, Undrst, and Ought *General Inquirer* dictionaries. Collectively, these variables reflect tweets that convey ethical content, positive content, emphatic content, and political and action content.

Next we measure four miscellaneous content variables. The first two are derived from "objects" in the tweet API: *Truncated*, which indicates tweets that have content truncated due to length; and *Possibly Sensitive*, which indicates tweets with "possibly sensitive" links.[4] Our next variable, *Chat Tag*, indicates tweets that contain a "chat" hashtag. Twitter chats are discussions held at specific days and times anchored by a specific hashtag (Budak and Agrawal 2013); they can be one-time events or occur on a weekly, monthly, or yearly basis. Twitter chats are indications of an active, temporally delimited back-and-forth conversation between the organization and members of the public and are therefore expected to be related to the level of public attention a message receives (Saxton 2016). Finally, *Celebrity Fishing* indicates tweets that seek to capture the attention of a highly followed celebrity on Twitter; if the celebrity "takes the bait," this tactic can result in a huge payoff in terms of geometrically increasing the diffusion of its message or call to action (see Guo and Saxton 2014b). We thus code a binary variable, *Celebrity Fishing,* to indicate those messages that reference (using an @USER mention) any Twitter user with one million or more followers.

Advanced Tweet Features

Our next category comprises 23 variables that relate to a variety of advanced tweet characteristics. Many of these variables proxy for tweet "sophistication," or the sophistication with which the user is able to use Twitter. The first two variables, *geo* and *coordinates*, indicate geographical coordinates linked to the tweets and as returned by the tweet API. Also returned by the API is *Withheld in Countries,* which is a field returned by the Twitter API to indicate countries in which the tweet (and/or tweet sender's account) is "withheld" (censored). We generate a binary variable to indicate tweets that were withheld in any country. *Symbols* and *Number of Symbols,* meanwhile, are binary and continuous variables, respectively, generated from the "symbols" field of the *entities* object in the Twitter API.

Next, the binary variable *Place* indicates the 2.3% of tweets that contained a geotagged "place" (such as a city, tourist site, restaurant), while *Place Type—Admin, Place Type—City, Place Type—Country, Place Type—Neighborhood,* and *Place Type—POI* (point of interest) indicate the type of place as indicated in the *place* object returned by the tweet API.

Finally, all tweets contain a *source* object indicating the "source" (or specific application) from which the tweet was sent. We created the following 12 binary variables for these sources, placing low-frequency sources in an "OTHER" category: *Source—Buffer, Source—Facebook, Source—Hootsuite, Source—HubSpot, Source—Other, Source—Sprout Social, Source—Thingie, Source—TweetDeck, Source—Twitter Ads, Source—Twitter Web Client, Source—Twitter for Android,* and *Source—Twitter for iPhone.*

As far as we are aware, the above tweet feature variables have not been examined in studies of public reactions and no literature exists that can be tapped to generate deductive insights. Instead, our insights are inductively derived. We argue it is plausible that, for instance, geocoding a tweet, tagging a "place," or using symbols may signal a more "sophisticated" tweet and/or Twitter user, and that "sophisticated" users and messages could be more likely to generate audience attention. We similarly believe it plausible that some of the "sources" could signal greater sophistication. Our feature selection analyses will show whether these assumptions are valid.

Account-Level Variables

Taking into account recent evidence that *who* sends a message is an important determinant of public reactions (e.g., Saxton et al. 2019; Xu and Saxton 2019), we next examined 34 account-level variables. All are derived from data in the "user" object returned by the Twitter API, and all save for three (*Number of Likes*, *Time on Twitter in Days*, and *Description Length*) are binary. We start with a description of the continuous variables. First, *Number of Likes* is a count of the cumulative number of tweets to date the organization has "liked"; it reflects the level of activity and is a rough proxy for the level of sophistication of the organization's social media use. Similarly, *Time on Twitter in Days* is a count of the number of days since the organization initiated its Twitter account, based on information in the user's *created_at* object (see Saxton 2016). Next, *Description Length* is a count of the number of words in the user's profile description.

We then generate two other variables based on the profile description that similarly serve as proxies for account sophistication: *Description Hashtags*, which indicates descriptions that include one or more hashtags; and *Description @*, which indicates descriptions that include one or more @USER mentions. Both variables were developed in response to novel behaviors we had seen in our analyses of the organizations' Twitter profiles.

The binary variable *Screen Name Change* indicates accounts that have undergone a change in their Twitter screen name since 2013. Our inductive reasoning is that we saw a number of organizations that made changes to their Twitter handles, and felt that plausibly a name change could cause a change in the level of public attention an account receives.

The remaining 28 variables are derived directly from the *user* API object: *Location, Description, Default Profile, Default Profile Image, Geo Enabled, Extended Profile, Translation Enabled, Profile Background Tile, Profile Use Background Image, Verified, Profile Banner URL, Display URL, EST* (Eastern Standard Time), *Contributors Enabled, Is Translator, Protected, Notifications,*

Profile Background Color, Profile Background Image URL, Profile Background Image URL HTTPS, Profile Image URL, Profile Image URL HTTPS, Profile Link Color, Profile Sidebar Border Color, Profile Sidebar Fill Color, Profile Text Color, Translator Type, and *Contributors.* For each of these variables, we convert the respective object into a binary variable indicating accounts where the respective object exists or is "True." For instance, if the account has a non-null value in the *description* field of the user API object, then it is coded as "1" on our variable *Description.* Similarly, an organization is given a value of "1" on *Translation Enabled* if the account has a value of "True" in the *is_translation_enabled* object of the *user* API. These 28 objects are all included based on the intuition that "account sophistication" is a likely driver of attention. Admittedly, here we come closest to "data fishing." We analyze all of these features because we do not know which of these 28 features best captures sophistication, nor are we certain account-level sophistication is in fact an important factor in driving attention. Despite the uncertainties, the potential payoff is increased understanding of our phenomenon of interest. Indeed, one of the core benefits of our method is the capacity to explore a great many more "hunches" and intuitive and inductive insights in our model-building efforts. In the end, if the new variables are not important, they will be dropped during the feature selection stage and we will have lost only some analytical and data-generating effort.

Organizational Characteristics

As our final category, we considered 37 "offline" organizational variables. The logic is similar to that outlined for account-level characteristics: that *who* is talking has a bearing on how much attention is paid to what is said. The difference is that these 37 features reflect non–social media characteristics that have been found to be important in the nonprofit literature.

The first two, *Revenue* and *Age,* were similarly included as controls in Chapter 3 and our 2018 *NVSQ* article. *Revenue* served as a proxy for size; in order to check whether an alternative measure carries greater explanatory power, we also include two alternative measures of size: *Assets* and *Total Functional Expenses.*

We then include two variables that are common in the nonprofit financial literature (e.g., Gordon, Knock, and Neely 2009; Khumawala, Neely, and Gordon 2010; Saxton, Neely, and Guo 2014; Weisbrod and Dominguez 1986): *Program Expense Percentage* and *Fundraising Expenses.* The former is the program spending ratio that reflects the proportion of spending devoted to programs rather than fundraising or administration; it is a proxy for the level of organizational efficiency. The latter indicates the amount spent on fundraising. We argue more efficient organizations could be more likely to garner public attention, and organizations that spend more on fundraising could be more oriented toward boosting their public profile and level of public attention.

We next operationalize *Advisory* using data on "donor advisories" given by the third-party ratings agency *Charity Navigator.* Donor advisories indicate potential organizational mismanagement (Saxton and Neely 2019), which could affect other areas of organization such as social media usage.

A series of nine binary variables then indicate the "industry" or "subsector" in which the organization is operating, based on the NTEE "major groups" categories (http://nccs.urban.org/classification/national-taxonomy-exempt-entities).

Finally, as with NTEE categories, state is commonly included in nonprofit organizational studies as a control (e.g., Harris, Petrovits, and Yetman 2017; Saxton and Neely 2019); we include it to tap potentially different levels of social media usage patterns across states, which might in turn affect levels of public attention accorded to the organizations. We thus include 21 state (as well as the District of Columbia) dummy variables indicating the state in which the organization is located.

Feature Selection

Guided by existing theory and available data, in the previous stage 133 variables were generated for potential inclusion in our theoretical model. In the second stage, *feature selection*, what we are seeking to do is identify the variables with the greatest explanatory and/or predictive power, while removing those that are unnecessary, irrelevant, or redundant.

Feature selection (Blum and Langley 1997; Guyon and Elisseeff 2003; Yu and Liu 2004) is one of the fundamental tasks of machine learning. To recall, "features" are what social scientists would typically call "variables," and feature selection comprises numerous procedures, steps, and algorithms for one key purpose: to take a large number—often thousands—of features (variables) and reduce them to a more manageable or parsimonious or informative level. Feature selection, which in the social sciences literature is known as variable selection, is part of the broader *model selection* process (see Saeys, Inza, and Larrañaga 2007).[5]

To conduct feature selection we utilize a suite of quantitative machine learning techniques conducted in the Python programming language. In particular, we rely heavily on the Python Data Analysis Library (PANDAS, https://pandas.pydata.org/) and Python's machine learning library *scikit-learn* (Pedregosa et al. 2011).[6]

At the beginning of the feature selection stage, and following machine learning convention, we use an 80/20 train/test split and split the data into *training* (n = 208,901 observations) and *testing* (n = 52,226) data sets (e.g., Amani and Fadlalla 2017; Guyon and Elisseeff 2003). The feature selection stage uses the training portion of the data, while the model testing stage uses the testing portion of the data.

In line with our methodological approach outlined earlier, feature selection proceeds in three main steps: (1) univariate, (2) bivariate, and (3) multivariate.

Univariate Feature Selection

The first step is to conduct *univariate* feature selection. In machine learning terminology, univariate techniques focus on characteristics of each explanatory variable in isolation. The meaning is thus analogous to what is found in typical social scientific terminology with, for instance, univariate statistics such as mean and standard deviation. Our focus here is on an initial "filtering" (Blum and Langley 1997; Guyon and Elisseeff 2003; John, Kohavi, and Pfleger 1994) of the features by removing all zero-variance and low-variance features.

For smaller data sets, identifying such variables is not troublesome. With Big Data, however, it becomes increasingly problematic to systematically identify such features as the size of the data grows. Accordingly, for univariate feature selection we use the *VarianceThreshold* class that is found in the Python package *scikit-learn*'s *feature_selection* module. We found 19 account-level and tweet-level variables had zero variation and all were thus omitted at this stage (see Table A.2 for detailed list).

We also use the *VarianceThreshold* class to identify variables with extremely low variation. Six variables are omitted for this reason. To start, the variables *geo* and *coordinates* are omitted because there were only 24 observations. The organizations in this sample essentially chose not to geotag their tweets with precise coordinates. There were also only 155 tweets with a *possibly_sensitive* tag; however, this variable is deleted chiefly because the organization has no control over it and thus could not manipulate it in order to garner attention. An additional three variables (two indicating geotagged "places," namely *Place Type—Country, Place Type—Neighborhood*, and one the state of Connecticut, *CT*) were selected for omission when using a threshold of 0.0001 in the *VarianceThreshold* class. For instance, there were only four tweets with a value of 1 for *Place Type—Neighborhood*, which is insufficient variation in a data set with several hundred thousand observations.

In sum, as shown in Table A.2, a total of 25 variables are omitted in this univariate stage, leaving us with 108 variables to consider for bivariate feature selection.

Bivariate Feature Selection

We now take our 108 remaining variables and conduct bivariate[7] feature selection techniques. Specifically, we incorporate two types of bivariate feature selection techniques (see Guyon and Elisseeff 2003). First we conduct a series of bivariate "feature importance" tests, which are helpful for screening variables for *relevance* (Yu and Liu 2004). We then employ bivariate correlations, which are useful for helping identify *redundancy* (Yu and Liu 2004) in the nascent theoretical model.

What differs from the univariate stage is that we now consider the statistical relationship between the dependent variable *Retweeted*, which indicates whether the organization's message received one or more retweets, and each individual explanatory feature. In this stage we are thus getting at *feature importance*. As with the univariate techniques, these bivariate techniques constitute "filter" methods (Blum and Langley 1997; Guyon and Elisseeff 2003) insofar as they can be used to select or drop variables before a multivariate *induction algorithm* (e.g., a multivariate feature selection algorithm) is run. The bivariate methods do not, in effect, attempt to identify useful subsets of variables (John, Kohavi, and Pfleger 1994). Because they do not consider the effects on the outcome variable of more than one algorithm at a time, these methods are not good for identifying redundancy nor interactions among variables. At the same time, bivariate techniques are useful for the calculation of basic relevance for each variable, which facilitates initial filtering and serves as a baseline against which multivariate selection results can be compared (Guyon and Elisseeff 2003). Taking a conservative approach, at this stage we drop only the 19 features that are highly nonrelevant or are redundant with respect to other, more relevant features. Below we provide further details on the various bivariate feature selection techniques we conducted.

Bivariate Feature Importance Tests: Determining Relevance

Before running correlations to look for redundancy, we ran a series of five feature importance tests to filter variables for relevance. Before describing each of these tests, we should point out that a researcher interested in using machine learning algorithms will find what can seem a confusing array of possible techniques. As with the decision to run an ordinary least squares (OLS) versus logistic versus negative binomial regression in typical quantitative social scientific research, it is crucial to understand both the data and which techniques are appropriate for the data. With regard to feature selection, the first step is understanding whether the problem is one of "regression" (a continuous dependent variable) or of "classification" (a binary dependent variable). Given our binary dependent variable *Retweeted*, all of these techniques represent "classifier" algorithms. In effect, the machine learning models employed in the feature selection process are attempting to classify each tweet as "likely to receive a retweet" or "likely to not receive a retweet."

Given how new the data science field is, our approach is not to pick a single bivariate classifier. Instead, we select five data-appropriate classifiers and "triangulate" the results. To start, we employ a relatively new algorithm, *Maximal Information Coefficient* (MIC), which is designed to elucidate bivariate relationships regardless of whether the relationship is linear or nonlinear; moreover, it is designed for application to very high-dimensional data sets.[8] We implement the algorithm in Python using the *minepy* package (http://minepy.readthedocs.io/en/latest/). Our next two tests are likely familiar to quantitative social scientists. Specifically, we conduct chi-square tests using scikit-learn's *chi2* algorithm and a classification-appropriate ANOVA *F* test using scikit-learn's *f_classif* algorithm. Our fourth algorithm is a "mutual information" algorithm run using the *mutual_info_classif* algorithm in scikit-learn. In referring to two variables (here, an independent and a dependent variable), mutual information (also called "information gain") refers to the "mutual dependence" between the two variables (Cang and Yu 2012; Kraskov, Stögbauer, and Grassberger 2004) as indicated by an *entropy*-based measure of information content. Given that entropy can be considered a measure of uncertainty, the algorithm can be seen as measuring the "loss of uncertainty" that information about one variable can bring to another. It is related to the

MIC algorithm and, like MIC, is (in contrast to the correlation coefficient, for instance), suitable for relationships in any functional form, whether linear or nonlinear (Krier et al. 2006). Finally, we run a Random Forest technique using scikit-learn's *RandomForestClassifier* algorithm. This is a "decision tree" method that ranks features based on their importance in a series of randomly selected subsets and decision tree splits (Rodriguez-Galiano et al. 2012).[9]

It is also important to recognize which classifiers are sensitive to variable ranges. For instance, many algorithms require normalization (e.g., z scores) or standardization (e.g., [0,1]) in order to return valid results. Given that most of our variables are binary in nature and therefore not normally distributed, for our tests we first normalize all 108 features on a 0–1 scale using scikit-learn's *MinMaxScaler*.[10]

Table A.3 shows scores for the 108 variables on each of the five algorithms. In order to make the scores across algorithms comparable, we normalized scores on each algorithm using the *MinMaxScaler*, which transforms values to be in the 0–1 range.[11] We then generate an overall score for each variable based on the mean of the five algorithm scores. Table A.3 shows the 108 variables ranked according to their mean score. The key point is that these features are ranked in the table based on *relevance*. *Number of Lists* can thus be considered the most relevant feature based on our suite of bivariate feature selection algorithms.

The chief purpose of the five bivariate classification algorithms in Table A.3 is to determine relevance. We found that nine features had scores of 0 on all five feature selection algorithms: *Advisory, Place Type—POI,* and seven state indicators (*MN, MT, WA, AZ, FL, GA, PA*). As summarized in the "Redundant/Low Relevance" column of Table A.3, we dropped all nine of these low-relevance features. While we could be more stringent at this stage, we opted to remove only the least relevant features during this stage, for the multivariate techniques are better suited to selecting features by taking the interactions among variables into account.

Bivariate Correlations: Determining Redundancy

The bivariate tests for feature selection discussed above were used to determine the relevance of each of the 108 features that remained after the univariate feature selection tests. As noted earlier, we also examined correlation matrices to help identify *redundancy* (Guyon and Elisseeff 2003, 1173) among pairs of explanatory features. Specifically, we use the relevance tests summarized in

TABLE A.3   Scores on five bivariate feature selection techniques for 108 variables, ranked by mean score (descending order)

Rank	Variable	Redundant/ Low Relevance	Mean score	MIC	Chi2	F	Mutual Information	Random Forest
1	No. of Lists		0.64	0.95	0.07	0.23	0.95	1
2	@ Message		0.636	0.35	1	1	0.34	0.49
3	No. of Followers		0.612	1	0.05	0.16	1	0.85
4	No. of Statuses		0.534	1	0.01	0.15	1	0.51
5	No. of Friends		0.472	0.98	0.02	0.05	0.97	0.34
6	Revenue		0.466	0.92	0.02	0.1	0.94	0.35
7	No. of Likes		0.456	0.97	0.01	0.06	0.97	0.27
8	Assets	redundant	0.434	0.92	0.04	0.09	0.93	0.19
9	Total Functional Expenses	redundant	0.416	0.91	0.02	0.08	0.9	0.17
10	Fundraising Expenses		0.414	0.91	0	0.02	0.91	0.23
11	PDM	redundant	0.396	0.22	0.56	0.55	0.22	0.43
12	Time on Twitter in Days		0.382	0.82	0	0.08	0.82	0.19
13	@/.@ Message	redundant	0.38	0.2	0.48	0.47	0.19	0.56
14	Verified		0.358	0.23	0.18	0.46	0.39	0.53
15	Program Expense %		0.324	0.68	0	0.06	0.68	0.2
16	PDR	redundant	0.198	0.1	0.26	0.24	0.1	0.29
17	Description Length		0.196	0.41	0	0	0.41	0.16
18	POLIT		0.18	0.04	0.03	0.07	0.17	0.59
19	No. of Mentions		0.174	0.05	0.01	0.07	0.07	0.67
20	No. of Hashtags		0.168	0.02	0	0	0.06	0.76
21	Age		0.156	0.32	0	0	0.33	0.13
22	Ovrst		0.15	0.01	0.01	0.02	0.08	0.63
23	Means		0.144	0	0	0.01	0.08	0.63
24	Virtue		0.142	0	0	0	0.08	0.63
25	Profile Banner URL		0.126	0.06	0.01	0.13	0.37	0.06
26	No. of URLs		0.126	0.04	0	0.05	0.26	0.28
27	User Mention	redundant	0.124	0.05	0.07	0.09	0.09	0.32
28	Source—HubSpot		0.122	0.07	0.21	0.18	0.06	0.09
29	URL	redundant	0.118	0.04	0.01	0.07	0.28	0.19
30	Undrst		0.118	0	0	0	0.03	0.56
31	Vice		0.118	0.02	0.03	0.03	0.04	0.47
32	Business Hours		0.102	0	0	0.01	0.18	0.32
33	Business Day EST		0.1	0.01	0	0.02	0.26	0.21
34	Our		0.1	0	0	0	0.01	0.49
35	Business Hours/Business Day EST	redundant	0.098	0.01	0.01	0.02	0.14	0.31
36	Intrj		0.092	0.01	0.01	0.01	0.02	0.41
37	You		0.088	0.01	0.03	0.03	0.03	0.34
38	Truncated		0.088	0.01	0.01	0.01	0.03	0.38

(*continued*)

Rank	Variable	Redundant/ Low Relevance	Mean score	MIC	Chi2	F	Mutual Information	Random Forest
39	Value Framing		0.084	0.01	0.01	0.01	0.02	0.37
40	Hashtag	redundant	0.082	0.01	0.01	0.02	0.08	0.29
41	DC		0.074	0.05	0.06	0.09	0.11	0.06
42	Description		0.072	0.01	0	0.01	0.34	0
43	Location		0.072	0.01	0	0.03	0.31	0.01
44	Display URL		0.066	0	0	0	0.33	0
45	Default Profile		0.064	0.04	0.11	0.09	0.05	0.03
46	VA		0.062	0.04	0.1	0.09	0.05	0.03
47	Negate		0.06	0	0.01	0.01	0.01	0.27
48	Source—Twitter Web Client		0.056	0.01	0.02	0.02	0.03	0.2
49	EST		0.048	0.01	0	0.01	0.19	0.03
50	.@ Message		0.048	0.01	0.01	0.01	0.01	0.2
51	Source—TweetDeck		0.046	0.02	0.04	0.04	0.05	0.08
52	Geo Enabled		0.044	0	0	0	0.17	0.05
53	Ought		0.044	0	0	0	0	0.22
54	Photo		0.044	0	0	0	0.01	0.21
55	Source—Facebook		0.036	0.02	0.05	0.05	0.01	0.05
56	Quote Status		0.036	0	0	0	0	0.18
57	Profile Use Background Image		0.034	0	0	0	0.15	0.02
58	Celebrity Fishing		0.034	0	0.01	0.01	0	0.15
59	Description @		0.032	0.03	0.04	0.04	0.03	0.02
60	Translation Enabled		0.032	0.03	0.05	0.04	0.03	0.01
61	TX		0.032	0.02	0.05	0.04	0.01	0.04
62	MI		0.03	0.02	0.05	0.04	0.02	0.02
63	Yes		0.03	0	0	0	0	0.15
64	CO		0.028	0.02	0.05	0.04	0.02	0.01
65	NTEE—Public, Societal Benefit		0.026	0	0	0	0.1	0.03
66	Source—Sprout Social		0.026	0.01	0.02	0.02	0.02	0.06
67	Source—Hootsuite		0.026	0	0	0	0.02	0.11
68	AL		0.024	0.03	0.03	0.03	0.03	0
69	Source—Twitter for Android		0.024	0.01	0.03	0.03	0.01	0.04
70	Extended Profile		0.02	0.01	0.02	0.02	0.02	0.03
71	Source—Twitter for iPhone		0.02	0	0	0	0	0.1
72	Profile Background Tile		0.02	0	0	0	0.05	0.05
73	NTEE—Education		0.018	0.02	0.03	0.02	0.02	0

nk	Variable	Redundant/ Low Relevance	Mean score	MIC	Chi2	F	Mutual Information	Random Forest
	NTEE—Arts, Culture and Humanities		0.018	0.01	0.02	0.02	0.02	0.02
	NTEE—Human Services		0.018	0.01	0.01	0.02	0.01	0.04
	No		0.016	0	0	0	0	0.08
	NTEE—Environment and Animals		0.014	0.01	0.03	0.02	0.01	0
	Screen Name Change		0.014	0.01	0.02	0.01	0.02	0.01
	NTEE—International, Foreign Affairs		0.012	0.01	0.02	0.02	0.01	0
	Place Type—Admin		0.012	0.01	0.02	0.02	0	0.01
	IL		0.01	0.01	0.01	0.01	0.01	0.01
	MA		0.01	0.01	0.01	0.01	0.01	0.01
	Source—Other		0.01	0	0	0	0	0.05
	NY		0.008	0	0	0.01	0.01	0.02
	Source—Thingie		0.008	0.01	0.01	0.01	0.01	0
	NTEE—Health		0.008	0	0.01	0.01	0.01	0.01
	NTEE—Religion Related		0.008	0.01	0.01	0.01	0	0.01
	Place	redundant	0.008	0	0	0	0	0.04
	Place Type—City		0.006	0	0	0	0	0.03
	Source—Buffer		0.006	0	0	0	0	0.03
	WI		0.006	0.01	0.01	0.01	0	0
	Description Hashtags		0.006	0	0	0	0.01	0.02
	MD		0.006	0	0	0	0.01	0.02
	CA		0.004	0	0	0	0.01	0.01
	NTEE—Unknown, Unclassified		0.004	0	0.01	0	0	0.01
	Video		0.004	0	0	0	0.01	0.01
	MS		0.002	0	0	0	0.01	0
	Chat Tag		0.002	0	0	0	0	0.01
	Source—Twitter Ads		0.002	0	0	0	0	0.01
00	MN	low relevance	0	0	0	0	0	0
01	MT	low relevance	0	0	0	0	0	0
02	WA	low relevance	0	0	0	0	0	0
03	Advisory	low relevance	0	0	0	0	0	0
04	AZ	low relevance	0	0	0	0	0	0
05	FL	low relevance	0	0	0	0	0	0
06	GA	low relevance	0	0	0	0	0	0
07	PA	low relevance	0	0	0	0	0	0
08	Place Type—POI	low relevance	0	0	0	0	0	0

e: This table shows average relevance scores for the 108 variables remaining after the univariate feature selection stage. Varies are ranked in descending order according to their Mean Score, which is the average of the scores on the five bivariate feature
ction algorithms. Redundant/Low Relevance indicates variables that were dropped during the bivariate feature selection stage.

Table A.3 in conjunction with correlation tests in order to identify the most relevant of each redundant pair of features. For instance, Table A.3 shows three organizational features that, as explained in the feature engineering section, are related to organizational size: *Revenue*, *Assets*, and *Total Functional Expenses*. All three are highly correlated, and because *Revenue* is the most "relevant" of the three (as indicated by its higher ranking in Table A.3), it is retained and the two redundant variables are dropped. Using this process, we identified and dropped the 10 redundant variables indicated by the Redundant/Low Relevance column of Table A.3. In effect, we use correlation matrices to identify the redundant features and then omit (referring back to the above rank orderings of relevance) the least relevant feature in each pair of redundant features. Below we elaborate on the process that was used to identify redundant variables. We searched for redundancy by conceptual category, beginning with *Network Characteristics*.

Network Characteristics. For each category we generated a correlation matrix and looked for any correlation above 0.50.[12] To start, we examined the correlations among the three network variables: *Number of Lists*, *Number of Followers*, and *Number of Friends*. We found the *Number of Lists* is correlated at 0.88 with *Number of Followers*, which is relatively high. However, we retain it in the model given the conceptual difference between the two features.

Communication Strategy: Targeting and Connecting. As listed earlier, we examined 12 *targeting and connecting* variables. We found two sets of potentially redundant features. First, @ *Message* is correlated with @/.@ *Message* as well as *PDR* and *PDM*. The variables are redundant insofar as all four are based on the @*USER* tool in tweets. Accordingly, and in line with the method we outlined above, we select the most relevant of these correlated features—@ *Message*—and drop @/.@ *Message*, *PDR*, and *PDM*.

We also see three other pairs of (unsurprisingly) correlated features: *Hashtag* with *Number of Hashtags*, *URL* with *Number of URLs*, and *User Mention* with *Number of Mentions*. In all three cases the binary version of the variable is less relevant. We thus drop *URL*, *Hashtag*, and *User Mention* from further analysis.

Timing and Pacing. We next look at our four *timing and pacing* variables: *Cumulative Number of Messages Sent*, *Business Hours*, *Business Day*, and *Busi-*

ness Hours/Business Day. Not surprisingly, *Business Day* is highly correlated with *Business Hours/Business Day.* The latter is less relevant and is therefore dropped.

Content. Next we examined the correlations for the six visual and "miscellaneous" content variables followed by correlations for the 14 textual content variables. There does not appear to be substantial redundancy. The highest correlation coefficient found was 0.48 between the *No* and *Negate* textual content features.

Advanced Tweet Features. For the six *place* features we found a high correlation (0.92) between the binary indicator of a *place* object (*Place*) and *Place Type—City.* *Place* is dropped due to its lower relevance score. For the 12 *source* features, in turn, there were no meaningful redundancies as reflected in the correlation coefficients.

Organizational Variables. We did not run correlations on the NTEE and state binary variables given that all industry-level variables and state variables are mutually exclusive. Of the seven remaining organizational features, we found that *Assets* is correlated at 0.70 with *Revenue.* Both are common indicators of nonprofit size and are thus conceptually redundant. *Revenue* has the higher relevance score as shown in Table A.3; therefore *assets* is dropped from further consideration. Likewise, *Total Functional Expenses* is dropped because of its conceptual and empirical overlap with *Fundraising Expenses,* which was shown to be more relevant in our bivariate feature importance tests.

Account Variables. Of the 18 account-level variables that remain after the above univariate and bivariate feature selection step, the highest correlation is 0.35 between *Time on Twitter in Days* and *Profile Banner URL.* In effect, there do not appear to be any meaningful redundancies in these account variables.

Bivariate Chi-Squared and Logistic Regression Results

Not discussed in Chapter 4 are additional series of bivariate chi-square tests and logit tests we ran between *Retweeted* and each feature. These tests can be seen to capture the direction of the relationship. The online appendix Section A contains 11 supplementary tables used during the feature selection process. Specifically, the tables show the bivariate relationships between the independent and dependent variables. Chi-square analyses are used for the binary independent variables and logit analyses for the continuous independent variables. Compared to other information presented in Chapter 4 and this methodological appendix, the key information these tables provide is the directionality of the relationship (positive, negative, or none) between each of our explanatory variables and our dependent variable *Retweeted*.

Multivariate Feature Selection

In our third stage we employ four types of *multivariate* feature selection methods on the remaining 89 variables: recursive feature elimination (RFE), linear support vector classification with L_1 penalty, linear support vector classification with L_2 penalty, and stochastic gradient descent classifier (SGDC) with *elastic-net* penalty. Throughout these tests our outcome variable is whether the tweet receives one or more retweets.

Some further background might be helpful for understanding these techniques. To start, there are three main types of feature selection algorithms: *filter, embedded,* and *wrapper* (Guyon and Elisseeff 2003; John, Kohavi, and Pfleger 1994). Filter methods were exclusively employed in the univariate and bivariate stages; the chief shortcoming of those filter approaches is that they do not consider combinations of or interactions among features, and thus ignore the effects of subsets of features (Bi et al. 2003).[13] In this section we thus concentrate on more advanced multivariate *embedded* and *wrapper* techniques.[14]

We specifically employ four types of multivariate feature selection methods on the remaining 89 variables. Our first algorithm, *recursive feature elimination* (RFE), is one of the *wrapper* methods, which "consider the selection of a set of features as a search problem, where different combinations are prepared, evaluated and compared to other combinations. A predictive model is used to evaluate a combination of features and assign a score based on model accuracy" (Brownlee 2014a). RFE is an example of a *backward elimination* feature selection technique, meaning it starts with all features and eliminates less useful variables one at a time, estimating model accuracy at each step: "The wrapper method searches through the space of variable subsets using the estimated accuracy from an induction algorithm as the measure of 'goodness' for a particular variable subset. Thus, the variable selection is being 'wrapped around' a particular induction algorithm" (Bi et al. 2003, 1230). In our case, the RFE is implemented with the *RFE* algorithm in scikit-learn and is "wrapped around" a logistic regression classifier (scikit-learn's *LogisticRegression* algorithm).

Our remaining three algorithms are *embedded* methods; these methods "learn which features best contribute to the accuracy of the model while the model is being created" (Brownlee 2014a). The most common embedded methods are what are known as *regularization* or *shrinkage* or *penalization* methods, so called because they introduce constraints that bias the solution to select fewer features.[15] Differently put, regularization methods apply a "penalty" that helps push less relevant features toward zero with the goal of achieving a *sparse* (or what we might more typically refer to as a "parsimonious") model.

All three of our embedded methods are in the support vector machine (SVM) family of techniques. Our first two embedded methods are two forms of linear support vector classification (SVC) methods using scikit-learn's *linearSVC* algorithm. Namely, we employ linear SVC first with the standard $L2$ norm penalty (Ho and Lin 2012) and then with the $L1$ norm penalty. The former, L2 regularization, is commonly known as *Ridge* classification/regression. The L1 model, meanwhile, is also commonly known as the Least Absolute Shrinkage and Selection Operator (LASSO) method (Tibshirani 1996). Both the LASSO and Ridge are "shrinkage" (also called "regularization") methods with subtle differences. In Ridge regression, a penalty is imposed on the size of the coefficients; it does "a proportional shrinkage" (Hastie, Tibshirani, and Friedman 2009, 69). LASSO, in turn, imposes a type of thresholding on the coefficients, pushing nonrelevant features closer to zero (and therefore to being dropped).[16]

Our final algorithm uses scikit-learn's *SGDClassifier* algorithm with an *elasticnet* penalty. As with the two other embedded algorithms, this implements a linear SVM model.[17] It is a linear classifier with stochastic gradient descent (SGD) learning. As with the two preceding algorithms, this classifier also uses a regularizer, called the *elasticnet*. The elasticnet regularizer is intended to be a type of "compromise" between the L1 and L2 norms. In effect, the employment of classifiers with the L1, L2, and elasticnet regularizers serves as a way to triangulate our findings.

To recap, we employ four types of multivariate feature selection methods on the remaining 89 variables: recursive feature elimination (RFE), linear support vector classification with L1 penalty, linear support vector classification with L2 penalty, and a stochastic gradient descent SVM classifier with

TABLE A.4 Scores on 4 multivariate feature selection techniques for 89 variables, ranked mean score

Variable	Rank	MEAN	RFE	LinearSVC (l1 penalty)	LinearSVC (l2 penalty)	SGDC (elasticnet penalty)
No. of Lists	1	0.980	1	1	1	0.92
@ Message	2	0.808	1	0.65	0.58	1
AL (Alabama)	3	0.743	1	0.55	0.53	0.89
Source—HubSpot	4	0.723	1	0.51	0.5	0.88
Description	5	0.675	1	0.09	0.69	0.92
NTEE—Environment and Animals	6	0.590	1	0.51	0.5	0.35
Program Expense %	7	0.575	1	0.36	0.35	0.59
No. of Friends	8	0.540	1	0.34	0.35	0.47
Display URL	9	0.440	1	0.2	0.15	0.41
Cumulative No. of Messages Sent	10	0.418	1	0.32	0.26	0.09
Revenue	11	0.403	1	0.27	0.23	0.11
No. of Mentions	12	0.375	1	0.15	0.14	0.21
MI (Michigan)	13	0.375	1	0.24	0.18	0.08
Age	14	0.373	1	0.13	0.14	0.22
Source—Facebook	15	0.370	1	0.2	0.21	0.07
No. of Followers	16	0.368	1	0.12	0.19	0.16
No. of Likes	17	0.363	1	0.14	0.12	0.19
No. of URLs	18	0.353	1	0.15	0.14	0.12
Default Profile	19	0.353	1	0.2	0.14	0.07
Place Type—Admin	20	0.350	1	0.17	0.16	0.07
Translation Enabled	21	0.340	1	0.11	0.11	0.14
Fundraising Expenses	22	0.338	1	0.14	0.11	0.1
Chat Tag	23	0.325	1	0.11	0.1	0.09
Screen Name Change	24	0.320	1	0.1	0.09	0.09
Time on Twitter in Days	25	0.310	1	0.12	0.12	0
CO	26	0.308	1	0.08	0.08	0.07
WI	27	0.308	1	0	0.11	0.12
EST	28	0.305	1	0.07	0.08	0.07
Description Hashtags	29	0.303	1	0.08	0.07	0.06
Verified	30	0.303	1	0.08	0.08	0.05
NTEE—Education	31	0.303	1	0.05	0.03	0.13
NTEE—Health	32	0.298	1	0.08	0.11	0
NTEE—Unknown, Unclassified	33	0.298	1	0.07	0.1	0.02
MD	34	0.295	1	0.1	0.07	0.01
Video	35	0.290	1	0.05	0.06	0.05
NTEE—Human Services	36	0.288	1	0.06	0.09	0

Variable	Rank	MEAN	RFE	LinearSVC (l1 penalty)	LinearSVC (l2 penalty)	SGDC (elasticnet penalty)
NTEE—Public, Societal Benefit	37	0.285	1	0.06	0.08	0
Truncated	38	0.285	1	0.05	0.05	0.04
Celebrity Fishing	39	0.285	1	0.06	0.05	0.03
Description Length	40	0.280	1	0.05	0.04	0.03
Description @	41	0.280	1	0.04	0.04	0.04
Location	42	0.278	1	0.04	0.05	0.02
IL	43	0.275	1	0.06	0.04	0
CA	44	0.270	1	0.05	0.03	0
Vice	45	0.270	0.98	0.03	0.03	0.04
Business Day	46	0.265	0.93	0.05	0.04	0.04
You	47	0.260	0.96	0.04	0.04	0
Photo	**48**	**0.255**	**0.8**	**0.06**	**0.05**	**0.11**
Source—Twitter Web Client	49	0.250	0.84	0.03	0	0.13
Source—Twitter for iPhone	50	0.248	0.87	0.03	0	0.09
Source—Twitter Ads	51	0.248	0.89	0.02	0.01	0.07
Profile Banner URL	52	0.245	0.73	0.08	0.07	0.1
Quote Status	53	0.243	0.91	0.03	0.03	0
Source—TweetDeck	54	0.235	0.82	0.03	0	0.09
No. of Hashtags	**55**	**0.233**	**0.71**	**0.07**	**0.1**	**0.05**
Geo Enabled	56	0.228	0.76	0.04	0.04	0.07
Place Type—City	57	0.225	0.78	0.05	0.04	0.03
Value Framing	**58**	**0.195**	**0.69**	**0.03**	**0.03**	**0.03**
Negate	59	0.188	0.64	0.04	0.03	0.04
POLIT	60	0.185	0.62	0.03	0.03	0.06
DC	61	0.183	0.6	0.05	0.06	0.02
Source—Twitter for Android	62	0.178	0.53	0.06	0.07	0.05
Source—Thingie	63	0.168	0.67	0	0	0
TX	64	0.165	0.47	0.04	0.05	0.1
Source—Sprout Social	65	0.165	0.49	0.03	0.06	0.08
Source—Buffer	66	0.163	0.51	0.01	0.04	0.09
Business Hours	67	0.155	0.58	0.02	0.02	0
Ovrst	68	0.150	0.56	0.02	0.02	0
Profile Use Background Image	69	0.135	0.44	0.03	0.03	0.04
Intrj	70	0.118	0.38	0.02	0.02	0.05
.@ Message	71	0.118	0.42	0.02	0.02	0.01
NTEE—Religion Related	72	0.113	0.33	0.07	0.01	0.04

(*continued*)

TABLE A.4 (*continued*)

Variable	Rank	MEAN	RFE	LinearSVC (l1 penalty)	LinearSVC (l2 penalty)	SGDC (elasticnet penalty)
Ought	73	0.110	0.4	0.02	0.02	0
Extended Profile	74	0.103	0.36	0	0	0.05
NY	75	0.095	0.29	0.04	0.05	0
Means	76	0.093	0.31	0.01	0.01	0.04
Source—OTHER	77	0.088	0.24	0	0.03	0.08
VA	78	0.075	0.27	0	0.03	0
MA	79	0.070	0.22	0	0.02	0.04
NTEE—Arts, Culture and Humanities	80	0.063	0.18	0	0.05	0.02
MS	81	0.058	0.09	0.12	0.02	0
Source—Hootsuite	82	0.055	0.13	0	0.03	0.06
Profile Background Tile	83	0.053	0.2	0.01	0	0
NTEE—International, Foreign Affairs	84	0.053	0.16	0	0.03	0.02
Undrst	85	0.035	0.11	0.01	0.01	0.01
Yes	86	0.023	0.07	0.01	0.01	0
Our	87	0.010	0.04	0	0	0
No	88	0.005	0.02	0	0	0
Virtue	89	0.000	0	0	0	0

NOTE: Highlighted variables indicate the 24 variables chosen for inclusion in the final theoretical model. Variables in bold are those that were included in the organizational-level analyses in Chapter 3.

elasticnet penalty. As in the bivariate feature selection, before running the algorithms all 89 features are normalized on a 0–1 scale using scikit-learn's *MinMaxScaler*.

Table A.4 shows the relevance/importance scores for all 89 variables on our four multivariate feature selection algorithms. As in Table A.3, we normalize scores on the four algorithms[18] and generate a mean score for each variable (see *MEAN* column in Table A.4). The features are ranked from most to least relevant based on this mean score. As in the bivariate stage, the *Number of Lists* feature is most relevant. The reader will notice that we have highlighted the first 20 variables as well as four others. As we describe in Chapter 4, these are the variables chosen for our final theoretical model.

The third and final stage of our analysis is model testing. This stage is covered in detail in Chapter 4.

NOTES

CHAPTER 1

1. For ease of exposition, for the remainder of the chapter our discussion focuses on US-based nonprofit organizations.

2. These organizations refer to US-based nonprofits that work abroad in the sector broadly defined as humanitarian relief and development.

3. The short essay cited here is adapted from a speech presented by Pablo Eisenberg to the Minnesota Council of Nonprofit Organizations in St. Paul, Minnesota, on October 14, 2004.

4. A good part of the discussion in this section is adapted from our article, "Speaking and being heard: How nonprofit advocacy organizations gain attention on social media" (Guo and Saxton, 2018).

CHAPTER 2

1. The World Wide Web and email are *services* that operate over the Internet.

2. "On 30 April 1993, CERN put the World Wide Web software in the public domain. Later, CERN made a release available with an open licence, a more sure way to maximise its dissemination. These actions allowed the web to flourish" (CERN, The birth of the Web, https://home.cern/science/computing/birth-web).

3. Even in 2005 most community foundations' websites were static "brochureware," Saxton and Guo (2011) found.

4. While these "precursors" to social media presaged a qualitative shift in communicative potential beyond that possible through email or websites, they are not generally considered "social media" given the constrained social networking features.

5. Given that the Obar, Zube, and Lampe (2012) survey was of social media use, it is not surprising to see such high rates of social media adoption in this study.

6. Because it is likely some organizations choose not to list a social media account on their GuideStar profile, the percentages shown likely underestimate somewhat the social media adoption rates of these 4,847 organizations. We thank Erica Harris for sharing the Guidestar data.

7. While there are minor differences in the set of organizations included over time, the size and focus of the organizations facilitate an "apples-to-apples" comparison.

8. Alternatively, Toms (2002, 855) defines information architecture as "a blueprint and navigational aid to the content of information-rich systems. As such information architecture performs an important supporting role in information interactivity."

9. Early relationship-building literature (e.g., Bortree and Seltzer 2009) underplayed or missed the conceptual recognition that these organizational choices were *architectural*—related to static choices regarding the venue—rather than dynamic efforts at fostering dialogue and public engagement. In concentrating on profile-type information, these perspectives also missed those architectural choices that are more closely related to two-way communication.

10. Such ties also serve as a mechanism by which organizations gain access to new information (Parise, Whelan, and Todd 2015).

11. For example, in a non-advocacy-specific sample of organizations, Saxton and Waters (2014) found the average *NonProfit Times* (NPT) Top 100 organization followed 8,373 other Twitter users in 2013, with a range from 43 to 194,840. This represented a jump from 2009, where the average organization followed 2,842 users and ranged from 3 to 46,723.

12. The hyperlink included at the end of the tweet is to an article by the *Dayton Daily News*. Most Twitter users will see an abbreviated version of the news article rather than the link. To see the tweet in its native format visit https://twitter.com/OpenSecretsDC/status/915016299734032385.

13. On Facebook, mentions of other users within a post have been possible since September 2009, and appeared in only 0.02% of all status updates in a fall 2009 sample of NPT Top 100 organizations, yet by 2013, 23% of all statuses contained one or more user mentions. User mentions (@ messages) are more popular on Twitter: 46% of all tweets in 2009 contained a user mention, while in 2013 they were the most widely used connecting tool, being found in 64% of all tweets sent.

14. On Facebook, for example, full hashtag support did not begin until June 12, 2013.

15. If there are multiple likes, the users who most recently liked the message will be visible. For example, the tweet "We'll see you in court" in Figure 2.2 earlier showed that the sample organizational tweet received 285,808 likes, with Twitter users being able to click on the "285,808 Likes" in order to see a detailed view of who the users were that liked the tweet.

16. To see the full tweet visit https://twitter.com/richardmelcher/status/111180 1447979593730.

17. This paragraph is adapted from our article "Social media capital: Conceptualizing the nature, acquisition, and expenditure of social media-based organizational resources" (Saxton and Guo in press).

18. Two key factors in the success of the #IceBucketChallenge are, first, the extensive celebrity involvement and, second, the way the challenge allowed each user to take center stage in the viral spread of the challenge through the creation of the user's own video.

19. In academia we see a similar shape with, for instance, the citation of academic papers (Redner 1998; S. Yang et al. 2012).

20. A careful reader will notice that in Chapter 5 of this book, we use the number of followers on Twitter as a proxy for "social media capital," a concept we introduced in Chapter 1. Please go to Chapter 5 for a discussion of the relationship between attention and social media capital.

21. The variable range is from 54 (National Child Safety Council, @Safetypup) to 1,409,521 (@ACLU).

CHAPTER 3

1. Other approaches include examining new moderators of existing relationships or proposing different relationships among existing variables. More incremental approaches would include replicating existing data, applying existing theory to new contexts, and measuring existing variables in new ways.

2. Deduction should, in our opinion, be a central part of the process.

3. Scholars in certain fields likewise search for variables deductively by drawing on any number of existing *fundamental theories*—such as those found in economics or psychology—and extrapolating to their current context. In certain contexts this is a valid approach.

4. The online appendix is available at http://social-metrics.org/quest-for-attention.

5. The RcEthic dictionary is one of many that have come to form part of what is known as the Harvard IV/Lasswell psycho-social dictionaries. The RcEthic dictionary contains 151 words related to moral rectitude, virtue, ethics, and values as described in Namenwirth and Weber (1987). As in previous research (e.g., Suddaby, Saxton, and Gunz, 2015; Tetlock, 2007; Tetlock, Saar-Tsechansky, and Macskassy, 2008), we accessed the Harvard IV/Lasswell dictionaries via the General Inquirer data files (see http://www.wjh.harvard.edu/~inquirer/).

6. In an unpublished study Saxton performed on the *NonProfit Times* Top 100 organizations, hyperlinks were the most common type of connection tool used by these organizations in 2008, with 68% of all tweets and 81% of all Facebook statuses containing a hyperlink. By 2013, the proportion of messages with a URL had dropped to 55% and 71% on Twitter and Facebook, respectively, reflecting the increased employment of other connecting tools.

7. This is higher than the proportions found in an earlier study of NPT Top 100 organizations. On Twitter, retweets comprised 16% of all tweets in a 2009 sample and 24% in 2013. On Facebook this feature is newer, with none in the 2009 sample and just under 3% of all status updates in 2013. At the time, Twitter thus appeared to be a more powerful dissemination network, whereas Facebook was more likely to feature original information.

CHAPTER 4

1. We believe the terms *data science* and *data analytics* are more or less synonymous, with *artificial intelligence* and *machine learning* referring to more specific subsets of tools used by the data scientist or data analytics professional.

2. See the methodological appendix for a more detailed discussion of the three stages.

3. The methodological appendix contains an in-depth discussion of this point.

4. https://developer.twitter.com/en/docs/tweets/data-dictionary/overview/user-object

5. The machine learning community generally refers to these techniques as "univariate" techniques given that they examine the relationship with the dependent variable of a single variable at a time. In the social sciences, however, such $X \rightarrow Y$ examinations are considered "bivariate."

6. Forward stepwise selection is generally considered a "computationally efficient alternative to best subset selection" (James et al., 2013, 207).

7. We ran four different regressions to directly test our model and show in Table 4.4 only the "best" model. Specifically, Model 1 represents the "best" model in the statistical sense in terms of how it conforms with standard research practice. Three other models (not shown) were run that (1) included only the top 20 variables, (2) replaced the limited state (*Alabama* and *Michigan*) and NTEE (*Environment and Animals*) variables chosen by the feature selection process with a full complement of state and NTEE fixed effects, and (3) included the top 24 variables without state or NTEE fixed effects and standard errors clustered on organization. Results were substantively similar to those shown in Model 1 in Table 4.4 and thus are omitted.

CHAPTER 5

1. It should be noted that our message-level analysis tells a different story: the more user mentions, URLs, or hashtags are included in a given message, the lower the amount of attention the message receives. This message-level finding suggests that, while user mentions provide a way of targeting and interacting with a focused user or a small subset of users, it is not necessarily the best way to garner widespread attention to the message itself in terms of retweets, likes, and replies. Those users that are mentioned in the tweet or included in the hashtag tend to pay more attention to this particular message as it is a direct communication to them; other users might feel less compelled to respond as the message is not directly relevant to them. Taken together, we can infer that although an increased use of connecting tools such as user mentions and hashtags in a message may reduce the popularity of the particular message, collectively they serve to increase public attention to a focal organization.

2. In December 2018, we gathered the maximum amount of data for each of the three organizations. Specifically, the Twitter API limits access to the last 3,200 tweets (including original and retweeted messages) sent per organization. Because the frequency of tweeting varies across organizations, the time periods covered are different for Alpha, Beta, and Gamma. In addition, the data presented are based on the original messages sent by the organizations and ignore retweeted messages. Specifically, statistics presented are based on the 2,058, 1,536, and 1,294 original tweets that were sent by Alpha, Beta, and Gamma, respectively, during the study period for each organization.

3. The same message was sent twice during the day.

METHODOLOGICAL
APPENDIX TO CHAPTER 4

1. Some consider feature selection to be a subset of feature engineering (Dong and Liu 2018), while others consider feature engineering to be separate from feature selection (Feature engineering vs feature selection, January 4, 2018, Feature Labs, https://www.featurelabs.com/blog/feature-engineering-vs-feature-selection/), and consider *feature engineering* to be more or less synonymous with *feature generation, feature construction,* or *feature extraction.* We conform to this second view and consider feature engineering to be a chiefly separate process that occurs before feature selection.

2. The term *data mining* refers to a broad range of techniques devoted to the identification of patterns in large-scale databases in order to acquire actionable or valuable insights, such as classifying financial transactions as either fraudulent or nonfraudulent (Albanese et al. 2017).

3. For details see https://developer.twitter.com/en/docs/tweets/data-dictionary/overview/user-object.

4. Specifically, when the tweet object returns a *possibly_sensitive* value of *True,* "it is an indicator that the URL contained in the Tweet may contain content or media identified as sensitive content." For a data dictionary for this and other Twitter API variables, see Table A.2 as well as the Twitter developer site (https://developer.twitter.com/en/docs/tweets/data-dictionary/overview/tweet-object).

5. In machine learning parlance, *model selection* involves not only feature selection but also the choice of a specific machine learning algorithm and associated "hyperparameters." We also note that feature selection is not the same as *dimensionality reduction* as in principal component analysis (PCA) or singular value decomposition (SVD): "Both methods seek to reduce the number of attributes in the dataset, but a dimensionality reduction method does so by creating new combinations of attributes, where as [*sic*] feature selection methods include and exclude attributes present in the data without changing them" (Brownlee 2014a).

6. For more details visit http://scikit-learn.org/

7. The machine learning community generally refers to these techniques as "univariate" techniques given that they examine the relationship with the dependent variable of a single variable at a time. In the social sciences, however, such $X \rightarrow Y$ examinations are considered "bivariate."

8. For an overview of MIC, see Albanese et al. (2017).

9. This is the most apparently "multivariate" of the algorithms used in this section. Yet it is important to recognize that the Random Forest technique does not take into account interactions among variables or combinations of variables.

10. Standardized scores (such as those achieved by scikit-learn's *StandardScaler*) could also be used in cases where all variables have a normal distribution.

11. Before normalization, *MIC* (absolute) scores ranged from 0 to 0.1667, *mutual _info_classif* scores ranged from 0 to 0.1149, *f_classif* (absolute) scores ranged from 0 to

27079.09, *chi2* scores ranged from 0 to 22468.09, and RandomForestClassifier scores range from 0 to 0.0532.

12. See Section B of the online appendix for the correlation tables. The online appendix is available at http://social-metrics.org/quest-for-attention.

13. "The main disadvantage of the filter approach is that it totally ignores the effects of the selected variable subset on the performance of the induction algorithm" (Bi et al. 2003, 1230).

14. Wrapper methods use learning techniques to assess the usefulness of the features, while embedded methods combine the feature selection stage with classifier construction.

15. "The regularizer is a penalty added to the loss function that shrinks model parameters towards the zero vector using either the squared euclidean norm L2 or the absolute norm L1 or a combination of both (Elastic Net)" (http://scikit-learn.org/stable/modules/generated/sklearn.linear_model.SGDClassifier.html).

16. The LASSO and Ridge methods "may also be considered algorithms with feature selection baked in, as they actively seek to remove or discount the contribution of features as part of the model building process" (Brownlee 2014b).

17. The loss function we use ("hinge") gives a linear SVM.

18. Prior to normalization, the *RFE* scores range from 1 (most relevant/"selected" for 44 variables) to 46. *LinearSVC* (with L1 penalty) ranges from 7.328 to -3.3441 while *LinearSVC* with L2 penalty ranges from 1.9398 to -1.1245. *SGDC* scores range from 1.9043 to -2.0596. To make these scores comparable, absolute values are taken and then normalized on a 0–1 range. RFE scores are first reversed so that larger values are given to the most relevant features.

REFERENCES

Albanese, D., Riccadonna, S., Donati, C., & Franceschi, P. 2017. "A Practical Tool for Maximal Information Coefficient Analysis." *bioRxiv*. https://doi.org/10.1101/215855.

Alexander, J., Nank, R., & Stivers, C. 1999. "Implications of Welfare Reform: Do Nonprofit Survival Strategies Threaten Civil Society?" *Nonprofit and Voluntary Sector Quarterly* 28: 452–475.

Allen, B. R., & Boynton, A. C. 1991. "Information Architecture: In Search of Efficient Flexibility." *MIS Quarterly* 15: 435–445.

Allport, G. W. 1961. *Pattern and Growth in Personality*. New York: Holt, Rinehart, & Winston.

Almog-Bar, M., & Schmid, H. 2014. "Advocacy Activities of Nonprofit Human Service Organizations: A Critical Review." *Nonprofit and Voluntary Sector Quarterly* 43: 11–35.

Amani, F. A., & Fadlalla, A. M. 2017. "Data Mining Applications in Accounting: A Review of the Literature and Organizing Framework." *International Journal of Accounting Information Systems* 24: 32–58.

An, S. 2019. "Attention Strategies for Nonprofit Advocacy on Social Media: Results from a National Study of Homelessness Nonprofits in the United States." PhD diss., University of Pennsylvania, Philadelphia.

Anderson, C. 2004. *The Long Tail*. Retrieved from https://www.wired.com/2004/10/tail/.

Anderson, C. 2006. *The Long Tail: Why the Future of Business Is Selling Less of More*. New York: Hachette Digital.

Andrews, K. T., & Edwards, B. 2004. "Advocacy Organizations in the U.S. Political Process." *Annual Review of Sociology* 30: 479–506.

Anger, I., & Kittl, C. 2011. "Measuring Influence on Twitter." Paper presented at the 11th International Conference on Knowledge Management and Knowledge Technologies, Graz, Austria.

Antheunis, M. L., & Schouten, A. P. 2011. "The Effects of Other-Generated and System-Generated Cues on Adolescents' Perceived Attractiveness on Social Network Sites." *Journal of Computer-Mediated Communication* 16: 391–406.

Auger, G. A. 2013. "Fostering Democracy through Social Media: Evaluating Diametrically Opposed Nonprofit Advocacy Organizations' use of Facebook, Twitter, and YouTube." *Public Relations Review* 39: 369–376.

Avner, M. 2002. *The Lobbying and Advocacy Handbook for Nonprofit Organizations: Shaping Public Policy at the State and Local Level.* St. Paul: Amherst H. Wilder Foundation.

Bakshy, E., Hofman, J. M., Mason, W. A., & Watts, D. J. 2011. "Everyone's an Influencer: Quantifying Influence on Twitter." In *Proceedings of the Fourth ACM International Conference on Web Search and Data Mining,* 65–74. New York: ACM.

Barabási, A. L., & Albert, R. 1999. "Emergence of Scaling in Random Networks." *Science* 286: 509–512.

Bass, G. D., Arons, D. F., Guinane, K., & Carter, M. F. 2007. *Seen But not Heard: Strengthening Nonprofit Advocacy.* Washington, DC: Aspen Institute.

Baumgartner, F. R., & Jones, B. D. 2010. *Agendas and Instability in American Politics.* Chicago: University of Chicago Press.

Bellah, R. N., Madsen, R., Sullivan, W. M., Swidler, A., & Tipton, S. M. 1991. *The Good Society.* New York: Knopf.

Benford, R. D., & Snow, D. A. 2000. "Framing Processes and Social Movements: An Overview and Assessment." *Annual Review of Sociology* 26: 611–639.

Benkler, Yochai. 2006. *The Wealth of Networks.* New Haven, CT: Yale University Press.

Bennett, D., & Fielding, P. 1999. *The Net Effect: How Cyber-Advocacy Is Changing the Political Landscape.* Merrifield, VA: E-Advocates Press.

Berry, J. M. 1977. *Lobbying for the People: The Political Behavior of Public Interest Groups.* Princeton, NJ: Princeton University Press.

Berry, J. M., & Arons, D. F. 2003. *A Voice for Nonprofits.* Washington, DC: Brookings Institution.

Bi, J., Bennett, K., Embrechts, M., Breneman, C., & Song, M. 2003. "Dimensionality Reduction Via Sparse Support Vector Machines." *Journal of Machine Learning Research* 3: 1229–1243.

Blackwood, A., Wing, K. T., & Pollak, T. H. 2008. *The Nonprofit Sector in Brief.* Washington, DC: Urban Institute.

Blum, A. L., & Langley, P. 1997. "Selection of Relevant Features and Examples in Machine Learning." *Artificial Intelligence* 97: 245–271.

Bodrunova, S. S., Litvinenko, A. A., & Blekanov, I. S. 2016. "Influencers on the Russian Twitter: Institutions vs. People in the Discussion on Migrants." In *Proceedings of the International Conference on Electronic Governance and Open Society: Challenges in Eurasia,* 212–222. New York: ACM.

Boles, B. 2013. "Technology's Role in the Nonprofit Sector: Increasing Organizational Effectiveness and Efficiency through Technology Innovations." *Columbia Social Work Review* 4: 69–79. https:// doi.org/10.7916/D88P5Z1B.

Bond, R. M., Fariss, C. J., Jones, J. J., Kramer, A. D., Marlow, C., Settle, J. E., & Fowler, J. H. 2012. "A 61-Million-Person Experiment in Social Influence and Political Mobilization." *Nature* 489: 295–298.

Bonk, K. 2010. "Strategic Communications." In *The Jossey-Bass Handbook of Nonprofit Leadership and Management*, 3rd ed., edited by D. Renz, 329–346. San Francisco: Wiley.

Boris, E., & Mosher-Williams, R. 1998. "Nonprofit Advocacy Organizations: Assessing the Definitions, Classifications, and Data." *Nonprofit & Voluntary Sector Quarterly* 27: 488–506.

Bortree, D. S., & Seltzer, T. 2009. "Dialogic Strategies and Outcomes: An Analysis of Environmental Advocacy Groups' Facebook Profiles." *Public Relations Review* 35: 317–319.

Bourdieu, P. 2002. "The Forms of Capital." In *Readings in Economic Sociology*, edited by N. W. Biggart, 280–291. Malden, MA: Blackwell.

boyd, d. m., & Ellison, N. B. 2007. "Social Network Sites: Definition, History, and Scholarship." *Journal of Computer-Mediated Communication* 13: 210–230.

Brady, S. R., Young, J. A., & McLeod, D. A. 2015. "Utilizing Digital Advocacy in Community Organizing: Lessons Learned from Organizing in Virtual Spaces to Promote Worker Rights and Economic Justice." *Journal of Community Practice* 23: 255–273.

Briggs, C. L., & Bauman, R. 1992. "Genre, Intertextuality, and Social Power." *Journal of Linguistic Anthropology* 2: 131–172.

Broom, G. M., Casey, S., & Ritchey, J. 1997. "Toward a Concept and Theory of Organization-Public Relationships." *Journal of Public Relations Research* 9: 83–98.

Brownlee, J. 2014a. "An Introduction to Feature Selection." *Machine Learning Mastery.* Updated June 3, 2019. https://machinelearningmastery.com/an-introduction-to-feature-selection/.

Brownlee, J. 2014b. "Discover Feature Engineering, How to Engineer Features and How to Get Good at It." *Machine Learning Mastery.* Updated May 22, 2019. https://machinelearningmastery.com/discover-feature-engineering-how-to-engineer-features-and-how-to-get-good-at-it/.

Bruning, S. D., Dials, M., & Shirka, A. 2008. "Using Dialogue to Build Organization–Public Relationships, Engage Publics, and Positively Affect Organizational Outcomes." *Public Relations Review* 34: 25–31.

Bruns, A., & Burgess, J. E. 2011. "The Use of Twitter Hashtags in the Formation of Ad Hoc Publics." Paper presented at the 6th European Consortium for Political Research, Reykjavik conference, 25–27.

Bruns, A., & Stieglitz, S. 2012. "Quantitative Approaches to Comparing Communication Patterns on Twitter." *Journal of Technology in Human Services* 30: 160–185.

Brynjolfsson, E., Hu, Y. J., & Smith, M. D. 2006. "From Niches to Riches: Anatomy of the Long Tail." *Sloan Management Review* 47: 67–71.

Budak, C., & Agrawal, R. 2013. "On Participation in Group Chats on Twitter." In *Proceedings of the 22nd International World Wide Web Conference Committee (IW3C2)*, 165–176.

Bürger, T. 2015. "Use of Digital Advocacy by German Nonprofit Foundations on Facebook." *Public Relations Review* 41: 523–525.

Calder, B. J., Malthouse, E. C., & Schaedel, U. 2009. "An Experimental Study of the Relationship Between Online Engagement and Advertising Effectiveness." *Journal of Interactive Marketing* 23: 321–331.

Cameron, A. F., & Webster, J. 2005. "Unintended Consequences of Emerging Communication Technologies: Instant Messaging in the Workplace." *Computers in Human Behavior* 21: 85–103.

Campbell, D. A., & Lambright, K. T. 2019. "Are You Out There? Internet Presence of Nonprofit Human Service Organizations." *Nonprofit and Voluntary Sector Quarterly* 48: 1296–1311.

Campbell, D. A., Lambright, K. T., & Wells, C. J. 2014. "Looking for Friends, Fans, and Followers? Social Media Use in Public and Nonprofit Human Services." *Public Administration Review* 74: 655–663.

Cang, S., & Yu, H. 2012. "Mutual Information Based Input Feature Selection for Classification Problems." *Decision Support Systems* 54: 691–698.

Carboni, J. L., & Maxwell, S. P. 2015. "Effective Social Media Engagement for Nonprofits: What Matters?" *Journal of Public and Nonprofit Affairs* 1: 18–28.

Casey, J. P. 2011. "Understanding Advocacy: A Primer on the Policy Making Role of Nonprofit Organizations." New York: Baruch College, City University of New York, Center for Nonprofit Strategy. Retrieved from: http://www.baruch.cuny.edu/mspia/ centers-and institutes/center-for-nonprofit-strategy-and management/documents/ Casey_UnderstandingAdvocacyaPrimeronthePolicyMakingRoleofNonoprofit Organizations.pdf.

Casey, J. P., & Mehrotra, A. 2011. "Solid Waste Management and Environmental Justice: Building and Sustaining Coalitions." *New York City Nonprofit Advocacy Case Studies (Series of Three Case Studies and Background Paper)*. New York: Baruch College, City University of New York, Center for Nonprofit Strategy and Management. Retrieved from: www.baruch.cuny.edu/spa/researchcenters/nonprofitstrategy/ CaseStudies.php.

Castells, M. 1996. *The Rise of the Network Society*. Cambridge, MA: Blackwell.

Cha, M., Haddadi, H., Benevenuto, F., & Gummadi, P. K. 2010. "Measuring User Influence in Twitter: The Million Follower Fallacy." In *Proceedings of the Fourth International AAAI Conference on Weblogs and Social Media*, 10–17.

Chang, H. 2010. "A New Perspective on Twitter Hashtag Use: Diffusion of Innovation Theory." In *Proceedings of the American Society for Information Science and Technology* 47: 1–4.

Chen, K. K. 2018. "Interorganizational Advocacy Among Nonprofit Organizations in Strategic Action Fields: Exogenous Shocks and Local Responses." *Nonprofit and Voluntary Sector Quarterly* 47: 97S–118S.

Chen, T., & Dredze, M. 2018. "Vaccine Images on Twitter: Analysis of What Images Are Shared." *Journal of Medical Internet Research* 20: e130. doi: 10.2196/jmir.8221.

Child, C. D., & Gronbjerg, K. A. 2007. "Nonprofit Advocacy Organizations: Their Characteristics and Activities." *Social Science Quarterly* 88: 259–281.

Clark, W. R., & Golder, M. 2015. "Big Data, Causal Inference, and Formal Theory: Contradictory Trends in Political Science?" *PS: Political Science & Politics* 48: 65–70.

Clear, A., Paull, M., & Holloway, D. 2018. "Nonprofit Advocacy Tactics: Thinking Inside the Box?" *VOLUNTAS: International Journal of Voluntary and Nonprofit Organizations* 29: 857–869.

Cleveland, W. 2015. "The Lessons of the Philanthropy 400: Investing in Fundraising Matters in a More Competitive World." *Chronicles of Philanthropy*. Retrieved from: https://www.philanthropy.com/article/The-Lessons-of-the/234029.

Cnaan, R. A., & Handy, F. 2005. "Towards Understanding Episodic Volunteering." *Vrijwillige Inzet Onderzocht* 2: 29–35.

Dalenberg, A. 2015. "Jesse Jackson Reminds Social Media Week that Some Things Are Bigger than Social Media." Retrieved from: https://www.bizjournals.com/bizjournals/news/2015/02/25/jesse-jackson-reminds-social-media-week-that-some.html.

Davenport, T. H., & Beck, J. C. 2001. *The Attention Economy: Understanding the New Currency of Business*. Cambridge, MA: Harvard Business Press.

Davis, R. 1999. *The Web of Politics: The Internet's Impact on the American Political System*. New York: Oxford University Press.

Debreceny, R. S., Rahman, A., & Wang, T. 2017. "Corporate Network Centrality Score: Methodologies and Informativeness." *Journal of Information Systems* 31: 23–43.

Denhardt, J. V., & Denhardt, R. B. 2015. *The New Public Service: Serving, not Steering*. New York: Routledge.

Deschamps, R., & McNutt, K. 2014. "Third Sector and Social Media." *Canadian Journal of Nonprofit and Social Economy Research* 5: 29–46.

de Tocqueville, A. 1838. *On Democracy in America*. New York: George Dearborn.

de Vries, L., Gensler, S., & Leeflang, P. S. H. 2012. "Popularity of Brand Posts on Brand Fan Pages: An Investigation of the Effects of Social Media Marketing." *Journal of Interactive Marketing* 26: 83–91.

Doerfel, M. L., Atouba, Y., & Harris, J. L. 2016. "(Un)obtrusive Control in Emergent Networks: Examining Funding Agencies' Control Over Nonprofit Networks." *Nonprofit and Voluntary Sector Quarterly* 46: 469–487.

Domo. 2018. *Data Never Sleeps 6.0*. Retrieved from: https://www.domo.com/learn/data-never-sleeps-6.

Dong, G., & Liu, H. 2018. *Feature Engineering for Machine Learning and Data Analytics.* Boca Raton, FL: CRC Press.

Downing, J., Fasano, R., Friedland, P., McCollough, M., Mizrahi, T., & Shapiro, J., eds. 1991. *Computers for Social Change and Community Organization.* New York: Haworth Press.

Edwards, H. R., & Hoefer, R. 2010. Are Social Work Advocacy Groups Using Web 2.0 Effectively? *Journal of Policy Practice* 9: 220–239.

Eisenberg, P. 2004. "Citizen Engagement: The Nonprofit Challenge." *Nonprofit Quarterly.* Retrieved from: https://nonprofitquarterly.org/citizen-engagement-the-nonprofit-challenge.

Eisenhardt, K. M. 1989. "Building Theories from Case Study Research." *Academy of Management Review* 14: 532–550.

Ellison, N. B., Steinfield, C., & Lampe, C. 2007. "The Benefits of Facebook "Friends": Social Capital and College Students' Use of Online Social Network Sites." *Journal of Computer-Mediated Communication* 12: 1143–1168.

Ellison, N. B., Vitak, J., Gray, R., & Lampe, C. 2014. "Cultivating Social Resources on Social Network Sites: Facebook Relationship Maintenance Behaviors and Their Role in Social Capital Processes." *Journal of Computer-Mediated Communication* 19: 855–870.

Elman, R. J., Ogar, J., & Elman, S. H. 2000. "Aphasia: Awareness, Advocacy, and Activism." *Aphasiology* 14: 455–459.

Eng, T. Y., Liu, C. Y. G., & Sekhon, Y. K. 2012. "The Role of Relationally Embedded Network Ties in Resource Acquisition of British Nonprofit Organizations." *Nonprofit and Voluntary Sector Quarterly* 41: 1092–1115.

Eppler, M. J., & Mengis, J. 2004. "The Concept of Information Overload: A Review of Literature from Organization Science, Accounting, Marketing, MIS, and Related Disciplines." *Information Society* 20: 325–344.

Equal Measures 2030. n.d. Advocates Survey 2018. Accessed December 8, 2019. https://www.equalmeasures2030.org/products/advocate-survey/.

Evans, M. S. 2014. "A Computational Approach to Qualitative Analysis in Large Textual Datasets." *PloS ONE9,* e87908. https://doi.org/10.1371/journal.pone.0087908.

Faiola, A., & Matei, S. 2005. "Cultural Cognitive Style and Web Design: Beyond a Behavioral Inquiry into Computer-Mediated Communication." *Journal of Computer-Mediated Communication* 11: 375–394.

Farrar-Myers, V. A., & Vaughn, J. S., eEds. 2015. *Controlling the Message: New Media in American Political Campaigns.* New York: NYU Press.

Forman, G. 2003. "An Extensive Empirical Study of Feature Selection Metrics for Text Classification." *Journal of Machine Learning Research* 3: 1289–1305.

Frumkin, P. 2002. *On Being Nonprofit: A Conceptual and Policy Primer.* Cambridge, MA: Harvard University Press.

Fyall, R., & McGuire, M. 2015. "Advocating for Policy Change in Nonprofit Coalitions." *Nonprofit and Voluntary Sector Quarterly* 44: 1274–1291.

Gais, T., & Walker, J., Jr. 1991. "Pathways to Influence in American Politics." In *Mobilizing Interest Groups in America*, edited by J. Walker, Jr., 103–121. Ann Arbor: University of Michigan Press.

Galaskiewicz, J., & Bielefeld, W. 1998. *Nonprofit Organizations in an Age of Uncertainty: A Study of Organizational Change*. New York: de Gruyter.

Gilbert, E., & Karahalios, K. 2009. "Predicting Tie Strength with Social Media." Paper presented at the SIGCHI Conference on Human Factors in Computing Systems, Boston.

Gilens, M., & Page, B. I. 2014. "Testing Theories of American Politics: Elites, Interest Groups, and Average Citizens." *Perspectives on Politics* 12: 564–581.

Gladwell, M. 2010. "Why the Revolution Will Not Be Tweeted." *New Yorker* 4: 1–9.

GlobalWebIndex. 2018. *Social: GlobalWebIndex's Flagship Report on the Latest Trends in Social Media*. Retrieved from: http://www.globalwebindex.com.

Goffman, E. 1974. *Frame Analysis: An Essay on the Organization of Experience*. New York: Harper & Row.

Goldkind, L. 2014. "E-advocacy in Human Services: The Impact of Organizational Conditions and Characteristics on Electronic Advocacy Activities Among Nonprofits." *Journal of Policy Practice* 13: 300–315.

Goldkind, L., & McNutt, J. G. 2014. "Social Media and Social Change: Nonprofits and Using Social Media Strategies to Meet Advocacy Goals." In *ICT Management in Non-profit Organizations*, edited by A.-M. José Antonio & L.-C. Ana María, 56–72. Hershey, PA: IGI Global.

Gollust, S. E., Niederdeppe, J., & Barry, C. L. 2013. "Framing the Consequences of Childhood Obesity to Increase Public Support for Obesity Prevention Policy." *American Journal of Public Health* 103: 96–102.

Gordon, T. P., Knock, C. L., & Neely, D. G. 2009. "The Role of Rating Agencies in the Market for Charitable Contributions: An Empirical Test." *Journal of Accounting and Public Policy* 28: 469–484.

Gormley, W. T., & Cymrot, H. 2006. "The Strategic Choices of Child Advocacy Groups." *Nonprofit & Voluntary Sector Quarterly* 35: 102–122.

Granovetter, M. S. 1973. "The Strength of Weak Ties." *American Journal of Sociology* 78: 1360–1380.

Greenberg, J., & MacAulay, M. 2009. "NPO 2.0? Exploring the Web Presence of Environmental Nonprofit Organizations in Canada." *Global Media Journal—Canadian Edition* 2: 63–88.

Grenny, J., Patterson, K., Maxfield, D., McMillan, R., & Switzler, A. 2013. *Influencer: The New Science of Leading Change*. New York: McGraw-Hill Education.

Grogan, C. M., & Gusmano, M. K. 2009. "Political Strategies of Safety-Net Providers in Response to Medicaid Managed Care Reforms." *Journal of Health Politics, Policy & Law* 34: 5–35.

Gross, C. P., Anderson, G. F., & Powe, N. R. 1999. "The Relation Between Funding by the National Institutes of Health and the Burden of Disease." *New England Journal of Medicine* 340: 1881–1887.

Guetzkow, J. 2010. "Beyond Deservingness: Congressional Discourse on Poverty, 1964–1996." *Annals of the American Academy of Political and Social Science* 629: 173–197.

Guo, C. 2007. "When Government Becomes the Principal Philanthropist: The Effect of Public Funding on Patterns of Nonprofit Governance." *Public Administration Review* 67: 456–471.

Guo, C. 2012. "Literature Review: Elements of Successful Nonprofit Advocacy." In *Beyond the Cause: The Art and Science of Advocacy*, 15–23. Washington, DC: Independent Sector.

Guo, C., & Marietta, M. 2015. "Value of Voices, Voice of Values: Participatory and Value Representation in Networked Governance." In *Creating Public Value in Practice*, edited by J. M. Bryson, B. B. Crosby, & L. Bloomberg, 67–86. Boca Raton, FL: CRC Press.

Guo, C., & Saxton, G. D. 2010. "Voice-In, Voice-Out: Constituent Participation and Nonprofit Advocacy." *Nonprofit Policy Forum* 1 (1): Article 5. https://doi.org/10.2202/2154-3348.1000.

Guo, C., & Saxton, G. D. 2014a. "Attention Philanthropy: The Good, the Bad, and the Strategy." *Nonprofit Quarterly* 21: 42–47.

Guo, C., & Saxton, G. D. 2014b. "Tweeting Social Change: How Social Media Are Changing Nonprofit Advocacy." *Nonprofit and Voluntary Sector Quarterly* 43: 57–79.

Guo, C., & Saxton, G. D. 2016. "Social Media Capital for Nonprofits: How to Accumulate It, Convert It, and Spend It." *Nonprofit Quarterly* 23: 10–16.

Guo, C., & Saxton, G. D. 2018. "Speaking and Being Heard: How Nonprofit Advocacy Organizations Gain Attention on Social Media." *Nonprofit and Voluntary Sector Quarterly* 47: 5–26.

Guo, C., Webb, N. J., Abzug, R., & Peck, L. R. 2013. "Religious Affiliation, Religious Attendance, and Participation in Social Change Organizations." *Nonprofit and Voluntary Sector Quarterly* 42: 34–58.

Guo, C., Xu, J., Smith, D. H., and Zhang, Z. 2012. "Civil Society, Chinese Style: The Rise of the Nonprofit Sector in Post-Mao China." *Nonprofit Quarterly* 19: 20–27.

Guo, C., & Zhang, Z. 2014. "Understanding Nonprofit Advocacy in Nonwestern Settings: A Framework and Empirical Evidence from Singapore." *VOLUNTAS: International Journal of Voluntary and Nonprofit Organizations* 25: 1151–1174.

Gupta, K., Ripberger, J., & Wehde, W. 2018. "Advocacy Group Messaging on Social Media: Using the Narrative Policy Framework to Study Twitter Messages about Nuclear Energy Policy in the United States." *Policy Studies Journal* 46: 119–136.

Guyon, I., & Elisseeff, A. 2003. "An Introduction to Variable and Feature Selection." *Journal of Machine Learning Research* 3: 1157–1182.

Hanna, R., Rohm, A., & Crittenden, V. L. 2011. "We're All Connected: The Power of the Social Media Ecosystem." *Business Horizons* 54: 265–273.

Hargittai, E. 2007. "Whose Space? Differences Among Users and Nonusers of Social Network Sites." *Journal of Computer-Mediated Communication* 13: 276–297.

Harlow, S., & Guo, L. 2014. "Will the Revolution Be Tweeted or Facebooked? Using Digital Communication Tools in Immigrant Activism." *Journal of Computer-Mediated Communication* 19: 463–478.

Harris, E., Petrovits, C., & Yetman, M. H. 2017. "Why Bad Things Happen to Good Organizations: The Link Between Governance and Asset Diversions in Public Charities." *Journal of Business Ethics* 146: 149–166.

Hastie, T., Tibshirani, R., & Friedman, J. 2009. *The Elements of Statistical Learning: Data Mining, Inference, and Prediction*, 2nd ed. New York: Springer.

Heclo, H. 1978. "Issue Networks and the Executive Establishment." In *The New American Political System*, edited by A. King, 87–124. Washington, DC: American Enterprise.

Hermida, A. 2010. "From TV to Twitter: How Ambient News Became Ambient Journalism." *Media/Culture Journal* 13.

Hick, S., & McNutt, J. G. 2002. *Advocacy, Activism, and the Internet: Community Organization and Social Policy*. Chicago: Lyceum.

Hill, C., & Jones, T. 1992. "Stakeholder-Agency Theory." *Journal of Management Studies* 29: 131–154.

Hills, G. E., Lumpkin, G. T., & Singh, R. P. 1997. "Opportunity Recognition: Perceptions and Behaviors of Entrepreneurs." *Frontiers of Entrepreneurship Research* 17: 168–182.

Ho, C.-H., & Lin, C.-J. 2012. "Large-Scale Linear Support Vector Regression." *Journal of Machine Learning Research* 13: 3323–3348.

Homans, G. C. 2013. *The Human Group*, vol. 7. New York: Routledge.

Hopkins, B. 1992. *Charity, Advocacy and the Law*. New York: Wiley.

Horne, C. S. 2005. *Toward an Understanding of the Revenue of Nonprofit Organizations*. PhD diss., Georgia Institute of Technology, Atlanta.

Hou, Y., & Lampe, C. 2015. "Social Media Effectiveness for Public Engagement: Example of Small Nonprofits." In *Proceedings of the 33rd Annual ACM Conference on Human Factors in Computing Systems*, 3107–3116.

Howlett, M. 1998. "Predictable and Unpredictable Policy Windows: Institutional and Exogenous Correlates of Canadian Federal Agenda-Setting." *Canadian Journal of Political Science* 31: 495–524.

Hughes, A. L., & Palen, L. 2009. "Twitter Adoption and Use in Mass Convergence and Emergency Events." *International Journal of Emergency Management* 6: 248–260.

Hurwitz, J., & Peffley, M. 1987. "How Are Foreign Policy Attitudes Structured? A Hierarchical Model." *American Political Science Review* 81: 1099–1120.

Hyde, M. K., Dunn, J., Bax, C., & Chambers, S. K. 2016. "Episodic Volunteering and Retention: An Integrated Theoretical Approach." *Nonprofit and Voluntary Sector Quarterly* 45: 45–63.

Independent Sector. 2001. *The New Nonprofit Almanac in Brief: Facts and Figures on the Independent Sector*. Washington, DC: Independent Sector.

Jacobson, R. 2013. *Industry Insights: 2.5 Quintillion Bytes of Data Created Every Day. How Does CPG & Retail Manage It?* Retrieved from: https://www.ibm.com/blogs/insights -on-business/consumer-products/2-5-quintillion-bytes-of-data-created-every-day -how-does-cpg-retail-manage-it/.

Jacoby, W. G. 2006. "Value Choices and American Public Opinion." *American Journal of Political Science* 50: 706–723.

James, G., Witten, D., Hastie, T., & Tibshirani, R. 2013. *An Introduction to Statistical Learning: With Applications in R*. New York: Springer.

Jang, C. Y., & Stefanone, M. A. 2011. "Non-Directed self-Disclosure in the Blogosphere: Exploring the Persistence of Interpersonal Communication Norms." *Information, Communication & Society* 14: 1039–1059.

Jenkins, J. C. 2006. "Nonprofit Organizations and Political Advocacy." In *The Nonprofit Sector: A Research Handbook*, edited by R. Steinberg and W. W. Powell, 307–331. New Haven: Yale University Press.

Johansson, H., & Scaramuzzino, G. 2019. "The Logics of Digital Advocacy: Between Acts of Political Influence and Presence." *New Media & Society* 21(7): 1528–1545 .https://doi.org/10.1177/1461444818822488.

John, G. H., Kohavi, R., & Pfleger, K. 1994. "Irrelevant Features and the Subset Selection Problem." In *Proceedings of the Eleventh International Conference on Machine Learning*, 121–129. New Brunswick, NJ: Morgan Kaufmann.

Jones, B. D., & Baumgartner, F. R. 2005. *The Politics of Attention: How Government Prioritizes Problems*. Chicago: University of Chicago Press.

Kane, G. C., Alavi, M., Labianca, G. J., & Borgatti, S. 2014. "What's Different about Social Media Networks? A Framework and Research Agenda." *MIS Quarterly* 38: 274–304.

Kaplan, A. M., & Haenlein, M. 2010. "Users of the World, Unite! The Challenges and Opportunities of Social Media." *Business Horizons* 53: 59–68.

Karpf, D. 2010. "Online Political Mobilization from the Advocacy Group's Perspective: Looking Beyond Clicktivism." *Policy & Internet* 2: 7–41.

Karpf, D. 2012. *The MoveOn Effect: The Unexpected Transformation of American Political Advocacy*. New York: Oxford University Press.

Keane, W. 2011. "Indexing Voice: A Morality Tale." *Journal of Linguistic Anthropology* 21: 166–178.

Kenski, K., & Stroud, N. J. 2006. "Connections Between Internet Use and Political Efficacy, Knowledge, and Participation." *Journal of Broadcasting & Electronic Media* 50: 173–192.

Kent, M. L., & Taylor, M. 1998. "Building Dialogic Relationships through the World Wide Web." *Public Relations Review* 24: 321–334.

Ketchen, D. J., & Shook, C. L. 1996. "The Application of Cluster Analysis in Strategic Management Research: An Analysis and Critique." *Strategic Management Journal* 17: 441–458.

Khumawala, S., Neely, D., & Gordon, T. P. 2010. "The Cost and Benefits of Voluntary Disclosures by Nonprofit Organizations." Available at SSRN: https://ssrn.com/abstract=1611189

Kietzmann, J. H., Hermkens, K., McCarthy, I. P., & Silvestre, B. S. 2011. "Social Media? Get Serious! Understanding the Functional Building Blocks of Social Media." *Business Horizons* 54: 241–251.

Kim, M., & Mason, D. P. 2018. "Representation and Diversity, Advocacy, and Nonprofit Arts Organizations." *Nonprofit and Voluntary Sector Quarterly* 47: 49–71.

Kinder, D. R., & Sears, D. O. 1985. "Public Opinion and Political Action." In *The Handbook of Social Psychology*, edited by G. Lindzey & E. Aronson, 659–741. New York: Random House.

King, B. 2008. "A Social Movement Perspective of Stakeholder Collective Action and Influence." *Business & Society* 47: 21–49.

Kingdon, J. W. 1984. *Agendas, Alternatives, and Public Policies*. Boston: Little, Brown.

Kleinman, G., & Hossain, D. 2009. "Issue Networks, Value Structures and the Formulation of Accounting Standards: An Exercise in Theory Building." *Group Decision and Negotiation* 18: 5–26.

Kluckhohn, C. 1951. "Values and Value Orientation in the Theory of Action." In *Toward a General Theory of Action*, edited by T. Parsons & E. A. Shils, 388–433. New York: Harper.

Kockelman, P. 2004. "Stance and Subjectivity." *Journal of Linguistic Anthropology* 14: 127–150.

Kraskov, A., Stögbauer, H., & Grassberger, P. 2004. "Estimating Mutual Information." *Physical Review E* 69: 66138.

Krier, C., François, D., Wertz, V., & Verleysen, M. 2006. "Feature Scoring by Mutual Information for Classification of Mass Spectra." In *Applied Artificial Intelligence: Proceedings of the 7th International FLINS Conference*, edited by D. Ruan, P. D'hondt, P. F. Fantoni, M. De Cock, M. Nachtegael, & E. E. Kerre, 557–564.

Kwon, O. B., Kim, C.-R., & Lee, E. J. 2002. "Impact of Website Information Design Factors on Consumer Ratings of Web-based Auction Sites." *Behaviour & Information Technology* 21: 387–402.

Lanham, R. 2006. *The Economics of Attention*. Chicago: University of Chicago Press.

Lecy, J. 2010. "Sector Density, Donor Policy, and Organizational Demise: A Population Ecology of International Nonprofits." Dissertation/Thesis, Maxwell School of Citizenship and Public Affairs, Syracuse University.

Lecy, J., & Thornton, J. 2016. "What Big Data Can Tell Us about Government Awards to the Nonprofit Sector: Using the FAADS." *Nonprofit and Voluntary Sector Quarterly* 45: 1052–1069.

Lecy, J., Mergel, I. A., & Schmitz, H. P. 2014. "Networks in Public Administration: Current Scholarship in Review." *Public Management Review* 16: 643–665.

Ledingham, J. A., & Bruning, S. D. 1998. "Relationship Management in Public Relations: Dimensions of an Organization-Public Relationship." *Public Relations Review* 24: 55–65.

Lee, Y. J., Yoon, H. J., & O'Donnell, N. H. 2018. "The Effects of Information Cues on Perceived Legitimacy of Companies that Promote Corporate Social Responsibility Initiatives on Social Networking Sites." *Journal of Business Research* 83: 202–214.

LeRoux, K. 2009. "The Effects of Descriptive Representation on Nonprofits' Civic Intermediary Roles: A Test of the 'Racial Mismatch' Hypothesis in the Social Services Sector." *Nonprofit & Voluntary Sector Quarterly* 38: 741–760.

LeRoux, K., & Goerdel, H. T. 2009. "Political Advocacy by Nonprofit Organizations: A Strategic Management Explanation." *Public Performance & Management Review* 32: 514–536.

Li, H., Lo, C. W. H., & Tang, S. Y. 2017. "Nonprofit Policy Advocacy Under Authoritarianism." *Public Administration Review* 77: 103–117.

Lipsman, A., Mudd, G., Rich, M., & Bruich, S. 2012. "The Power of 'Like': How Brands Reach (and Influence) Fans through Social-Media Marketing." *Journal of Advertising Research* 52: 40–52.

Liu-Thompkins, Y., & Rogerson, M. 2012. "Rising to Stardom: An Empirical Investigation of the Diffusion of User-Generated Content." *Journal of Interactive Marketing* 26: 71–82.

Lovejoy, K., & Saxton, G. D. 2012. "Information, Community, and Action: How Nonprofit Organizations Use Social Media." *Journal of Computer-Mediated Communication* 17: 337–353.

Lovejoy, K., Waters, R. D., & Saxton, G. D. 2012. "Engaging Stakeholders through Twitter: How Nonprofit Organizations Are Getting More out of 140 Characters or Less." *Public Relations Review* 38: 313–318.

Lu, J. 2018. "Organizational Antecedents of Nonprofit Engagement in Policy Advocacy: A Meta-analytical Review." *Nonprofit and Voluntary Sector Quarterly* 47: 177S–203S.

Macias, W., Hilyard, K., & Freimuth, V. 2009. "Blog Functions as Risk and Crisis Communication During Hurricane Katrina." *Journal of Computer-Mediated Communication* 15: 1–31.

MacIndoe, H., & Whelan, R. 2013. "Specialists, Generalists, and Policy Advocacy by Charitable Nonprofit Organizations." *Journal of Sociology & Social Welfare* 40: 119–149.

Marietta, M. 2010. "Value Representation—the Dominance of Ends Over Means in Democratic Politics: Reply to Murakami." *Critical Review* 22: 311–329.

McKeever, B. S. 2018. *The Nonprofit Sector in Brief 2018: Public Charities, Giving, and Volunteering.* Washington, DC: Urban Institute.

McNutt, J. G. 2008a. "Advocacy Organizations and the Organizational Digital Divide." *Currents: New Scholarship in the Human Services* 7: 1–13.

McNutt, J. G. 2008b. "Web 2.0 Tools for Policy Research and Advocacy." *Journal of Policy Practice* 7: 81–85.

McNutt, J. G., & Boland, K. M. 1999. "Electronic Advocacy by Nonprofit Organizations in Social Welfare Policy." *Nonprofit and Voluntary Sector Quarterly* 28: 432–451.

McNutt, J. G., & Boland, K. 2007. "Astroturf, Technology and the Future of Community Mobilization: Implications for Nonprofit Theory." *Journal of Sociology and Social Welfare* 34: 165.

McNutt, J., Guo, C., Goldkind, L., & An, S. 2018. "Technology in Nonprofit Organizations and Voluntary Action." *Voluntaristics Review* 3: 1–63.

McNutt, J. G., & Menon, G. M. 2008. "The Rise of Cyberactivism: Implications for the Future of Advocacy in the Human Services." *Families in Society: The Journal of Contemporary Social Services* 89: 33–38.

Meeder, B., Karrer, B., Sayedi, A., Ravi, R., Borgs, C., & Chayes, J. 2011. "We Know Who You Followed Last Summer: Inferring Social Link Creation Times in Twitter." In *Proceedings of the 20th international conference on the World Wide Web*, 517–526. New York: ACM.

Merry, M. K. 2013. "Tweeting for a Cause: Microblogging and Environmental Advocacy." *Policy & Internet* 5: 304–327.

Merry, M. K. 2014. "Broadcast versus Interaction: Environmental Groups' Use of Twitter." *Journal of Information Technology & Politics* 11: 329–344.

Miles, M. B., & Huberman, A. M. 1984. *Qualitative Data Analysis: A Sourcebook of New Methods.* Beverly Hills: Sage.

Miller, M. 2014. "Celebrities and Citizens Alike Are Embracing the Ice Bucket Challenge and the Cause it Benefits." *Buffalo News.*

Monge, P. R., & Contractor, N. S. 2003. *Theories of Communication Networks.* New York: Oxford University Press.

Mosley, J. E. 2011. "Institutionalization, Privatization, and Political Opportunity: What Tactical Choices Reveal About the Policy Advocacy of Human Service Nonprofits." *Nonprofit & Voluntary Sector Quarterly* 40: 435–457.

Mosley, J. E. 2012. "Keeping the Lights On: How Government Funding Concerns Drive the Advocacy Agendas of Nonprofit Homeless Service Providers." *Journal of Public Administration Research and Theory* 22: 841–866.

Murray, M. 2019. "As Howard Dean's "Scream" Turns 15, its Impact on American Politics Lives On." NBC News. Retrieved from: https://www.nbcnews.com/politics/meet-the-press/howard-dean-s-scream-turns-15-its-impact-american-politics-n959916.

Myers, S. A., & Leskovec, J. 2014. "The Bursty Dynamics of the Twitter Information Network." In *Proceedings of the 23rd International Conference on World Wide Web,* 913–924. New York: ACM.

Namenwirth, J. Z., & Weber, R. P. 1987. *Dynamics of Culture.* Boston: Allen & Unwin.

Nelson, T. E., & Garst, J. 2005. "Value-based Political Messages and Persuasion: Relationships Among Speaker, Recipient, and Evoked Values." *Political Psychology* 26: 489–515.

Nelson, T. E., Wittmer, D. E., & Shortle, A. F. 2010. "Framing and Value Recruitment in the Debate over Teaching Evolution." In *Winning with Words,* edited by B. F. Schaffner & P. J. Sellers, 11 40. New York: Routledge.

Nesbit, R. 2017. "Advocacy Recruits: Demographic Predictors of Volunteering for Advocacy-Related Organizations." *VOLUNTAS: International Journal of Voluntary and Nonprofit Organizations* 28: 958–987.

Nesi, P., Pantaleo, G., Paoli, I., & Zaza, I. 2018. "Assessing the reTweet Proneness of Tweets: Predictive Models for Retweeting." *Multimedia Tools and Applications,* 1–26.

Neu, D., Saxton, G., Everett, J., & Shiraz, A. R. 2018. "Speaking Truth to Power: Twitter Reactions to the Panama Papers." *Journal of Business Ethics,* 1–13.

Neumayr, M., Schneider, U., & Meyer, M. 2015. "Public Funding and its Impact on Nonprofit Advocacy." *Nonprofit and Voluntary Sector Quarterly* 44: 297–318.

Obar, J. A., Zube, P., & Lampe, C. 2012. "Advocacy 2.0: An Analysis of How Advocacy Groups in the United States Perceive and Use Social Media as Tools for Facilitating Civic Engagement and Collective Action." *Journal of Information Policy* 2: 1–25.

Ocasio, W. 2011. "Attention to Attention." *Organization Science* 22: 1286–1296.

O'Connell, B. 1994. *People Power: Service, Advocacy, Empowerment.* New York: Foundation Center.

O'Connell, B. 1996. "A Major Transfer of Government Responsibility to Voluntary Organizations? Proceed with Caution." *Public Administration Review* 56: 222–225.

Onyx, J., Dalton, B., Melville, R., Casey, J., & Banks, R. 2008. "Implications of Government Funding of Advocacy for Third-Sector Independence and Exploration of Alternative Advocacy Funding Models." *Australian Journal of Social Issues* 43: 631–648.

Ory, J. 2017. "How Social Media has Changed Advocacy: A Lawmaker's Perspective." Phone2Action, June 27, 2017. https://phone2action.com/blog/social-media-has-changed-advocacy-joaquin-castro/.

Osili, U., & Zarins, S. 2018. "Fewer Americans Are Giving Money to Charity but Total Donations Are at Record Levels Anyway." Insights Newsletter, Indiana University Lilly Family School of Philanthropy. Retrieved from: https://philanthropy.iupui.edu/news-events/insights-newsletter/2018-issues/july-2018-issue1.html.

Parise, S., Whelan, E., & Todd, S. 2015. "How Twitter Users can Generate Better Ideas." *MIT Sloan Management Review* 56: 20–25.

Park, H. W., Barnett, G., & Nam, I. 2002. "Hyperlink–Affiliation Network Structure of Top Web Sites: Examining Affiliates with Hyperlink in Korea." *Journal of the American Society for Information Science and Technology* 53: 592–601.

Parks, M. R. 2014. "Big Data in Communication Research: Its Contents and Discontents." *Journal of Communication* 64: 355–360.

Pasek, J., More, E., & Romer, D. 2009. "Realizing the Social Internet? Online Social Networking Meets Offline Civic Engagement." *Journal of Information Technology & Politics* 6: 197–215.

Pedregosa, F., Varoquaux, G., Gramfort, A., Michel, V., Thirion, B., Grisel, O., Blondel, M., et al. 2011. "Scikit-Learn: Machine Learning in Python." *Journal of Machine Learning Research* 12: 2825–2830.

Petray, T. L. 2011. "Protest 2.0: Online Interactions and Aboriginal Activists." *Media, Culture & Society* 33: 923–940.

Pieters, R., & Wedel, M. 2004. "Attention Capture and Transfer in Advertising: Brand, Pictorial, and Text-Size Effects." *Journal of Marketing* 68: 36–50.

Prakash, A., & Gugerty, M. K. eds. 2010. *Advocacy Organizations and Collective Action.* New York: Cambridge University Press.

Quan-Haase, A., Cothrel, J., & Wellman, B. 2005. "Instant Messaging for Collaboration: A Case Study of a High-Tech Firm." *Journal of Computer-Mediated Communication* 10: article 13.

Quinn, J. B. 1988. "Strategies for Change." In *The Strategy Process: Concepts, Contexts, and Cases*, edited by J. B. Quinn, H. Mintzberg, & R. M. James, 2–9. Englewood Cliffs, NJ: Prentice-Hall.

Rainie, L., & Wellman, B. 2012. *Networked: The New Social Operating System.* Cambridge, MA: MIT Press.

Reddick, C. G., & Ponomariov, B. 2013. "The Effect of Individuals' Organization Affiliation on their Internet Donations." *Nonprofit and Voluntary Sector Quarterly* 42: 1197–1223.

Redner, S. 1998. "How Popular Is Your Paper? An Empirical Study of the Citation Distribution." *European Physical Journal B—Condensed Matter and Complex Systems* 4: 131–134.

Reid, E. 1999. "Nonprofit Advocacy and Political Participation." In *Nonprofits and Government: Conflict or Collaboration?*, edited by E. T. Boris & C. E. Steuerle, 291–325. Washington, DC: Urban Institute Press.

Ren, C. R., & Guo, C. 2011. "Middle Managers' Strategic Role in the Corporate Entrepreneurial Process: Attention-based Effects." *Journal of Management* 37: 1586–1610.

Rodriguez-Galiano, V. F., Ghimire, B., Rogan, J., Chica-Olmo, M., & Rigol-Sanchez, J. P. 2012. "An Assessment of the Effectiveness of a Random Forest Classifier for

Land-Cover Classification." *ISPRS Journal of Photogrammetry and Remote Sensing* 67: 93–104.

Rokeach, M. 1973. *The Nature of Human Values.* New York: Free Press.

Rooney, P., Steinberg, K., & Schervish, P. G. 2004. "Methodology Is Destiny: The Effect of Survey Prompts on Reported Levels of Giving and Volunteering." *Nonprofit and Voluntary Sector Quarterly* 33: 628–654.

Rose-Ackerman, S. 1982. "Charitable Giving and "Excessive" Fundraising." *Quarterly Journal of Economics* 97: 193–212.

Ryan, C. 1999. "Australian Public Sector Financial Reporting: A Case of Cooperative Policy Formulation." *Accounting, Auditing & Accountability Journal* 12: 561–582.

Rybalko, S., & Seltzer, T. 2010. "Dialogic Communication in 140 Characters or Less: How Fortune 500 Companies Engage Stakeholders Using Twitter." *Public Relations Review* 36: 336–341.

Saeys, Y., Inza, I., & Larrañaga, P. 2007. "A Review of Feature Selection Techniques in Bioinformatics." *Bioinformatics* 23: 2507–2517.

Salamon, L. M., Benevolenski, V. B., & Jakobson, L. I. 2015. "Penetrating the Dual Realities of Government–Nonprofit Relations in Russia." *VOLUNTAS: International Journal of Voluntary and Nonprofit Organizations* 26: 2178–2214.

Saxton, G. D. 2016. *CSR, Big Data, and Accounting: Firms' Use of Social Media for CSR-Focused Reporting, Accountability, and Reputation Gain.* PhD thesis, Schulich School of Business, York University. Retrieved from https://yorkspace.library.yorku.ca/xmlui/handle/10315/32708.

Saxton, G. D., Gomez, L. M., Ngoh, Z., Lin, C., & Dietrich, S. 2019. "Do CSR Messages Resonate? Examining Public Reactions to Firms' CSR Efforts on Social Media." *Journal of Business Ethics* 155: 359–377.

Saxton, G. D., & Guo, C. 2011. "Accountability Online: Understanding the Web-based Accountability Practices of Nonprofit Organizations." *Nonprofit and Voluntary Sector Quarterly* 40: 270–295.

Saxton, G. D., & Guo, C. 2014. "Online Stakeholder Targeting and the Acquisition of Social Media Capital." *International Journal of Nonprofit and Voluntary Sector Marketing* 19: 286–300.

Saxton, G. D., & Guo, C. In press. "Social Media Capital: Conceptualizing the Nature, Acquisition, and Expenditure of Social Media-based Organizational Resources." *International Journal of Accounting Information Systems.*

Saxton, G. D., Guo, C., & Brown, W. A. 2007. "New Dimensions of Nonprofit Responsiveness: The Application and Promise of Internet-based Technologies." *Public Performance & Management Review* 31: 144–173.

Saxton, G. D., & Neely, D. G. 2019. "The Relationship Between Sarbanes–Oxley Policies and Donor Advisories in Nonprofit Organizations." *Journal of Business Ethics* 158: 333–351.

Saxton, G. D., Neely, D. G., & Guo, C. 2014. "Web Disclosure and the Market for Charitable Contributions." *Journal of Accounting and Public Policy* 33: 127–144.

Saxton, G. D., Niyirora, J., Waters, R. D., & Guo, C. 2015. "#AdvocatingForChange: The Strategic Use of Hashtags in Social Media Advocacy." *Advances in Social Work* 16: 154–169.

Saxton, G. D., & Wang, L. 2014. "The Social Network Effect: The Determinants of Giving through Social Media." *Nonprofit and Voluntary Sector Quarterly* 43: 850–868.

Saxton, G. D., & Waters, R. D. 2014. "What Do Stakeholders "Like" on Facebook? Examining Public Reactions to Nonprofit Organizations' Informational, Promotional, and Community-Building Messages." *Journal of Public Relations Research* 26: 280–299.

Schaupp, L. C., & Bélanger, F. 2013. "The Value of Social Media for Small Businesses." *Journal of Information Systems* 28: 187–207.

Schemer, C., Wirth, W., & Matthes, J. 2012. "Value Resonance and Value Framing Effects on Voting Intentions in Direct-Democratic Campaigns." *American Behavioral Scientist* 56: 334–352.

Schlozman, K. L., Verba, S., & Brady, H. E. 2013. *The Unheavenly Chorus: Unequal Political Voice and the Broken Promise of American Democracy.* Princeton, NJ: Princeton University Press.

Schmid, H., Bar, M., & Nirel, R. 2008. "Advocacy Activities in Nonprofit Human Service Organizations: Implications for Policy." *Nonprofit & Voluntary Sector Quarterly* 37: 581–602.

Schwartz, E. 1996. *Netactivism: How Citizens Use the Internet.* Sebastopol, CA: O'Reilly & Associates.

Scurlock, R., Dolsak, N., & Prakash, A. 2020. "Recovering from Scandals: Twitter Coverage of Oxfam and Save the Children Scandals." *VOLUNTAS: International Journal of Voluntary and Nonprofit Organizations* 31: 94–110.

Shah, D. V., Kwak, N., & Holbert, R. L. 2001. "'Connecting' and 'Disconnecting' with Civic Life: Patterns of Internet Use and the Production of Social Capital." *Political Communication* 18: 141–162.

Shirky, C. 2003. "Power Laws, Weblogs, and Inequality." Retrieved from: http://www.shirky.com/writings/herecomeseverybody/powerlaw_weblog.html.

Shirky, C. 2011. "The Political Power of Social Media: Technology, the Public Sphere, and Political Change." *Foreign Affairs* 90: 28–41.

Simon, H. A. 1971. "Designing Organizations for an Information-Rich World." In *Computers, Communications and the Public Interest,* edited by M. Greenberger, 37–72. Baltimore, MD: Johns Hopkins University Press.

Simon, S., & Peppas, S. 2005. "Attitudes Towards Product Website Design: A Study of the Effects of Gender." *Journal of Marketing Communications* 11: 129–144.

Slater, M. D., & Gleason, L. S. 2012. "Contributing to Theory and Knowledge in Quantitative Communication Science." *Communication Methods and Measures* 6: 215–236.

Smith, B. G. 2012. "Public Relations Identity and the Stakeholder–Organization Relationship: A Revised Theoretical Position for Public Relations Scholarship." *Public Relations Review* 38: 838–845.

Sniderman, P. M., & Theriault, S. M. 2004. "The Structure of Political Argument and the Logic of Issue Framing." In *Studies in Public Opinion: Attitudes, Nonattitudes, Measurement Error, and Change*, edited by W. E. Saris & P. M. Sniderman, 133–165. Princeton and Oxford, NJ: Princeton University Press.

Snow, D. A., Rochford, E. B., Jr., Worden, S. K., & Benford, R. D. 1986. "Frame Alignment Processes, Micromobilization, and Movement Participation." *American Sociological Review*, 464–481.

Sproull, L. S. 1984. "The Nature of Managerial Attention." *Advances in Information Processing in Organizations* 1: 9–27.

Statista. 2019a. *Most Popular Social Networks Worldwide as of July 2019, Ranked by Number of Active Users (in millions)*. Retrieved from: https://www.statista.com/statistics/272014/global-social-networks-ranked-by-number-of-users/.

Statista. 2019b. *Percentage of U.S. Population who Currently Use any Social Media from 2008 to 2019*. Retrieved from: www.statista.com/statistics/273476/percentage-of-us-population-with-a-social-network-profile/.

Stieglitz, S., & Dang-Xuan, L. 2013. "Emotions and Information Diffusion in Social Media—Sentiment of Microblogs and Sharing Behavior." *Journal of Management Information Systems* 29: 217–248.

Stivers, C. 1994. "The Listening Bureaucrat: Responsiveness in Public Administration." *Public Administration Review* 54: 364–369.

Strauss, A., & Corbin, J. 1998. *Basics of Qualitative Research*, 2nd ed. Thousands Oaks, CA: Sage.

Suárez, D. F. 2009. "Nonprofit Advocacy and Civic Engagement on the Internet." *Administration & Society* 41: 267–289.

Suárez, D. F., & Hwang, H. 2008. "Civic Engagement and Nonprofit Lobbying in California, 1998–2003." *Nonprofit & Voluntary Sector Quarterly* 37: 93–112.

Suchman, E. 1968. *Evaluative Research: Principles and Practice in Public Service and Social Action Programs*. New York: Russell Sage Foundation.

Suddaby, R. 2006. "From the Editors: What Grounded Theory Is Not." *Academy of Management Journal* 49: 633–642.

Suddaby, R., Saxton, G. D., & Gunz, S. 2015. "Twittering Change: The Institutional Work of Domain Change in Accounting Expertise." *Accounting, Organizations and Society* 45: 52–68.

Swani, K., Milne, G., & P. Brown, B. 2013. "Spreading the Word through Likes on Face-book: Evaluating the Message Strategy Effectiveness of Fortune 500 Companies." *Journal of Research in Interactive Marketing* 7: 269–294.

Taber, C. S., & Lodge, M. 2006. "Motivated Skepticism in the Evaluation of Political Beliefs." *American Journal of Political Science* 50: 755–769.

Taylor, M., & Doerfel, M. 2011. "Evolving Network Roles in International Aid Efforts: Evidence from Croatia's Post War Transition." *VOLUNTAS: International Journal of Voluntary and Nonprofit Organizations* 22: 311–334.

Taylor, M., Kent, M. L., & White, W. J. 2001. "How Activist Organizations Are Using the Internet to Build Relationships." *Public Relations Review* 27: 263–284.

Teles, S., & Schmitt, M. 2011. "The Elusive Craft of Evaluating Advocacy." *Stanford Social Innovation Review* 9: 40–43.

Tetlock, P. C. 2007. "Giving Content to Investor Sentiment: The Role of Media in the Stock Market." *Journal of Finance* 62: 1139–1168.

Tetlock, P. C., Saar-Tsechansky, M., & Macskassy, S. 2008. "More than Words: Quantify-ing Language to Measure Firms' Fundamentals." *Journal of Finance* 63: 1437–1467.

Thornton, J. 2006. "Nonprofit Fundraising in Competitive Donor Markets." *Nonprofit and Voluntary Sector Quarterly* 35: 204–224.

Tibshirani, R. 1996. "Regression Shrinkage and Selection Via the Lasso." *Journal of the Royal Statistical Society. Series B (Methodological)* 58: 267–288. Retrieved from: http://www.jstor.org/stable/2346178.

Toms, E. G. 2002. "Information Interaction: Providing a Framework for Information Architecture." *Journal of the American Society for Information Science and Technol-ogy* 53: 855–862.

Trussel, J. M., & Parsons, L. M. 2007. "Financial Reporting Factors Affecting Donations to Charitable Organizations." *Advances in Accounting* 23: 263–285.

Tufekci, Z. 2013. "'Not This One': Social Movements, the Attention Economy, and Mi-crocelebrity Networked Activism." *American Behavioral Scientist* 57: 848–870.

Tufekci, Z. 2018. "YouTube, the Great Radicalizer." *New York Times* 12: 15 (March 10, 2018). Retrieved from: https://www.nytimes.com/2018/03/10/opinion/sunday/youtube-politics-radical.html.

Unerman, J., & Bennett, M. 2004. "Increased Stakeholder Dialogue and the Internet: Towards Greater Corporate Accountability or Reinforcing Capitalist Hegemony?" *Accounting, Organizations and Society* 29: 685–707.

Valenzuela, S., Park, N., Kee, K. 2009. "Is There Social Capital in a Social Network Site? Facebook Use and College Students' Life Satisfaction, Trust, and Participation." *Journal of Computer-Mediated Communication* 14: 875–901.

Vasarhelyi, M. A., Kogan, A., & Tuttle, B. M. 2015. "Big Data in Accounting: An Over-view." *Accounting Horizons* 29: 381–396.

Verba, S., Schlozman, K. L., & Brady, H. E. 1995. *Voice and Equality: Civic Voluntarism in American Politics*. Cambridge, MA: Harvard University Press.

Vergeer, M., Lim, Y. S., & Park, H. W. 2011. "Mediated Relations: New Methods to Study Online Social Capital." *Asian Journal of Communication* 21: 430–449.

Verikas, A., Gelzinis, A., & Bacauskiene, M. 2011. "Mining Data with Random Forests: A Survey and Results of New Tests." *Pattern Recognition* 44: 330–349.

Voss, G. B. 2003. "Formulating Interesting Research Questions." *Journal of the Academy of Marketing Science* 31: 356–359.

Wallace, T., & Porter, F. 2013. "Introduction—Aid, NGOs and the Shrinking Space for Women: A Perfect Storm." In *Aid, NGOs and the Realities of Women's Lives: A Perfect Storm*, edited by T. Wallace, F. Porter, & M. Ralph-Bowman, 19–29. Rugby, Warwickshire: Practical Action Publishing.

Waters, R. D., Burnett, E., Lamm, A., & Lucas, J. 2009. "Engaging Stakeholders through Social Networking: How Nonprofit Organizations Are Using Facebook." *Public Relations Review* 35: 102–106.

Waters, R. D., & Jamal, J. Y. 2011. "Tweet, Tweet, Tweet: A Content Analysis of Nonprofit Organizations' Twitter Updates." *Public Relations Review* 37: 321–324.

Webster, J. G. 2011. "The Duality of Media: A Structurational Theory of Public Attention." *Communication Theory* 21: 43–66.

Weisbrod, B. A., & Dominguez, N. D. 1986. "Demand for Collective Goods in Private Nonprofit Markets: Can Fundraising Expenditures Help Overcome Free-Rider Behavior?" *Journal of Public Economics* 30: 83–96.

Wellman, B. 2002. "The Rise (and Possible Fall) of Networked Individualism." *Connections* 24: 30–32.

Westerman, D., Spence, P. R., & Van Der Heide, B. 2012. "A Social Network as Information: The Effect of System Generated Reports of Connectedness on Credibility on Twitter." *Computers in Human Behavior* 28: 199–206.

Wittig, M. A. & Schmitz, J. 1996. "Electronic Grassroots Organizing." *Journal of Social Issues* 52: 53–69.

Wood, B. D., & Vedlitz, A. 2007. "Issue Definition, Information Processing, and the Politics of Global Warming." *American Journal of Political Science* 51: 552–568.

Worrell, J., Wasko, M., & Johnston, A. 2013. "Social Network Analysis in Accounting Information Systems Research." *International Journal of Accounting Information Systems* 14: 127–137.

Xu, W., Sang, Y., Blasiola, S., & Park, H. W. 2014. "Predicting Opinion Leaders in Twitter Activism Networks: The Case of the Wisconsin Recall Election." *American Behavioral Scientist* 58: 1278–1293.

Xu, W., & Saxton, G. D. 2019. "Does Stakeholder Engagement Pay Off on Social Media? A Social Capital Perspective." *Nonprofit and Voluntary Sector Quarterly* 48: 28–49.

Xu, Y., & Ngai, N.-P. 2011. "Moral Resources and Political Capital: Theorizing the Relationship between Voluntary Service Organizations and the Development of Civil Society in China." *Nonprofit and Voluntary Sector Quarterly* 40: 247–269.

Yang, S., Han, R., Ding, J., & Song, Y. 2012. "The Distribution of Web Citations." *Information Processing & Management* 48: 779–790.

Yerxa, S. W., & Moll, M. 1994. "Notes from the Grassroots: On-line Lobbying in Canada." *Internet Research* 4: 9–19.

Yu, L., & Liu, H. 2004. "Efficient Feature Selection Via Analysis of Relevance and Redundancy." *Journal of Machine Learning Research* 5: 1205–1224.

Zhan, X., & Tang, S. Y. 2013. "Political Opportunities, Resource Constraints and Policy Advocacy of Environmental NGOs in China." *Public Administration* 91: 381–399.

Zhang, C. 2018. "Nongovernmental Organizations' Policy Advocacy and Government Responsiveness in China." *Nonprofit and Voluntary Sector Quarterly* 47: 723–744.

Zhang, Z., and Guo, C. In press. "Still Hold Aloft the Banner of Social Change? Nonprofit Advocacy in the Wave of Commercialization." *International Review of Administrative Sciences.*

INDEX